MICHAEL HONE

HOMOSEXUAL HEROS

The cover picture: a detail of Michelangelo's immortal *David*.

ALL PICTURES ARE IN THE PUBLIC DOMAIN

Expanded 2022 Edition

My books include: *Cellini; Caravaggio; Cesare Borgia; Renaissance Murders; TROY; Greek Homosexuality; ARGO; Alcibiades the Schoolboy; RENT BOYS; Roman Homosexuality; Renaissance Homosexuality; Homoerotic Art* [in full color]; *Sailors and Homosexuality; The Essence of Being Gay; John [Jack] Nicholson; THE SACRED BAND; German Homosexuality; Gay Genius; SPARTA; Charles XII of Sweden; Mediterranean Homosexual Pleasure; CAPRI; Boarding School Homosexuality; American Homosexual Giants; HUSTLERS; Omnisexuality, the Death of Gay and Straight Sex; Y.M.C.A. Homosexual Haven; All-Boy Porn Stars; All-Male Pornography; VINTAGE The Golden Age of All-Male Erotica; Sebastian* and *The History of British Homosexuality.*
I live in the South of France.

DEDICATION
This book is dedicated to Willem Arondeus
who shouted out in front of a Nazi firing squad,
''Let it be known that homosexuals are not cowards.''

CONTENTS

INTRODUCTION

The men within these pages were the world's foremost heroes, among them the greatest military leaders ever known, Alexander the Great, seconded by his lover Hephaestion. Spartans at Thermopylae saved Western civilization from Eastern barbarism under Darius and Xerxes, while in Thebes the Sacred Band of 300 lovers defended the law that proclaimed it illegal for anyone to maintain that sex between men was *not* beautiful. Rome was less male-oriented than Greece, but two heroic emperors, Trajan and Hadrian, although married, may never have *known* their wives, women at the time satisfied enough with marriage to a man of wealth and social standing, while during the Renaissance poisonous religion found its antidote in the Medici who unearthed the texts of Ancient Greece, bringing forth the rebirth responsible for the masterpieces of homosexuals Michelangelo, Cellini and the greatest man to have ever lived, Leonardo da Vinci. Over the tomb of homosexual Frederick the Great, Napoleon declared to his generals, following their conquest of Prussia, ''Gentlemen, if this man were still alive, we would not be here.'' Richard I, born in England but raised in France, from whence comes his name Richard Coeur de Lion, took the crusades to the walls of Jerusalem, alongside the man who shared his bed, King Philippe II. T.E. Lawrence fought for Arab independence, bringing the troops of King Faisel up to and through the gates of Damascus, a fitting gift, he wrote, for the people of the boy he loved, Dahoum, and John Nicholson led British forces over the fortifications of Delhi in retribution for the greatest massacre of English men, women and children that Britain had ever endured, the Mutiny of 1857, his lover Herbert Edwardes the only man who knew of Nicholson's secret devotion for the soldiers he led.

And so on to our own day, heroes in every walk of life, *Homosexual Heroes* ending with Jack Mackenroth, swimmer, Outgames competitor, menswear designer, gay-rights defender and magnificently sexy pornstar. Yet despite the valiant men within these pages, despite same-sex marriages and the Great Liberator--Internet--heroism is still required for a boy to admit, to his locker-room buddies, that he prefers them to the chirping maidens in the adjoining showers.

This revised and enlarged edition is priced at the lowest cost permitted by the editors so that young readers can discover, with profound pride, the lives of the heroes who have cleared the path for us, pride shared by Apple president Tom Cook who stated, ''I'm proud to be gay and I consider being gay among the greatest gifts God has given me'', seconded by CNN's Anderson Cooper who proclaimed, ''I think being gay is a blessing, and it's something I am thankful for every single day.''

ACHILLES AND PATROCLUS
The Foremost Heroes of Homer's *Iliad*
1200 B.C.

In the union of Achilles and Patroclus, Homer has offered us the greatest love story the world has known, one that took place is the mists of time when the lives of mortals were inseparable from those of the gods. Some doubt that a love of such beauty and intensity could have existed, as they doubted too the existence of the Trojan War, or ever that of Troy itself until Schliemann discovered the site and adorned his wife with the gold jewelry perhaps worn by Helen of Sparta herself, over 3,000 years ago.

Achilles was called up to participate in the War because a Trojan priest, Calchas, predicted that it would not be won without him, while Patroclus was obliged to go because he had been one of Helen of Sparta's suitors, men set on killing each other for her hand until King Odysseus of Ithaca had them all take an oath to support the man chosen for her mate, and to come to their aid in times of peril. The Trojan Paris abducted Helen when Aphrodite herself promised he would possess her, in exchange for a Golden Apple on which was etched For the Fairest. The Apple had been disputed between Aphrodite and two other goddesses, Athena and Zeus's wife Hera. Their desire for revenge for the loss of the Apple spurred them to exhort all of Hellas to sail to the shores of mighty Troy where Paris had taken Helen, a welcome interlude for the Spartan queen whose husband Menelaus was sensually piteous in comparison to Paris, Paris young and virile, a swordsman whom Aphrodite had already presented to Helen in dreams, Paris confirming Aphrodite's assurance to the queen that none were better endowed than Trojans, an encouragement to her boarding the boat.

On the shores of mighty Troy the war waged on and disagreements between the leaders became rampant during the nine years of stalemate, the most serious of which was between Achilles and the Greek commander Agamemnon, Menelaus's brother. Following one such dispute Achilles refused to enter combat. His lover Patroclus convinced his belovèd to let him wear his armor in the belief that when the Trojans saw it, they would give up the fight:

"You can take my armor and chariot and lead the Myrmidons into combat," said Achilles, "but you've promised to do no more than drive the Trojans away from the boats."

"When they see me dressed as you, they'll clear out quickly enough," answered Patroclus. "No one's so crazy as to come up against the mighty Achilles--they'll scatter like a bunch of eunuchs."

"Under no condition are you to go farther than the ships," insisted Achilles gravely. "When you see that the Trojan's have turned back, you return."

Achilles helped his friend don his golden breastplate and greaves with their silver buckles, the everlasting workmanship of Immortal Hephaestus. He fitted the gold shield to Patroclus' arm and strapped the silver-handled bronze sword over his left shoulder. Then, for an uneasy moment, they stood in silence facing each other. At last Achilles made a movement forward. Patroclus bit his lower lip, stopping his friend by grasping his right wrist. Achilles saw the trickle of blood run from the corner of Patroclus' mouth and understood. He took his friend's wrist in his own hand and through the mystery of touch begged him to return unharmed. He then put his golden helmet into Patroclus' hands and led him to the camp of the Myrmidons. There, the troops--ready for combat after months of wintry inaction--were entrusted to Patroclus' care. Achilles, wanting to take no chance with the lives of his troops and friend, repeated his orders that they were only to chase the Trojans away from the ships. The driver Automedon came up with Achilles' chariot and Patroclus stepped on behind him. Achilles handed up two spears and bade him farewell.

The moment the men pulled away, Achilles went into his hut and took a carved chalice from out the chest his mother had packed for him. He washed his hands and the chalice, filled it with his finest wine and went out into the courtyard to speak to Zeus. He slowly spilt his offering on the sand as he spoke.

"Dearest Father, I commit the precious life of my friend into your hands. He has taken my place in battle to bring help to our retreating troops, and to uphold my pledge not to fight as long as Agamemnon remains their commander. Patroclus is more to me, Father, than I am to myself. Without his presence, death would surely be a sweeter refuge than this world which brings only burdens as we approach the futility of old age. For the warmth of the sun, the blue horizon, the tepid waters that caress our homeland, the swaying fields of golden wheat that fill our stomachs at the end of a day's labor, the soft breeze that cools our brow, and the hills of grapes that soothe our dry lips, all these suffice when one is young and the earth is seen through the eyes of youth. But when one shares one's life with another, there is need of a deeper meaning, a greater understanding.

"You so decreed at the Beginning of Time that Man was not to live alone, Wise Father, and through your wisdom came the supreme happiness: life by the side of one's belovèd. By living your word we are whole, Father, and in our minds and hearts you exist. For such is our hallowed pact: through your will we walk the bountiful Earth; and through our worship--and the prayers of our children and their children--you continue to endure, Father, forever and ever. You have offered us the gift of love, and we have granted you Immortality. One day I will cease, Father, but you will go on. The fruit of my love will continue to call you Father, and worship your name. I will fulfill my duty, and you must fulfill yours. But let it not be now, the coming of the dark. Let me and my friend live on to know the depths of our love, and to continue to sing your praise.

"As a child, Father, Patroclus came to our house an orphan. Soon he was a friend and then a brother. Later, in the absence of my father Peleus, he became my companion and guide. He has only me, and I him. Please dear god, Father of Justice, keep him from harm's touch. Show mercy to two of your children. I am not asking for eternity, Father, but just a final, fleeting moment of happiness."

Achilles poured out the last of the wine, and Olympian Zeus on high heard his prayer. Through the heavy folds of sleep the words reached his ears. He rose from the love-bed he shared with Ganymede, cast away the curtains of willow bows and pierced the bank of swirling clouds that hid Troy. Golden rays lit up the plain for the first time that day, and revealed Patroclus riding along the beach toward the place where the Trojans had breached the mound and set fire to the ships. Almighty Father wrapped the belovèd friend of Achilles in a blaze of protective light and promised that it was not there that he would meet his end.

Patroclus had nearly reached the ships. Zeus caused the Earth to shake and the mountains to explode in fire. The sun was blackened and the sea poured onto the beaches. Trojans and Greeks fell to their knees in awe and fear, each man with a fast prayer to Zeus-Savior on his lips. Only Patroclus was undaunted. Enveloped in light and with a bloodcurdling war cry resounding from his high-plumed helmet, he led the Myrmidons in attack. The Trojans mistook him for the mighty Achilles and scampered in full panic back over the Greeks' hastily flung-up walls. Father Zeus took pride in the noble Patroclus, and held his scales of Justice up for all the gods to witness his immutable decision to make Achilles' courageous friend the day's victor. How great, then, was his own deception when Zeus saw the scales tip slowly but immutably downward in opposition to Achilles' companion. It suddenly became clear that above glorious life, with all awesome beauty and heartrending disappointment, hovered motherly Clotho, Aunt Lachesis and grandmotherly Atropos, spinning, measuring and snipping, and not even Zeus had sway over their eternal labor.

Father sat heavily on a nearby hill and put his great head in his weathered hands. "I cannot weep for Man," he thought. "To do so would be to continually flood the Earth. And how can I relieve Man's agony if everyone plots behind my back and bribes me with their love? Even the final decisions of life and death are beyond my power. All I can do, and do it I shall," he said, rising, "is make this day the most valiant in Patroclus' short life, and one that will bring him eternal renowned for his bravery, while defending the honor of his friend."

So saying, Zeus snapped his orders to all concerned that Patroclus was to have his own way. And even the Fates, he hinted darkly, would be wise to slow up their work until the waning of the day.

On went the Trojans towards their own walls with Patroclus hot on their heels, slaying to the right and to the left. Pronoos was the first to be brought down and then Thestor, as Patroclus' spear broke through his jaw. Next came Erylaos whose head Patroclus split in two. Then fell Erymas, Amphoteros, Epaltes, Tlepolemos, Echos, Pyris, Ipheus, Euppos and Polymelos, valiant Trojans every one. Even Zeus's own son Sarpedon was killed by a javelin thrown through the heart. This grieved Almighty Father for he had greatly loved Laodemeia, Sarpedon's mother, and had carefully supervised his love-child's upbringing. Zeus dispatched Apollo to cleanse the blood-splattered body in the crystal waters of the Scamander. The boy was anointed with ambrosia and dressed in the finest garments before being handed over to Death. Zeus allowed himself a tear, since Sarpedon was half-immortal, and wished to curb Patroclus, his murderer, who meant less to him than his own blood. But bound by his word, he let the slaughter go on until Patroclus--forgetting Achilles' warning--came up to the citadel's mighty walls. So certain was his invincibility that even Hector took cover behind the Scaian Gates. Stragglers were cut down and left dying in the dust. Adrestos, Autonoos, Echeclos, Perimos, Megades, Epistor, Melanippos, Elasos, Mulios and Pylartes all met death within reach of the lofty doors the Trojans had closed and barred in fear of Patroclus' dripping sword. When the last of those abandoned had been dispatched, the Greeks prepared to climb Troy's walls. Already siege ladders had been brought up and Patroclus led the Myrmidons to the top of the west ramparts.

And it was then and there that Zeus turned his back on the man he had brought within a hair's breadth of victory. He returned to Olympus to mourn Sarpedon, who had once told Zeus, "I would gladly have avoided the war if immortality and not old age and death were the prize offered the survivors. But since no one can escape Death, let honors come in glory, the glory that we can give to others, or the glory others can give to us." Father left the outcome in the hands of the only god still on the field, Apollo, the Trojans' friend.

Three times Patroclus climbed to the top of the ramparts, and three times Apollo pushed him back. And so they would have continued until the arrival of Night if the Fates hadn't signaled Apollo from afar that the end of Patroclus' allotted length of wool was nearing the snippers. The god shoved the ladder away one last time and went down to find Hector. Taking the form of one of the guards, Asios, Apollo addressed the prince: "There's no reason to be afraid, Hector. That's not Achilles out there, it's Patroclus."

"It may be Patroclus as you say, my friend, but only a fool would go up against him as invincible as he is now."

"You won't be alone," insisted Asios. "Apollo will be there to disarm him."

"How do you know that?" demanded Hector, turning towards the guard.

"It was Apollo who stopped Patroclus from getting a foothold on the ramparts. Put your faith in him, Prince Hector. He loves the Trojans and won't let them down."

Hector saw from the piercing eyes that the speaker was Apollo himself. He therefore set off immediately through the Scaian Gates to confront Patroclus.

Outside, the Myrmidons were joined by reinforcements. Agamemnon, Menelaus, and Odysseus came up with their troops, as did Nestor, Idomeneus, Diomedes and the other captains. To their surprise, they saw that the Trojans, who were fleeing from them just hours before, were now coming out to engage battle. Neither side had time to form up into correct formations before becoming involved in a deadly melee. Spears were impossible in such close quarters and even swords were used with difficulty. Daggers were more efficient, but the soldiers used them badly, through lack of practice, and most of the thrusts produced superficial injuries rather than mortal wounds. For that reason Apollo decided to cut Patroclus off from his troops.

Under the cloak of invisibility he came up and pulled Patroclus, a final time, from the walls. Patroclus hit the ground, shattering Achilles' spear and breaking the shield. He tried to regain his feet but Apollo gave him another slap that sent him sprawling back into the trodden dust. Achilles' breastplate rolled gently from Patroclus' side. Still again the young prince sought to rise, but in vain. Apollo gave him one last shove that drove him clear of his fighting comrades and knocked the golden helmet from his stunned head. The boy's matted hair lay in ripples over his brow, and sweat blurred his half-closed eyes. Numbly he pushed himself to his hands and knees, but the blows from the Immortal god had overwhelmed him.

Never again would he ride by Achilles' side, or listen for his friend's familiar steps coming up the beach, or hold him when fear swept his restive dreams. Already Death was ascending to claim the body, still warm and unmarked. Death regretted the work the Fates had dealt him, yet his role was not the worst: for it was not he, nor Man, nor the Immortals, nor Helios, nor any living thing that would see Patroclus lose his beauty and fall into dust: the final witness would be the still, solitary, anonymous grave.

Patroclus tried to rise; Death drew nearer; and Hector broke away from the entangled pack and approached the prince on running feet, his spear poised tightly against his side. Patroclus turned his chest and arched his body towards the blurred warmth of the midday sun which enclosed his head in a halo, his arms outstretched as if to welcome Achilles, not the quickly advancing Trojan. And it was then, on his knees, his body open to the sun and his friend, that Hector planted his spear in the taut muscles of the abdomen, at the place where he had first received precious life.

Menelaus saw Patroclus fall the moment that Atropos snipped his cord. He sent Antilochos to tell Achilles. Antilochos rode across the plain and after an hour arrived in front of Achilles' hut. He was crying, poor man, for he had loved his companion, and he was afraid for his own life lest Achilles in a wild frenzy of agony cut his throat for being the bearer of such news.

Achilles came from out his hut and stood glassy-eyed as Antilochos bore the evil tidings. Achilles stared unspeaking for seemingly endless moments and then collapsed to the beach like a marionette cut from its strings. A groan, wrenching and hollow, formed within the deepest recesses of his soul as he became aware of the full horror of his loss. And the wail that left his lips sounded the death keel for a thousand men and heralded the end of a nation, a friendship, a love and the will to live. Antilochos knelt before his stricken commander and grasped Achilles' hands tightly in his for fear that in his fury Achilles would do himself or Antilochos harm.

"Weep for Patroclus, Antilochos," cried Achilles, "not for your own life. It is not you who will feel the brunt of my sword!"

Automedon came in from battle on Achilles' chariot behind the two immortal steeds, Xanthos and Balios. Achilles jumped on to go after Patroclus' body. Naked but for a borrowed sword that hung from a strap over his right shoulder and two spears, one in hand and one strapped to the chariot, Achilles swept across the beach and headed inland with such haste that his chargers' hooves scarcely grazed the ground.

The gods would never forget the slaughter seen that day. At its end a thousand lads lay obscenely exposed to flies that dropped their maggots into festering sword gashes and vulture-torn muscle; all honor and decency-- even the modesty of the tomb--were denied them.

Before the gates of Troy Menelaus and Aias succeeded in wresting the body of Patroclus away from Hector. Back to the shore they rode, past Trojans running blindly before the approach of Achilles. Achilles saw Menelaus' chariot racing by and guessed at its hapless passenger. He broke off the fighting and followed it to the Greek camp. Menelaus wished to spare him the sight of Patroclus' disfigured body, mercilessly fought over by Greeks and Trojans, the latter who wished to parade it naked and broken through the steep, winding streets of Troy. But Achilles forced his way to his friend, taking Patroclus in both arms and drawing him tightly to his chest. Sobbing, waving back and forth with his friend held against him like a nursing child, Achilles watched over him throughout the cold, bitter night.

Dawn found Achilles bent unmoving over Patroclus' corpse. In the raw, white light both bodies had so much the same waxen hue that his mother Thetis, coming up from her cave in Ocean, took them both for dead.

"Achilles?" she asked, tentatively.

"And so it is, Mother, that when the desire to live is most insatiable, we are called upon to die. My heart is broken from the loss of my friend; what a simple matter it now will be to wrench what remains of my soul from my breast. The shadow of the tomb is upon me. Were it not for the revenge that is Patroclus' right, I would accompany him now to the Elysian Fields. But I must first meet with Hector and make him regret his crime. I hope he has lived well, for there will be no comfort for him beyond the grave."

Achilles rose to his feet. I must release Patroclus to the maidens who will clean and wrap him in linen," he said. "We shall raise a pyre so his body will be spared defilement, and his soul will fly unhampered to the Kingdom of Hades and Persephone. Then will I meet Hector before Troy's invincible gates; then will our destinies unfold. No more will Achilles feel the comfort of a mother's embrace; no more will Hector know the love of a faithful wife. The cold earth will claim its due; into dust and oblivion our brief moment of existence--vital to us, so trivial to the gods--will ebb; and we will be no more. I am a coward Patroclus; would I have died before you, than live to avenge your loss."

The camp began to stir. From Nestor's tent came Agamemnon, Calchas, Menelaus, Odysseus and the other captains, all of whom had held a wake for Patroclus throughout the long night. Each looked wan and unkempt. They bent with difficulty as they passed through the tent flaps, and straightened uncomfortably. They did not stand around, for they had worked out a plan throughout the weary hours. None dared to approach Achilles except Calchas, who had been delegated to the duty. He went to the young warrior and whispered quiet, tender words in his ear. The old priest's usual excitability had been drained by the numbing lack of sleep. He placed his hands-on Achilles' arm, as much to support himself as to reassure the boy, and led him up the beach to the narrow path that led to Apollo's temple. Together they would spend the morning in prayer.

Nestor had Patroclus' corpse taken to the enclosure of waist-high stalks that surrounded the old king's tent. A group of servant maidens washed and oiled his skin, rinsed and combed his hair, dressed him in a white tunic and wrapped him in a sheet of wool. The maidens had done what they could in the absence of his natural warmth, and the sweetness of his breath and the fragrance of his skin.

Odysseus was sent to the verdant lap of Mount Ida with a large detail to bring back logs for a funeral pyre. The trees were rapidly felled, branched and dragged back behind the soldiers' horses.

On a gently sloping plain behind the shore Aias and Teucer supervised the digging of a shallow pit in which the funeral pyre was to be raised and in which the offerings were to be burned. Agamemnon had given himself the job of getting together the sacrifice. He had requisitioned jars of honey, vine and oil; sheep, cattle and a covey of partridges; four horses, one of which had belonged to Patroclus; and two of Patroclus' hounds. Twelve Trojan captives were also to be slain. Agamemnon hoped that the amplitude of the endowment would persuade Achilles to renounce his decision to not commit himself and the Myrmidons to the siege of Troy.

Menelaus supervised the building of the pyre. The logs were placed in the shallow pit and crisscrossed to form a giant square the length and width of a ship. On the top, ten feet from the earth, a platform was built of planks.

From the heights of Olympus the Ruling Twelve descended on joyless clouds to the plain of Troy where they hung suspended in the darkened sky high above the site. The Winds, the Furies and the Planets joined them, as did Night, Day and Mother Earth; the Fates, the Cyclopes and the Dactyls; plus uncountable other lesser gods like the Stars, Moon and, alas!, Death. Looking down on the plain that was wrapped in a warm blanket of autumn orange and gold, they saw the funeral procession drawing near the pyre.

The men marched slowly, each step in time to the haunting beat of the soldiers' swords striking against their shields. The Myrmidons led the procession. Six abreast and four hundred deep, they were dressed in full battle regalia. Patroclus was carried gently on the shoulders of Agamemnon, Odysseus, Diomedes, Idomeneus, Nestor, Calchas, Aias and Menelaus. Achilles led the Myrmidons. The rest of the troops took up the rear, forming a line a mile long.

From Troy's walls watched Priam, Hecabe, Antenor, Eiphobus, Helen and … Paris. Did it ever occur to the young fool that it was he the agent of such misery?

At the pyre, Achilles gave his eternal farewell to Patroclus. He did it simply, respecting even in death his lover's modesty. The corpse was lifted onto the platform. Below, into the gutters between the edge of the pit and the logs, the animals were sacrificed, the jars of food, oil and wine were emptied and the captured Trojans were condemned to die. Each of the twelve was on his knees facing the logs. Each had his hands roped behind his back. All waited their turn as Achilles himself passed behind, pushed his knee into their spines, pulled back their heads by the hair, and slit their throats with Patroclus' own dagger. Their lives, valiant manhood and beauty ebbed rapidly down their chests and formed puddles where they fell after being shoved into the pit. All the gods looked on sadly except Death, who was busy flittering from one victim to the next.

Then came the soldiers, each throwing in a gift or libation. Finally Achilles stood alone before the pyre with Antilochos to his right. He took

Patroclus' dagger and cut off the sprig of his own hair. He climbed to the platform and laid it in Patroclus' folded hands. Antilochos stepped forward and handed Achilles a torch that he immediately threw into the straw between the logs. The Winds blew down from the clouds to help the fire get a sure start. Moments later it was a roaring blaze and in Hades, Patroclus, free at last, crossed over the Styx and onto the Elysian Fields.

Achilles does avenge Patroclus by killing Hector, turning over the body to Hector's aged father Priam, who prepared his son's dirge and funeral pyre. Achilles then confronted his own death in Apollo's temple, where Achilles had confided the secret to his immortality to Hector's sister Polyxena, and where her little brother Troilus had thrown himself against Achilles' sword when Achilles proved an obstacle in Troilus' possession of Helen, with whom the boy had fallen in love.

And while a dirge went up behind the city's gates, Achilles kept his rendezvous with the Three Fates. He wandered through the brilliant morning--fresh and still--up to Apollo's temple on the nearby hill. Heroic Patroclus had found eternal rest; valiant Hector had passed Mankind's conclusive test; and now the final retribution was required: the death of the young god that Peleus had sired. For wise Achilles had embraced a life of worth; his every act had been nobly planned from birth. The end of the well-trodden path was now in sight; he had to step from hallowed Life into dreadful Night. Within the temple came Polyxena's command: the time to pay back Troilus was now at hand. Her brother Paris was supplied the secret key, to bold Achilles' godlike immortality.

Achilles was before the altar to be blessed; where Troilus had fallen, he too would find rest. For lurking in the shadows of the temple's room, were the foul, treacherous phantoms that meant his doom. He knelt before the statue that was cold and grim; Had all the gods forgotten and abandoned him? He asked Apollo if he knew his fearsome name; behind him Paris raised his bow and took firm aim. Achilles was aware of the uncanny still; his body trembled as he felt a piercing chill. Then came a sudden noise that shattered the vile dark; the lethal arrow went directly to its mark. Apollo guided it to stunned Achilles' heel: no one could change Apollo's hard, unbending will. Achilles, son of Thetis, was abruptly killed; and his Destiny everlastingly fulfilled.

Courageous Nestor found the body lost to Sleep; he bent his head uncaring of who would see him weep. The Myrmidons conveyed their king away on shields; aloft, they carried him across the autumn fields. No more would great Achilles feel the sun's presence; no more would brave Patroclus know love's sweet essence; no more would noble Hector watch his children bloom: the tomb would hold all three in its eternal gloom. The gods beheld Achilles be consumed by fire; in Troy, old Priam put the torch to Hector's pyre. Over the plain two funnels of smoke filled the air; both nations fell upon their knees in mournful prayer. The gods from Mount Olympus saw the rising flames; in the immortal stars they carved the heroes' names. Then Zeus, their souls, to Heaven did finally commend; and the Age of the Demigods came to an end. (24)

Patroclus and Achilles

HARMODIUS AND ARISTOGEITON
514 B.C.

Hippias and Hipparchus, brothers, were joint dictators in Athens, having come to power following the death of their father Peisistratus, tyrant of Athens. Hipparchus fancied the wondrous Harmodius who refused his advances. To gain revenge, Hipparchus invited Harmodius' sister to take part in the Panathenaea Games, and then publicly refused her entry, accusing her of not being a virgin, a requirement for participation and insult because virginity was a marital necessity. Harmodius and his lover Aristogeiton decided to rid Athens of the dictatorship and thusly redeem the honor of Harmodius' sister. With daggers hidden in their chitons, the boys fell on Hipparchus at the foot of the Acropolis, stabbing him to death. Hipparchus' guards immediately killed Harmodius, and Aristogeiton was captured. While being tortured to reveal any coconspirators, Aristogeiton agreed to tell the truth if Hippias would promise him clemency, sealed with a handshake. When Hippias complied, Aristogeiton laughed at his having shaken the hand of his own brother's murderer. Hippias, mad with fury, thrust his dagger into Aristogeiton's throat.

A boy's chiton.

After the death of his brother, Hippias set up a more drastic form of dictatorship, the catalyst for his overthrown and the rise of the democratic reformist Cleisthenes. Harmodius and Aristogeiton were declared heroes and liberators, and countless statues were raised in their names, one of which was later captured by Xerxes who took it to Susa where Alexander the Great found it and returned it to Athens. The legend of the two boys, and the sanctity of their love, was of such importance that even in Roman times statues of them continued to be sculpted. Their ancestors received vast privileges, such as free meals and front-row theater seats (23).

Heroes Harmodius and Aristogeiton, killed by Hippias in 514 B.C. Aeschines, Herodotus, Thucydides and Demosthenes used them as examples of the beneficial effects of same-sex love, comparing both to Achilles and Patroclus.

LEONIDAS
Hero of the Battle of Thermopylae
480 B.C.

Leonidas
Golden Gate Historic Park, San Francisco
Sculpture by George Geefs

Spartan military training was the most vigorous since the advent of warfare, the result a people of such indomitable strength that their capital, Sparta, was without walls, as was Persian Persepolis, while in Athens fortifications not only encircled the city, but were extended to include the port of Piraeus. Yet despite the rigors, Spartan lovers were the most loyal in homoerotic history, equal to Thebans in devotion and intensity, Spartan discipline in no way lessoning the fervor of Spartan attachments. It was Leonidas, at the head of 300 Spartan lovers, men and their young companions, who so weakened the invading Persians at Thermopylae, headed by Xerxes, that Athenians under Themistocles and Aristides were able to decapitate them at Salamis. We owe the freedom we enjoy today to the men who halted the invading barbarians in 490 and 480 B.C.

Leonidas was co-king of Sparta. There were always two kings, one of whom had to remain home when the other left on military or diplomatic adventures. Kingship passed from father to son, but only to sons born after his father had been named king. The kings were priests who solemnized sacrifices, and supreme commanders of the army. In the field they had absolute power of life and death. The kings were aided by a council of 28, whose members were age 60 or over, an oligarchy chosen by the people but only from the ranks of the nobility. There was an assembly of citizens over age 30 who could only debate proposals offered by the kings or ephors, and voted by acclamation. The ephors, five in number, represented the people and made sure the kings protected the people's interests. Anyone could be elected ephor. In this way there were near-perfect checks and balances: the kings checked each other; the council represented the nobility and the assembly the people; and the ephors maintained correct rapport between the kings and their citizens. In time, only the kings and the ephors would count. Later still, it was the ephors who detained power, perhaps because the kings, competing against each other, were often in deadlock. Two ephors always accompanied the king who took the field. It was also they who decided foreign policy.

All of Sparta was a giant military camp. When a child was born it was washed in wine in the belief that this would fortify it. It was then examined. If found wanting, it was exposed on Mount Taygetus, in a chasm known as the apothetae. It was more common for boys than girls to be killed in this way, as boys had to be perfect. Trials for babies included bathing them in cold river water and exposing them to the elements, insuring that only the strongest would survive and procreate.

At age seven the survivors were trained to endure pain and hardships through incredibly difficult discipline, making them invincible and totally dedicated to the state. From the age of twelve they were watched over by older men who were their lovers, with whom they assuaged their passion where they could, outside the barracks. The young boys were obliged to request this form of friendship, entering into it totally voluntarily.

The Spartans never hung around oil or perfume shops as did Athenian youths, but in their extremely limited lifespan, says Plutarch, ''They at times relaxed from the severity of their training or even, as at Thermopylae, during times of war. Then they beatified their hair and clothing, prancing around like horses, a true delight to the eyes.''

An ephebe, boys who pranced about like yearlings, proud of their strength, beauty and virility.

The training center where the boys were enrolled at age seven was called the agoge (meaning ''rearing''). They lived in groups called herds, under the authority of whip-bearing older boys known as boy-herders. They were given a red cloak and told to make their beds out of reeds, pulled up by hand as they were not allowed knives. They were underfed as an encouragement to go foraging--stealing--food to supplement their diet. There was no obesity under the Spartans, and thanks to this early training they could sustain hunger when on military campaigns. They could enter a pedagogic relationship with older men at age twelve if they so chose, voluntary relationships in which the boys were sexually dominated, as older boys and men had to prove their strength and mastery in this practice as they did in all others, a bond that was both exceedingly intimate and yet known by all--there being no secrets in the barracks they shared. The boy was expected to endure the man's lust, although there were most probably moments of great tenderness among certain pairs. In exchange, the men made men of the boys, imparting that which was most precious to the boy, the men's knowledge. They learned enough math and reading to get by, and besides their daily training and hunting expeditions, they played ballgames and took up dancing and singing. At eighteen they became reserve members in the Spartan army and at age twenty they were voted into one of the messes by their peers, but all had to agree to their entry, a requisite that must have been an enormous incentive for them to prove themselves loyal comrades at all times. Incredibly, they were allowed ten years during which they could attempt to be admitted into a mess; if they failed to do so they were denied Spartan citizenship. At age thirty they could marry. Childbearing was certainly limited by the fact that they married late and then had to sneak into the women's quarters to do their duty, although they could, if they so chose, have a home where they could raise a family. As boys had only a slight degree of literacy, they were encouraged to develop their reading and oratorical skills if they become diplomats or generals later on.

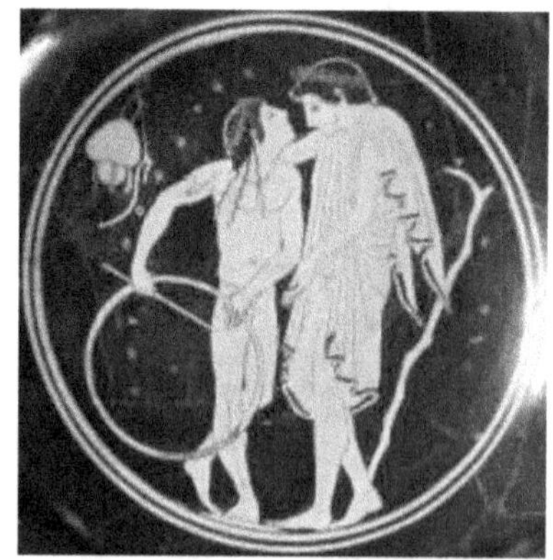

Belovèd and lover

In Athens and Sparta one had to be very careful in how one treated a citizen boy. There was a code that had to be respected before a lover could penetrate his belovèd. The lover had to show himself worthy, valiant, protective, a good teacher in terms of knowledge and the handling of arms. Gifts were appreciated: a new cloak, a chiton, a cup, a sword, a dagger, perhaps even body armor. While awaiting the moment for the boy to give himself completely, sex was mutual manipulation and intercrural (between the thighs), represented on vases, stated historian Kenneth Dover, as both standing ''bolt upright''.

The city-state was all-encompassing, and the people, wrote Plutarch, ''hadn't the time to live for themselves but like bees they slaved away for the benefit of the whole community.'' The Spartans had thusly engineered the most extreme militaristic society in recorded history.

Spartan women were trained like boys, and because they had to defend the city-state when the men were away, they were, paradoxically, better educated and better fed than other women in the Greek world, especially when compared to Athens that treated its women with Persian-style misogynic disregard, Athenian women there to cook and to bring forth boys. They were in the custody of their husbands, legally minors. A man caught having sex with them or any other woman in the household could be killed on the spot with total immunity. That men married in their late thirties and women married virgin when they were around 15, was an added incentive for boys to have sex among themselves.

If Spartan women couldn't produce offspring with their husbands, they bred for their country by being serviced by studs known for the fecundity of their seed. Husbands fully accepted this because they understood that they had to produce boys who would one day stand for them when they entered a room, as they now stood for their leaders.

A Spartan was a warrior from ages 20 to 60.

Most of what we know about Sparta comes through Xenophon who sent his sons there to be educated much as, today, a father sends his boys to a military academy in the hope that it will straighten them out. A Spartan boy had his admirers, who were many, and his lover, who was unique and with whom he exchanged emotive pledges. Nature being what it is, a boy may have wound up having many lovers, one at a time, and a lover many boys--*perhaps* one at a time. The boy then grew to become a man and took a boy, and the eternal cycle was repeated. It was good for a boy to have as many admirers as possible, good for his ego and for his future place in society, as each admirer would place a stone in the construction of the boy's ascendancy, all of which was good for his father's status too). The criteria were a beautiful face and a beautifully-made body, but these were often ephemeral in comparison to a boy's courage, intelligence, personality, charisma and sense of self-worth--not to mention his or his family's wealth and social status.

The boys crept out of their barracks to have intercourse with their wives, the stealthy stealing into the night firing the lust of their young, healthy loins, insuring the powerful inseminations that would bring forth sons of their own (who would one day, it has to be repeated, rise to their feet for them, as they now rose to their feet for their current commanders). The girls were said to have had shaved heads and to have worn cloaks like the boys. The men then returned to the barracks and their companions. Plutarch maintained that in many cases the men even had children before seeing what their wives looked like in daylight! Again, it's highly possible that this exceptional way of lovemaking--charging around in the dead of night like thieves--had been decided on in order to charge a boy's sexual libido to the maximum. Once they had children, Spartans could continue in this way or set up housekeeping in homes of their own. Sparta was a wild country of forests, meadows and mountains, all of which provided veils in acts of love and passion, although the usual sites for trysts between men and boys were just outside the barracks, gymnasia, training fields and campsites. As reported, a man too old to reproduce was obliged by law to get a young man whom he admired to do for his wife what he couldn't.

The Greek ideal.

Men impregnated boys but had to be discreet about it. The tyrant Periander was murdered because during a drinking bout he asked his belovèd, in front of numerous friends, whether by this time in their friendship the boy was not yet with child. The boy leaned over as if fiddling with his sandals, and when his lover bent to see what he was doing, he thrust his knife into his lover's chest. When word spread as to the reason he had acted as he did, he got off with the approbation of his peers, the other boys.

Xenophon describes a tender battle scene in which a certain Episthenes, seeing that a handsome enemy boy was about to be executed, ran to Xenophon and begged for the boy's life. Xenophon approached his general, Seuthes, in charge of Episthenes, to ask if the lad's life could be spared, as Episthenes had shown himself a valiant warrior. Seuthes asked

Episthenes if he would be willing to take the boy's place and be executed. Episthens stretched out his neck and told Seuthes to strike off his head. The boy rushed forward, dropped to his knees and begged that both their lives be spared. Episthenes rose and enfolded the lad in his arms, telling Seuthes that he would have to kill them or let them both go free. Seuthes laughed and, says Xenophon, winked at him. The story is certainly true as someone of Xenophon's value would never have recounted it otherwise.

A Spartan had no life of his own, he had no existential problems to solve, and who knows, perhaps there was something satisfying in the comradeship among men, knowing that when one awoke his day was planned, that he and his friends would eat, train and exercise together, march, sing and laugh in the fullness of men raised as brothers. Nothing to question, nothing to fear so long as they remained united. A visitor to their country must have been very surprised: an unwalled city of men and women who chose a healthy existence, one of bravery and simplicity, who followed the Apollonian ideal of moderation in all things.

Leonidas

At first Leonidas' mother didn't produce children. Her husband was therefore allowed to have a second wife, from whom came Cleomenes. The first wife then gave birth to a boy, followed by Leonidas. The children of Spartan kings who were eligible for the throne did not have to pass through the rigorous schooling of other Spartan boys, but because Leonidas was not considered as a possible heir to kingship, he was forced to go through the agoge like the other herds, a task which greatly hardened him and supremely prepared him for war. Then one brother died in Africa, another was declared insane and fled Sparta, which cleared the way for Leonidas come to power, one of the best-trained kings in Spartan history, and just in time, for Persian Xerxes crossed the Hellespont, at the head of an army of 2,000,000 (figures very *greatly*), bent on enslaving all of Hellas. Leonidas chose to lead 300 of Sparta's finest against Xerxes as Thermopylae, men and boys who had taken vows as lovers and belovèds, each of whom preferred death to a show of weakness.

The Spartans were convinced that Xerxes could be stopped at the hot sulfur springs called Thermopylae, a narrow pass between the sea and the mountains the Persians would be forced to go through on their way to Athens. King Leonidas went there at the head of the 300, as well as the forces of other allies. Leonidas knew it was a suicide mission, and when one of his friends murmured that the Persians would be so numerous that their arrows would block out the sun, Leonidas answered, ''Then we'll fight in the shade.

Xerxes' spies reported to him that the Spartans were exercising, bathing in the sea and caring for their hair. Xerxes asked a Spartan captive what was going on. He told the king that this was the Spartan way to prepare for death, and that the king should take care because the Spartan army was the greatest the world had ever known, for they were free men fighting freely. He added that the law was Sparta's only master, from which we have the incredibly moving Spartan epitaph known to every schoolboy, in honor of the 300: *Go tell the Spartans, stranger passing by, that here, obedient to Spartan law, we lie.*

Leonidas statue found at Thermopylae, along
with a full list of the Sacred 300.

The Persians at first held back, certain that the Spartans, seeing the enormous number of enemy troops, would end up fleeing. When they refused to budge, Xerxes sent an embassy to Leonidas, telling him that if he gave up his arms Xerxes would make him king of all of Greece. Leonidas answered, ''Come and get them yourselves!'' The Persians waited another five days before they finally attacked, their losses 20,000 men before withdrawing to lick their wounds, among them many of Xerxes' elite troops, the Immortals, while Spartans and their allies lost 2,500.

The Persians hesitated to make a further attempt until Leonidas was betrayed by a local, Ephialtes, who led the Persians along a mountain track that outflanked the Spartans. Aware of the hopelessness of his position, Leonidas dismissed the greater part of his troops, covering their escape with his 300. The Persians, still afraid of the Spartans and their remaining allies, shot thousands of arrows from a safe distance into the enemy ranks, killing them off one by one. When Leonidas fell, his men covered his body with their cloaks. When they too died, Xerxes had Leonidas beheaded and his body hung from a stake, to the eternal shame of the Persian king. The Persian troops then continued on to Athens, short of two of Xerxes' brothers who had been killed at Thermopylae, while Xerxes' ships sailed to Salamis … and the final countdown.

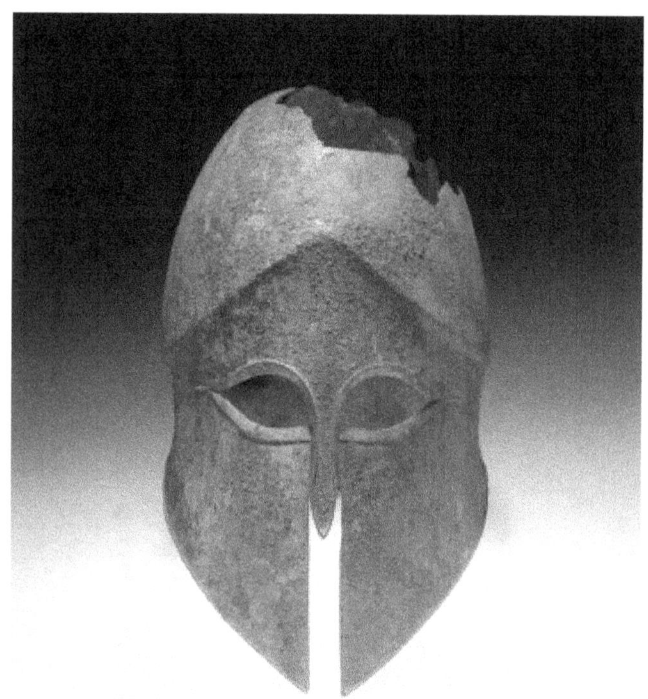

A Thermopylae helmet, a treasure from the hallowed 480 B.C. battle.

THEMISTOCLES – ARISTIDES – STESILAUS
The Battles of Marathon and Salamis
490 B.C. and 480 B.C.

As Xerxes approached Athens two leaders of unsurpassed importance to the Athenians were preparing for battle, battle against the king of the Persians and a battle against each other, for they both loved the same boy, Stesilaus of Ceos. The men were Themistocles and Aristides.

Themistocles grew up during the reign of Pisistratus. Pisistratus seized dictatorial power thanks to his influence over the poorer segments of the population. He was, in fact, the world's first known populist and as such popular. He did surprisingly well, putting Athens on the road to empire by taking certain islands and lands along the Hellespont, the most important being in Ionia on the western coast of today's Turkey. When he died his son Hippias, aided by his younger brother Hipparchus, took his place, their story, and that of Harmodius and Aristogeiton, recounted above.

Thanks to the intervention of the Spartan King Cleomenes, Hippias was forced to flee to the court of Darius in Persia. When Cleomenes suddenly went insane due to, some say, his fondness for taking wine Scythian-style--unwatered, he was replaced by Leonidas. Cleomenes then committed suicide by gnawing through his arms to his veins, following which, Plutarch tells us, his belovèd Panteus, ''the most beautiful and valorous youth in Sparta,'' killed himself out of faithfulness. Plutarch continues, ''When he found Cleomenes lying motionless, he gave him a push and, seeing that he could still knit his brows, he kissed him, and raised him. Holding the body next to him, he plunged his sword into his own breast.''

A lover's suicide

As a child, one of Themistocles' teachers told him, ''One day you will be great, but whether for good or for evil only the future will tell.'' He was known for his love of boys but also for ''honoring'' his wife, who produced numerous sons and daughters, one of which, his boy Neocles, died after being bitten by a horse. Before Themistocles rose to prominence, Cleisthenes took power. A democrat who introduced freedom of speech and action never known to the Athenians, he prepared the soil in which Themistocles grew to manhood. Cleisthenes introduced ostracism into Athens, something he hoped would reinforce democracy by allowing the Athenians, by a vote of 6,000 or more, to get rid of those they suspected of having tyrannical intentions. Themistocles would later misappropriate the system, using it to rid Athens and himself of his rival, Aristides, whose love for the boy they shared, Stesilaus, was becoming too invasive. But for the moment the reforms of Cleisthenes, says Plutarch, ''allowed Athenians to become a great power by according them the greatest equality and freedom of speech any other country had ever achieved.'' Themistocles used the new freedom, Plutarch continues, ''to become a first-class infighter, propagandist, always making himself visible to the people.'' He ''wooed the poor, courted the average Athenian in the taverns, on the docks and during his shopping in the markets. He canvassed as no politician before him, remembering the name of every man,'' says Plutarch. And the people loved him for it. He must have had a very common touch, because once any man rose even slightly above the masses, the Athenians, sooner or later, made him pay for it--often with his life.

The moment Themistocles gained power he put into movement the biggest ship-building project in the history of Athens, making the country a major naval force, placing it directly on the path to empire. Thanks to Themistocles Athens became a cornucopia and Athenians benefited from all the goods known to the known world. The Piraeus, Athens' port, was expanded and the walls that would eventually connect the city with its port were begun. In all of this Themistocles set a course for Athens that has made Greece the immense sea power it is today.

Then came the invasion of Greece by the Persian Darius and Athens turned to a man older and more experienced than Themistocles, the general Miltiades. Thanks to his decisiveness Athenian forces marched to Marathon, accompanied by 1,000 Plataeans. They should have been accompanied by Spartans, but the Spartans didn't participate because the Persians' arrival fell during one of their religious festivities. Before the battle Miltiades called on the memory of the lovers Harmodius and Aristogeiton to inspire the troops, saluting them as ''Athens' greatest heroes.'' The allies, a total of 10,000, engaged in a standoff against the Persians, numbering 20,000, until the Persian ships received a shield signal from a mysterious source beyond the beach, informing them that with Miltiades held down in Marathon, Athens itself was wide open. They therefore decided to leave. Seeing this, Miltiades attacked from the surrounding hills. His combined army slaughtered the Persians still on the coast, many of whom were bogged down in the coastal marshes, killing, according to Herodotus, 6,400. Miltiades lost 192 Athenians and Plataeans. The Athenians then ran back to Athens to warn the people of the arrival of the Persian fleet. When the enemy rounded Cape Sounion they saw the Athenians, in great numbers, coolly waiting to receive them. Darius gave orders to set sail for home.

The hallowed year of the Battle of Marathon was 490 B.C.

A youth present at Marathon.

No one knows the name of the traitor who sent the shield signal to Darius. But it was certainly not the Spartans who, arriving too late for battle, caught up with the Athenians left to guard the beach at Marathon. The Spartans examined the dead Persians, kicking them in verification. They congratulated their Athenian comrades, patted them on the back, told them ''well done'', and headed back to their mountain aerie.

In Athens Miltiades, after being so badly wounded in another campaign a year later when attacking Pyros that he would soon die, was dishonored by Athenians who charged him with treason for having let his injury stop him conquering Pyros. He was sent to prison where he died of gangrene. The great sculptor Phidias erected a statue in his honor, dedicated to Nemesis, whose role it is to destroy those who become too mighty. Incredibly, it is said that the Persians themselves built a marble memorial to Miltiades, in memory of Marathon!

Themistocles moved in to fill the vacuum left by Miltiades, but the nobility of Athens, perhaps tired of Themistocles' plebian ways, decided to nominate Aristides, a man all knew to be virtuous, honest and incorruptible, to confront him. Aristides' followers called him ''the just''. Plutarch maintains that the rivalry between Aristides and Themistocles took a bitter turn due to their adoration of the same boy. In Plutarch's words, ''They were rivals for the love of the beautiful Stesilaus of Ceos, and were passionate beyond all reason.'' The men fought over the boy by the intermediary of ships, Themistocles wanting more, Aristides wanting fewer. It ended in a close vote with the ostracism of Aristides, sent away from the city for ten years. Plutarch offers us a wonderful anecdote concerning what was, in reality, a referendum. An illiterate voter came up to Aristides whom he didn't know from sight and asked him to scratch the name of Aristides on the voting shard. When Aristides asked him how the man he was voting against had disappointed him, the voter replied, ''He didn't disappoint me but I'm sick and tired of hearing him always called 'the just.' '' Aristides duly inscribed his own name of the ballot.

The Persians returned, this time under Xerxes, at the head of 2,000,000 men, say some ancient historians. Following the death of Leonidas and the massacre of his troops at Thermopylae, Xerxes entered Athens which Themistocles had ordered evacuated, except for a group of warriors entrenched on the Acropolis. They held out for two weeks before being slaughtered. Xerxes landed men on the island of Salamis, telling them to kill the Greeks who would swim there once the Persians had sunk their ships, ships which were stationed in the bay of Salamis. Themistocles wanted the Persians to enter the bay, knowing that their less maneuverable vessels would be at a disadvantage there. To accomplish this, he sent his slave, Sicinnus, to the Persian camp to tell Xerxes that the Greeks, knowing they were outnumbered, would escape under darkness that night. He added that as the Athenians and Spartans hated each other, the Athenians had decided to go over to the great king's side.

The Persians thusly entered the bay and, as foreseen, hindered by their size and number, were boarded and their ships set afire. Defeated and fearing that the Athenians would sail to the Hellespont and destroy the pontoon bridges, thusly blocking his retreat, Xerxes made a mad dash back to Persia. The Athenian general Aristides, recalled from exile, sailed to the island of Salamis and massacred the Persians who were in wait to butcher them.

Afterwards the people only had eyes for Themistocles, but the Athenians were insatiably jealous of their heroes, and in this Themistocles did not help himself for, like Alcibiades, his life soon to be covered, he had the knack of making himself bigger than life. As Aristophanes put it, he farted higher than his ass. He was ostracized and died in exile, his life recounted in my book *Greek Homoexuality*.

As for Aristides, he died as he had lived, poor, honest and just.

And neither man got the boy. Stesilaus was, tragically, killed at Marathon.

ALCIBIADES
450 – 404 B.C.

The world loves a rogue, and there is no better example than Alcibiades. He was all things to those who crossed his path: intelligent, courageous, ambitious, eloquent in speech, charm personified, so handsome that it's the first adjective employed by biographers and historians alike, sexually versatile, the ideal top to men and women; he was totally amoral, as depraved as a teenager, as corrupt as a cop, as streetwise as a delinquent, as pampered as the son of a wallstreeter, as sexy as Brad Pitt; he was irreligious, treasonous, and the proof that the gods really do raise to dizzying heights those they wish to utterly destroy.

Today we have showmen, great orators, warriors and boys who are totally fearless. We have boys who are nearly superhuman in their beauty. There are arrogant boys, willful boys and, naturally, boys who's only interest is in themselves. There are lusty boys who live for sex, taking bodies and offering their own; boys who get off with girls, and boys who go with other boys or other boys and girls--the coalescence of it all in Alcibiades.

He sought ways to remain in the public eye, going so far as to cut off the tail of his dog, its most beautiful attribute. This caused the desired scandal among the Athenians to which he answered, ''Well, I got the attention I was looking for on the one hand, while taking their attention away from the really bad things I've been up to.''

Many men were thought to have slept with him as a boy, and every boy dreamed of his fine adolescent body nearing their own, his hand slipping beneath the chiton to pay homage to the lad's new juvenescence, grasping it while passing behind, the boy's silent assent obligatory before Alcibiades guided his tumescence between the thighs, just his thighs, a first release, a first compliance to later full--and fully consented--coition.

Once, when Alcibiades disappeared for over a week, Pericles' friends suggested that an alarm should be raised in order to find him. Pericles had been named the boy's guardian since the death of his father when the boy was ten. He now answered that if the lad were dead a general alarm would only find him a little earlier than if there were no alarm at all; if he were alive, on the other hand, the discovery that he had run away would only harm his reputation. Left unsaid was the certainty that if he had run away it was certainly with some man, as no woman could supply him--or would dare supply him--with the luxuries to which he was accustomed. When Alcibiades found out that his guardian, the most respected man in Athens, had defended him, he knew that from then on he could do exactly as he wished. ''For now on,'' he said to his companions, ''the Athenians can kiss my royal ass.''

Wrote Aristophanes in *The Birds*: ''You meet my son as he comes out of the gymnasium, all fresh from his bath, and you don't kiss him or fondle his balls.''
A boy's erect prong was a pleasant anchorage to grasp as a man reached around from behind.

Anytus, a rich lad, was very fond of him and invited Alcibiades to a meal among friends. Alcibiades arrived with companions but proceeded only to the dining room doorway from which he greeted Anytus and his guests, seated before a table with silver and gold tableware. Anytus was, asserts Athenaeus (who goes out of his way to do so), ''Alcibiades' lover.'' Alcibiades ordered his companions to gather up half of the tableware, after which he bade Anytus a good evening. When Anytus' friends, scandalized, asked what Anytus was going to do about the theft Anytus answered that, on the contrary, Alcibiades had shown great tenderness in not taking it all. As hope springs eternal in the human breast, Anytus certainly expected that Alcibiades would show other forms of tenderness at another time.

Alcibiades received gifts (or took gifts, as he did at Anytus' dinner) in exchange for love, the penalty for which, at certain times in Athens, was death. Athenian citizens could sell their bodies to whom they wished, but in doing so they could no longer benefit from the rights accorded to citizens. They could no longer speak before the Assembly. They could no longer use the courts for reparation should they in anyway be maligned. If they attempted to do so, they were in real danger of being stoned to death. All that was needed was for someone, anyway, to prove that the person had, at any time in his life, sold himself. A foreigner, on the other hand, someone who was not an Athenian citizen, could prostitute himself/herself without any juridical consequences of any sort. Many foreigners did so and perhaps the totality of male Athenians took advantage of their services at one time or another. When the boy Alcibiades left his bedroom at Pericles' home, it was to sleep with a man who had something to offer him, and the ''something'' in question was often money. Alcibiades, as a youth, was a high-class rent-boy who escaped punishment thanks to his guardian, Pericles.

Handsome lads were in great demand in Athens and as the competition to win their favors was fierce, it often cost their aspirants a small fortune, not to speak of the lengthy wooing. Life wasn't always easy for the boys either, as they couldn't show themselves too easy for fear of being treated as whores. Stringent laws tried to protect them, but it was clear that when boys wanted to amuse themselves, total surveillance was next to impossible. Foreigners and slaves could be put to death if they tried their hand at boy-love with Athenian citizens. Stringent punishment was reserved for teachers and trainers who had access to them in schools and gymnasiums, access forbidden to older boys over eighteen. Their fathers' male friends were especially carefully watched. If a guardian prostituted the boy he was supposed to protect, he could be stoned. If men couldn't get what they wanted from ''nice'' boys, there were always whorehouses. They flourished throughout Athens. The ones for boys had courts where the lads sunned themselves, naked, their wares in varying states of arousal. But whorehouses offered compensations. With ''nice'' boys, men often had to content themselves with intercrural sex, performed upright with the penis inserted between the thighs, while in whorehouses they could penetrate anally to their hearts' content. They could also get blown, otherwise a seemingly rare occurrence in antiquity.

Cruising areas at night were the market place, back streets, in cemeteries, along the quays of the Piraeus and in the Ciramicus--the potters' quarter, northwest of the Acropolis--as well as martial arts schools. Sex was mostly a hidden activity, although some amphorae and twin-handled cups show men fucking in groups in full view of other men.

Philemon (see Sources) tells us that the great lawgiver Solon, seeing that young men at times did very unlawful and foolish things due to their inability to find a sexual outlet, allowed prostitutes, male and female, to post themselves throughout Athens in front of their housing, totally naked so as not to fool the client. One paid one's obol and took one's pleasure. A person who sold himself could be used by the client in any way he wished, which is the definition of hubris, and therefore *presumably* against Athenian law.

For the Greeks making love to women was a source of pleasure, as was intercrural sex, full coition with both sexes, self-pleasuring, and circle-jerks were as common as boys pissing side by side.

Love between men has rarely been a long tranquil river. At times lovers fought, sword in hand, for the love of a boy. Plutarch tells us of Theron who chopped off his own thumb to show his love for his belovèd, and challenged a rival to do the same. Plutarch mentions, too, the case of Konon who killed himself, weary of the tasks imposed on him and never rewarded by a youth he wished to have as a belovèd.

Alcibiades had the image of Eros embossed on his shield that Athenaeus states was made of ivory and gold, leaving no doubt as to his amorous pretentions, to the loathing of virtuous Athenians. Having been brought up in the company of his guardian Pericles' friends--actors, statesmen, philosophers, as well as the whores Pericles frequented--there was little the boy didn't know and hadn't experienced from a very young age. The philosopher Bion suggests that he had indeed begun early on: ''Even as a child he made men unfaithful to their wives, and as a young man he made women unfaithful to their husbands.'' Aristophanes tells us in *The Frogs*, ''They love him and hate him, but cannot do without him.'' He wrote another play, lost, entitled *The Man with Three Dicks,* in which Alcibiades' erotic exploits were satirized. Alas, we know not in what way.

Statues of Hermes, god of travelers, were erected at crossroads. Their particularity was a fully engorged phallus with ample foreskin. As crossroads were places of encounter, the phalli took on erotic signification. Boys looking for adventure would stroke them for luck, girls searching for husbands did likewise, and women wanting children made pilgrimages to the sites--in fact, the phalli were polished to a luster. During the night preceding an expedition to capture Sicily, Hermes' phalli throughout Athens were vandalized, most probably by drunken pranksters, exactly the milieu frequented--and most often led--by Alcibiades, a youth known by all for his brilliant intellect and total absence of morality. As during our own times, in ancient Athens too people were unduly respectful of those of high birth and affluence, the reason they were reluctant to attack Alcibiades head on. The destruction was also heresy, as Hermes was an Olympian god. And it was the worst possible omen prior to a military enterprise. But there was a strong possibility that Alcibiades would escape punishment thanks to his connection with Pericles and his immense wealth.

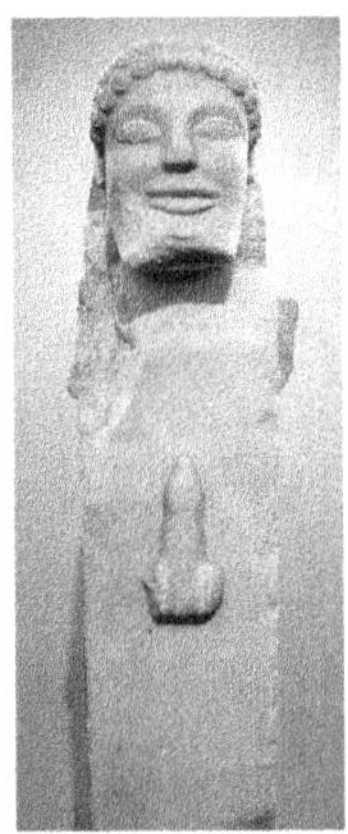

Hermes at the crossroads

The problem with Sicily began in 415 B.C.--the 17th year of the Peloponnesian war--when a delegation from the island came to tell Athenians that the time was ripe for them to conquer Syracuse, the most important city-state on Sicily. The people of Syracuse were ethnical Dorians, as were the Spartans, whereas the members of the delegation from the much smaller city-state of Segesta were ethnical Ionians, as were the Athenians. Syracuse, the island's principal city, was about the size of Athens. It was rich and the island richer. Its capture would supply Athens with immense wealth, resources and more wheat than Athens would ever need. Sicily was the breadbasket of the Greek world, as, later, Egypt would be for the Romans.

Alcibiades wanted to go to war and soon he had the Athenians on their knees, drawing sketches of the island in the sand, each vying to place the major island towns in their right places. Men and boys were forming lines to join up as members of the expedition, certain that they would reap gold through sacking the palaces and homes of the rich inhabitants. The delegation from Segesta arrived with 60 talents of silver (a talent weighed 26 kilos) and plates of solid gold. In addition, they declared that their temples and citizens possessed a treasure in solid gold vessels. The Athenians sent a delegation to assure itself that this was so; the members returned with smiles on their faces. This turned the heads of the Athenians, and especially that of the handsome Alcibiades who was always in need of lucre.

When the Athenian noble Nicias saw that Alcibiades had stirred up the blood of Athenians hungry for war and the riches reaped through war, he threw in his support, so long as he was named general and the size of the fleet and the number of warriors involved in Alcibiades' plan were at the very least doubled, thereby giving Athens a chance at success. He did warn his friends, however, to beware of Alcibiades who would one day endanger Athens in order to live a brilliant life of his own.

When the full Athenian force did finally arrive in Sicily, it discovered that the solid gold brought to Athens by the Segestaeans was only silver plated with gold, and the solid gold vessels the expedition had seen at Segesta had only been the same vessels passed from house to house and from temple to temple!

Alcibiades wanted to be judged for the crime against Hermes before setting sail for Sicily, aware that during his absence his enemies, were he not judged, would do what was necessary to turn heads and buy votes. After all, the penalty for heresy was death, Athenians as serious about offending the gods as were Europeans, later, under the Inquisition. Had his request to be judged before setting sail been accepted, he would have certainly been acquitted for the simple reason that the Athenians needed him for their intervention. But the request was refused, and he prepared to leave for Sicily as co-general with Nicias at the head of what Thucydides said was the greatest armada ever raised by a single Greek state, 134 triremes and a far greater number of smaller ships, as well as 30,000 men. Diodorus Siculus recounts that all of Athens--inhabitants, friends, lovers and children--traipsed behind the warriors as they made their way to the Piraeus, singing and waving fronds. The ships bobbing in the harbor had been fully decked out with banners, flags and pennants, their sides covered with the shields of all the participating countries, those furnishing soldiers or money. Perfume burners and fires in bronze vessels consumed incense in such quantity that the air was misty with it. Lovers kissed their friends goodbye and the boys went off to their fates.

Just after arrival at the island of Sicily, a ship, the *Salaminia*, came from Athens demanding that Alcibiades return to stand trial for the destruction of the Hermes' statues. Judging from the behavior of the emissaries sent to bring him back, Alcibiades knew what awaited him at home. He knew that the Athenians had perfected the art of using men for their own benefit, but that they would then humble and chasten them when the men became too powerful or too well known. This was a highly dangerous move on the part of the Athenians because the army and sailors favored Alcibiades, who had an uncanny way of winning over the men under his command; the Athenians therefore treated him with kid gloves, promising anything to get him aboard. Otherwise, they knew, the whole army would mutiny. Besides the army's love for him, the soldiers also felt that under someone indecisive like Nicias the war could drag on for an eternity, with no riches, as Alcibiades had promised, at the end. Alcibiades agreed to return but on his own ship.

Unknown to all, his true destination was Sparta. A Spartan nurse had cared for Alcibiades and had instilled the love of Sparta in the child's heart. Also, his family had had traditional connections with Sparta. When a Spartan delegation came to Athens in search of a peace agreement in 421 Alcibiades, thanks to his family, enjoyed privileged access to the ephors. Alcibiades didn't waste time in seducing the Spartans. He wore their coarse clothes, bathed in cold water, ate their disgusting broths, drank their inferior wines, and fucked their women, one of whom was King Agis' wife who bore Alcibiades' son Leotychides. Alcibiades counted on Leotychides to found a new Spartan race of Alcibiadesian origin. It didn't help matters much when Agis' wife went around calling her baby Alcibiades, the name she preferred to Leotychides. Alcibiades could play the role of the perfect Spartan, Plutarch tells us, because he was the perfect chameleon--all things to all men, displaying virtue or vice as the occasion called. It must have been marvelous to observe his technique because men really liked and appreciated him, and being a man's man is not an easy task. Plutarch goes on to say that in Sparta he devoted himself to athletic exercises; in Ionia he enjoyed the luxury of the baths, oiled and perfumed, at ease with the fondling of both sexes; in Thrace he drank to the dregs among the dregs; in Thessaly he awed all with his horsemanship; and in Persia he exceeded even the Persians in magnificence. He was thusly accused of playing a double game, but men have been known to willfully march to more than just one tune without having treacherous motives.

Alcibiades' sex with Spartan men would have been rapid and carnal, but with a Spartan boy he would have taken advantage of a hunting expedition when, sheltered probably by a rocky outcropping, he would have lain alongside the lad, both enrobed in the traditional wine-red Spartan cloak. He would have pressed his cloth-enclosed erection against the other's buttocks, perhaps occasionally reaching around to caress the lad through the folds of wool. At no time would skin come into contact with skin. Alcibiades would have ejaculated in this way, into the fabric. The boy too would have ejaculated thanks to the pushing of his penis against the tissue and rocky surface, or he would have brought himself off with his own hand, hidden in the folds of his own cloak. In this way historians have attempted to bring understanding to the multiple texts on the subject, each vague and contradictory, about how men had sex with young boys they called striplings. As usual with Sparta, nothing was ever crystal clear, even if common sense nods towards Spartan lads as randy as their Athenian counterparts, the sex, in reality, as rough as the Spartans themselves.

Alcibiades had been sentenced to death when he hadn't returned to Athens, and now he was again sentenced to death, this time by the cuckolded Agis. It seems that Agis had no difficulty in believing the rumors of his wife's unfaithfulness simply because for a period of ten months that followed an earthquake--the magnitude of which had scared him out of his wits while copulating with her--he hadn't dared approach her again. Leotychides had been conceived during this time. Luckily Alcibiades was forewarned, giving him an opportunity to flee to his supreme enemy's camp: the Persian Tissaphernes.

Tissaphernes was the governor (called a satrap) of the western part of Phrygia, Lydia and Caria, a diplomat, a general and a key advisor to King Darius II. And he was right up Alcibiades' alley in the sense that he too was a lover of guile, an admirer of rogues, as well as being wonderfully subtle. He was also 40, an age during which a man especially appreciates a boy's beauty, and a boy a man's. And there was no one more beautiful and intelligent than Alcibiades, possessor of behavior so smooth it anesthetized the Persians into believing everything he said. In fact, Tissaphernes named his most beautiful garden, containing streams and meadows, pavilions and baths, Alcibiades Park, the name it was referred to ever after, a pleasure retreat both men shared during Alcibiades' sojourn. The situation was indeed remarkable as Tissaphernes loathed the Greeks for the disaster they wrought on Darius I and Xerxes. He was also, Plutarch says, psychopathic and perverse. Yet he ended up flattering Alcibiades even more than Alcibiades--an expert--flattered him. Thucydides wrote that the real reason for Alcibiades' treason was the hope that the Athenians would, in desperation, recall him.

And this was a possibility as things were going very wrong for Athens. Inaction on the part of Nicias and his advisors gave the Sicilians time to build more ships and rearm. They were not accomplished sailors, far less so than the Athenians, but they were fighting for their lives and survival as a people, an incredibly strong incentive. During a first naval battle at Plemmyrion, a harbor very chose to Syracuse, the Athenians fought in a restricted space unfit for their large vessels but perfect for Syracuse's smaller ships. Reinforcements promised by Athens arrived late, held up by storms, after the Syracusans had inflicted great damage. Athenian land forces then tried to capture a Syracusan fort atop a cliff overlooking the harbor. When this failed the attackers tried to withdraw, which caused panic among those still climbing upwards. Men lost their footing and attempted to cling to what they could after flinging away their spears and shields. Most fell to their deaths, a reported 2,000 in all.

Nicias met with his advisers who all advised withdrawal back to Greece. But Nicias, perhaps fearful of the consequences when he confronted the citizens of Athens, perhaps suffering from the Trojan complex--he and his men called women as the Trojans had been when they lost their city-- decided to carry on. Alas, no one had the authority to stop him. He did decide, however, to abandon the Plemmyrion harbor. But before he could, an external event made him change his mind, which is sad because had he done so, he would have escaped with his life and ships. But Nicias was a superstitious man who believed in signs and omens. One such sign was a full eclipse of the moon, an omen that seemed to indicate that he should remain where he was. This gave the Syracusans time to block the entrance of the harbor with every ship and floating vessel at their disposal, all linked by heavy chains. On the hills surrounding the harbor local villagers turned out to watch from an incomparable bird's-eye view. Over the days that followed they saw one side win the battle, only to be undone the next day; the Athenians on board the ships cried victory one moment, while moaning their defeat the next. In the end the Athenians abandoned their ships in favor of an escape overland. But again Nicias changed his mind. This too was sad because historians believe that had they set off immediately, Nicias and his men would have been able to make their way, on foot, to Sicilian colonies that were still in their corner. But Syracusan spies infiltrated Nicias' ranks, telling the soldiers that the roads leading away from the harbor were blocked, and that they would do well to prepare themselves before confronting the enemy. This they believed and remained a day too long, the time needed for the Syracusans to really block the passages out. The Athenians had thusly to fight their way through the enemy, which caused damage in the ranks, but the worst destruction was reserved for laggards, consisting of the weak, the wounded and the sick. As usual on the battlefield, dysentery was a mortal enemy, emptying the body of its substance in the most despicable fashion known to men.

Nicias finally sued for peace, offering to pay the stupendous sum of a talent per man spared, a sum that would be guaranteed by Athens, putting the city-state in debt for years to come. The Syracusans refused, and the Athenians continued their death march. Hungry and dying of thirst, they made their way to the river Assinaros, one that would have a dreaded reputation for all time. Here the Athenians literally climbed over each other to gain access to the stream, while Syracusans, catching up with them on horseback, slaughtered them with arrows and spears from the banks, but even then the men drank water muddy and red with blood. The survivors were rounded up and sold into slavery, most of whom were sent to stone quarries where they disappeared from history. The lucky ones, those who were handsome, were handed over as sexual slaves, and there is at least a chance that they were well treated. Nicias, whom the Syracusans held responsible for the misery and death of so many Sicilian warriors, was tortured in the most miserable fashion, says Thucydides without going into detail, before his throat was slit. The Syracusans had been forced to fight for their survival, and as such must certainly not be blamed for wanting to keep their freedom. So content were they that from then on, each and every year, they organized festivities in honor of their victory, festivities known as the Assinarian Games.

Back in Athens the women went on the world's first sex strike, hoping to force the men to make peace before making love. But Greece being Greece (at that time, at least), this was hardly a hardship. There's an anecdote that comes down to us through a play by Aristophanes, *Lysistrata*. One of the women in the play, who had taken part in the sex strike, now complained about how impossible it was to get sex once a woman was old: "It's the same with men," a man answers. "Not at all," the woman continues. "Any grey-haired man can pick up a young girl, but a woman's season is short." (She didn't foresee the advent of cougars.)

It was at this moment that Alcibiades chose to reenter the scene. He sent negotiators to Samos to inform the Athenians stationed there with their fleet that he could arrange an alliance with Tissaphernes who was at the moment in favor of the Spartans. But Tissaphernes wanted an end to Athenian democracy, favoring an oligarchy headed by Alcibiades--whom Tissaphernes trusted--instead. The Athenian population on the island, believing themselves every bit as qualified to represent Athenians as were the Athenians in Athens, decided to forgive Alcibiades--with, perhaps, the ulterior motive that he would still be able to bring Tissaphernes over to their side, a sentiment that Alcibiades encouraged. The Athenian general Thrasybulus, stationed at Samos, was sent to bring Alcibiades to Samos where he was made general. The island was known for its beautiful boys, one of whom was sought out by all generals and politicians passing by. He was Bathylle and the poet Anacreon had his portrait painted, giving these instructions to the artist: "And between his charming, incendiary thighs, paint a noble member that aspires to be loved."

The men on Samos adored Alcibiades as he had been adored wherever he set foot. Right off the bat he won a series of victories so grand that the soldiers and sailors felt exalted and glorified. And Plutarch goes on: "The army directly under him felt so superior to the other soldiers that they wouldn't mix with them." He added that, "While others had known defeat, Alcibiades' men were invincible." Although Thrasybulus was responsible for many victories, "it was always Alcibiades," says Cornelius Nepos, "not Thrasybulus, who reaped the glory, thanks to his golden rhetoric and natural gifts." Luckily, a little later Alcibiades' superheroes found themselves in difficulty during another battle, and were saved by the rabble soldiers they had thumbed their noses at. The result was that they all kissed and made up, and had a huge barbeque during which bread and meat were thrown around, from one man to another, as a sign of friendship.

As general, Alcibiades led his ships into the Hellespont to gather money and sailors. He went from victory to victory, doing wonders for Athenian morale. Soon Alcibiades was Athens' uncontested leader. Before he personally returned to his homeland he sent his troops into the city to tell of his glorious victories, thereby assuring his triumphal arrival. Only then did he bring captured Spartan galleys into the Piraeus, loaded with spoils, bedecked with dancers, lyre players and drummers, his own ship rigged with his signature purple sails--the indisputable hero of his people. He made his way to the Acropolis through throngs of delirious well-wishers. Cornelius Nepos goes on to tell us that he gave a speech in which he blamed the Fates for his troubles, and not the Athenians, now shedding tears, who had nonetheless sentenced him to death. (The hypocrisy was, of course, mindboggling, but as usual he knew exactly what he was doing.) He emphasized the fact that he had influence over Tissaphernes who promised, said Alcibiades, to make sure that Athens and Athenians never lacked for food or money, even if it meant that he, Tissapernes, ''ended up selling his own bed.'' He was applauded, his estates were returned, and priests annulled the curses aimed at him. From here on the Athenians went from victory to victory until the entire Hellespont was theirs. Alcibiades was given complete charge over the war and carte blanche in any attempt to come to terms with Persia. But victory is an unfaithful mistress.

Alcibiades returned to Samos and tried to engage the Spartans, but they were too wary of his power. They bided their time until he went off to the Hellespont to again gather money and additional soldiers. The Spartan navy chose that moment to strike and win a series of battles. Alcibiades lost the backing of Athens, and rather than lose his life too, he retreated to a castle in Thrace that he had had the forethought to construct. The Athenians still outnumbered the Spartans in ships and tried to engage them in the Hellespont, in view of Alcibiades' fortification. The Athenians anchored in the harbor of Aegospotami, the Spartans at Lampsacus. Soon a daily routine set in. Day after day the Athenians would sail from Aegospotami to Lampsacus, but the Spartans always refused to leave their protective harbor to fight. The Athenians would then sail back to Aegospotami where they would disembark for a leisurely meal on the shore and horse around as boys and men are like to do at the beach. One day Alcibiades left his lair and came down to warn the leaders that they should be more on the lookout, and the army far more disciplined. The Athenians gazed on Alcibiades, atop his horse, his purple robe open to the navel, his skin oiled, his hair and beard carefully curled, and shook their heads in wonder at this man who had lorded it over Athens since his childhood, and who was now in self-exile. Some knew him, some knew him even very well. For them all, this was just Alcibiades being Alcibiades. They thanked him because it was conceivable he would live to reign again over them all. He rode away, his long robe spread over the horse's ass.

When the Spartans felt that the time was ripe, they set sail for Aegospotami where they attacked the Athenian forces, asleep in the shade of the afternoon sun. There was no battle. The men on shore scurried into the hinterland and those on the ships surrendered. Of the 180 vessels present, only 20 got away. Four thousand boys and men, then and there, had their throats cut, depriving them of their lust and their beauty and their already far-too-short lives.

Alcibiades, who had been deified a few short months before by the Athenians, was now, after the defeat, vilified for his arrogance and general depravity. The people knew about his castle on the Hellespont and hated him for it, wondering why such a fortification had been deemed necessary and how much of Athens' treasury its walls protected. The castle was located in Thrace, a land known for its barbarians. There, Alcibiades had his own private army which he used to despoil his neighbors. Cornelius Nepos tells us that, as in all the other countries Alcibiades had lived, in Thrace too he had seduced the local louts, drinking them under the table and screwing among what Thracians considered their nobility, as well as among the dregs. But as there is no honor among thieves, as soon as the Thracian brigands learned that the Athenians and the Spartans were set on Alcibiades' death, they began to plunder his wealth, daring him to do anything about it. He fled into the interior of Thrace but as the robbery of his possessions continued, he finally sailed back to Persia, to the satrap Pharnabazus. Bewitched by Alcibiades, now forty, who had lost none of his charm and little of his beauty, and who had known kings, princes, and generals, Pharnabazus offered him not only shelter but also the revenues from the town of Grynium. Believing he could do better, Alcibiades decided to see the great king himself, Artaxerxes II at Susa. He also knew of Lysander's contacts with Cyrus the Younger, and the attempts of both men to replace Artaxerxes with Cyrus. He felt he could advise Artaxerxes on how to avoid being overthrown by his younger brother, and how to avoid mounting problems with Sparta. Perhaps fearing that Alcibiades would enthrall Artaxerxes as he did Pharnabazus himself, Pharnabazus refused to help Alcibiades in his quest to travel to Susa. The Athenian left anyway. Lysander learned of his departure and informed Pharnabazus that if Alcibiades were not handed over alive or dead, Sparta would end all collaboration with Persia. Lysander, in turn, was being pressured by the oligarchy he had set up in Athens, men whose survival depended, they felt, on eliminating Alcibiades as a future menace to their very survival.

Alcibiades put in at a town along the way to Susa and, wanting company for the night, Cornelius Nepos tells us, took a young Arcadian, a loyal friend, to bed. Pharnabazus' men had followed him and very silently heaped brush around the habitation, which they then set on fire. Awoken by the light and crackling of the blaze, and guessing at its origin, Alcibiades flung his Spartan-style cloak around his left arm and took up his sword in his right hand. He and his friend threw as much clothing as possible on the blaze, making a narrow passage through the flames. They leaped through a window and, naked, confronted men who immediately backed away. But they were outnumbered, and even from a distance many of their enemies' numerous spears and arrows hit their marks. Dead, Alcibiades was decapitated and his head bagged for Pharnabazus. His companion for a night, younger and faster, managed to escape.

But Plutarch maintains that Alcibiades had been killed by the brothers of a girl whom Alcibiades had seduced, and so his death had nothing to do with either Lysander or Pharnabazus. Both Nepos and Plutarch agree on what followed: Another friend, a whore, Timandra, found the headless body that she wrapped in his Spartan cloak and had cast into the blaze, a pyre less worthy than that built for Achilles, Patroclus and Hector (10).

Exactly like the Sparta he loved and admired, Alcibiades is one of the strangest, most original, most enigmatic creatures to have adorned the Earth. Lustful, intelligent and beautiful, even in boyhood his admirers had made him aware of every erogenous zone on his body, far in advance of the friends his age. He knew human nature and weaknesses thanks to his enlightened guardian Pericles, whose home and bed were replenished by his whore mistress, Aspasia, and whose salon was graced by the greatest philosophers and dramaturges the world has known. Just as importantly he allowed his body to serve, valiantly in battle, erotically in sex. Charm, class, a come-hither regard that could stagger, an orator capable of enthralling an assembly, a manliness that inspired other men, a self-confidence that won over diamond-in-the-rough Spartans and cynically jaded Orientals. People were truly fond of him, they genuinely liked to be around him, and so exquisite did he know himself to be that when Socrates chose *not* to lie with him, he honestly admired the philosopher's unfathomable restraint before such perfection. In the whole world I can only think of the Florentine Lorenzo *Il Magnifico* who comes close, if one can make abstraction of beauty and military expertise, in which Lorenzo was lacking (4).

EPAMINONDAS AND PELOPIDAS
Founders of the Sacred Band of Thebes
371 B.C.

The Sacred Band of Thebes destroyed the Spartan army in 371 B.C., the first army to ever do so. The Spartans had been victorious against the Persians and had brought Athens to its knees during the Peloponnesian Wars. And now a group of Thebans destroyed its power forever. The cause of the war between the Spartans and Thebans was Spartan domination over a people that wanted its freedom, a people who had had enough of Spartans ever trying to force them into forming an oligarchy. The Thebans elected a general, Epaminondas, to confront them at the town of Leuctra. The outcome swung back and forth until Epaminondas gave the signal for his lover, Pelopidas, to enter the fray at the head of the Sacred Band, lovers and their belovèds, who would unhesitatingly fight to the death rather than show themselves cowards in front of their comrades, and, especially, before he who had been chosen as a life companion. The Thebans allowed the Spartan survivors to leave with their dead, including their king, Cleombrotus, and then raised a trophy to their victory. But here the real victory was not over the Spartans, the veritable victory was the loyalty and friendship--the pledge of eternal love--begun years prior when Epaminondas had met the young, handsome and valiant Pelopidas, a truly unique figure in Greek history. Born rich and dedicated to attaining the summits in athletics, Pelopidas squandered the family fortune on Theban poor. Plutarch tells us that when criticized for dilapidating his wealth, reminding him that money was a basic necessity, Pelopidas pointed to a blind and crippled pauper and said, ''Yes, it's necessary for him.'' He himself ate the simplest of foods and wore the plainest clothes. He rejoiced in the hardships of physical and militaristic training which took place in an atmosphere of soldierly friendships.

Epaminondas not only won at Leuctra, he and Pelopidas then entered the Peloponnese where they set free the Messenian helots, after generations of slavery. Naturally, Messenia became Thebes' most loyal and most grateful supporter (21).

The idea for the Sacred Band had been Pelopidas'. He modeled it after his friendship with Epaminondas, 150 lovers and 150 belovèds, men and boys who would never shy away from death if it meant betraying his lover's or his belovèd's faith in him. Polyaenus describes the Sacred Band as being composed of men "devoted to each other by mutual obligations of love" and Plato describes a lover as being ''a friend inspired by god.'' The Theban general Pammenes had criticized Nestor of Trojan War fame when he organized his troops by tribe and clan and not by lovers and belovèds because, says Plutarch, ''Friendship grounded in love is never to be broken and is invincible, since lovers and belovèds, to avoid shame, will rush into danger to rescue one another.'' The perfect example was given during the Battle of Leuctra when one of the Sacred Band, ambushed, asked his enemy to run him through at the breast so that his lover would not blush at seeing a wound to the back. The Sacred Band never sought death for itself. To the contrary, they entered battle protected with armor and armed with the finest weapons. They spent their days in the palaestra training and learning strategy, but also in philosophy and singing and dancing. There was much discussion on tactics, a science Epaminondas was already famous for. Their bodies were sleek, oiled and kept clean by their companion who scraped the oil from the toned muscles with a strigil. They sweated in huts warmed by fired stones over which they splashed water. Plato tells us that ''love between males was so special in Thebes that it was illegal for anyone to maintain that sex between men was *not* beautiful.'' The Sacred Band was stationed on the Acropolis. Their service started at around age twenty and ended around age thirty. Pelopidas turned them into shock troops whose main function was killing enemy leaders by any means possible, thereby crippling the enemy by depriving it of its head.

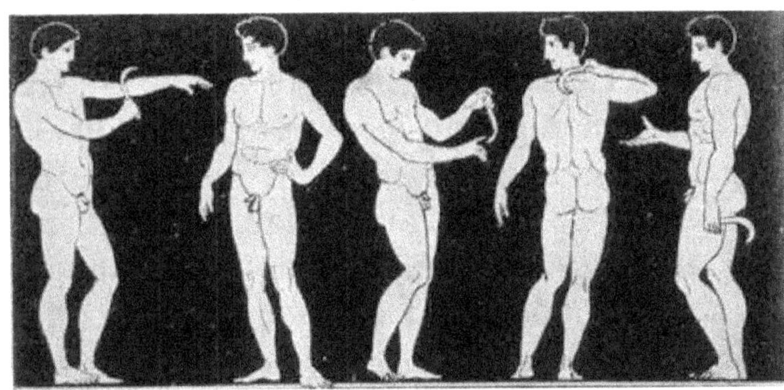

Athletes using a strigil.
During the Battle of Leuctra one of the Sacred Band, ambushed, asked his enemy to run him through at the breast so that his lover would not blush at seeing a wound to the back.

We know this about the Theban Pammenes, who had criticized Nestor as mentioned above. When Philip of Macedon was a boy he was sent to Thebes and placed under the care of the great general Pammenes, an ardent boy-lover, who immediately reserved the young and willing prince for his bed. Years later, when Philip was king of Macedon, his general Pausanias came to him with the complaint that he had been forcefully sodomized. Pausanias felt that he had the king's ear because they too had been lovers when young. Pausanias claimed that he had had relations with a boy who killed himself when Pausanias threw him over for another. The boy's former lover, a certain Attalus, decided to wreck vengeance on Pausanias by inviting him to a banquet, during which he forcefully raped Pausanian after getting him drunk. Pausanias hoped that King Philip would avenge the outrage by killing Attalus. But Attalus was both an essential general in Philip's army and the uncle of Philip's wife. So to placate Pausanias, Philip named him to his personal guard, affording Pausanias the proximity he needed to drive a dagger into Philip's chest-- thus opening the way for Philip's son, the Great Alexander. Pausanias, in turn, was cut down by Philip's guard. History can be crueler still: The Sacred Band liberated Thebes from Spartan domination and won its freedom until it was totally destroyed by Alexander, he who was said to have known defeat only once in his life, when confronting the thighs of his lover Hephaestion.

Cicero called Epaminondas "the first man of Greece." Centuries later Montaigne named Epaminondas one of three of the world's "worthiest men," the other two being Homer and Alexander the Great. We know of Epaminondas and Alexander's preferences, but nowhere in Homer's writings does he mention male-male relations. Most aspects of Epaminondas' reputation have been lost due to the fact that just a score of years after his passing Alexander obliterated Thebes, thusly destroying his and Pelopidas' heritage. He is also less known because we have, thanks to Plutarch, the life of Pelopidas, while that of Epaminondas was lost. But we do have traces of his past due to Cornelius Nepos and Diodorus Siculus. As a boy he favored wrestling, running and prowess in the handling of weapons. What the poets call the defining moment of his life occurred during the Battle of Mantinea, in 385 B.C., an earlier battle when Thebes fought on the side of Sparta. Here he saved Pelopidas' life. Epaminondas had noticed the boy in camp, and later he came upon him during the fighting, slumped on the ground amid the bodies of his comrades, apparently dead, as his body had been pierced in six places by sword and spear thrusts. Epaminondas now stood his ground above him, he too receiving wounds to the chest by a spear and on the arm by a sword. He in turn was saved by the Spartan king Agesipolis who arrived in the nick of time with his men. Times change as do alliances and Thebes found itself fighting innumerable skirmishes against the Spartans until the city-state was forced to bend to Spartan will. The Spartans occupied the Acropolis and set up a puppet regime but, incredibly, allowed Epaminondas to remain because he was poor and the Spartans equated his poverty with impotence. Other Thebans had been forced to leave, among them Pelopidas. Both men, one inside and one outside, now prepared those around them for a revolt against the Spartans. When ready, Pelopidas led his men into the city where, with the aid of his lover, they killed the city's governing body in their beds. They then set siege to the Acropolis. The Spartans, in a rare move for them, agreed to surrender if they could leave with their lives. This was granted and Thebes was again free. The victory was especially important because, for the first time, Sparta was seen as being assailable.

Epaminondas and Pelopidas then went to the shrine of Iolaus where they offered up thanks, Iolaus a member of the Argonauts and one of

Heracles' numerous lovers (29). The gymnasium in Thebes was called the Iolaus and athletic games to the boy were known as the Iolaeia. Plutarch states that men and their belovèds exchanged sacred vows of love at the shrine of Iolaus. And according to Aristotle, same-sex couples ''invoked his name to guarantee their oaths of faith and to punish faithless lovers.'' The lives of both men are fully covered in my book *Sparta*.

Epaminondas and Pelopidas, heroes who saved Thebes from the bondage of Sparta.

An epigram on a tombstone, concerning the Sacred Band, has been recently found with this inscription: ''Direct your arrows, dear Eros, at these bachelors, that, bold in the love they share they will defend their fatherland, for your arrows fire boldness and of all the gods you, Eros, are supreme at exalting front-line champions.''

ALEXANDER AND HEPHAESTION
356 – 323 B.C.

In 343 B.C. Philip II invited Aristotle to his court to give instruction to Alexander, age 13, and his inseparable companion Hephaestion, both boys born the same year, 356. Aristotle considered Hephaestion a far more assiduous student than Alexander and noted that Alexander shared all his secrets with the boy who was ''by far his dearest friend.'' As they were the same age they most probably shared each other's bodies in equal measure, neither one being predominantly the lover or the beloved, a couple open to other companions, underlined by Athenaeus who stated that Alexander ''had a boundless passion for beautiful boys.'' Physical relief from puberty, in the absence of girls whose virginity was kept intact in order to arrange marriages of social status and wealth, took all forms, the boys' love historically compared that of Achilles and Patroclus.

Alexander and Hephaestion, warriors and heroes of not only their times, but of all times.

Aristotle taught his students the art of medicine as he himself had been instructed before his father's early death, instruction that continued afterwards thanks to other members of his family who wanted to see Aristotle follow in his father's steps. Alexander always carried a copy of Homer's *Iliad* that he kept under his pillow with his dagger. Dionysius of Halicarnassus informs us that Alexander, Hephaestion and their companions were Aristotle's pupils for eight years. One has the impression that Alexander's mind was incredibly mobile, flashing from one philosophy to another, shifting from tutor to tutor, idea to idea, as he did sexually from boy to boy, although Hephaestion was most assuredly the love of his life, especially as Hephaestion was always, irrevocably, his staunchest pillar.

Alexander, the world's greatest strategist until the advent of Julius Caesar, his future as the greatest warrior of all time cut short by an early death.

Alexander and Hephaestion formed a partnership during which Hephaestion commanded troops, built bridges, went on diplomatic missions, founded new settlements, as well as the incredible multitude of other tasks necessary when one rode with Alexander. During the siege of Tyre Alexander turned over the fleet to him, a difficult enterprise as the men he commanded had been conquered by Alexander's army and were thusly not the most responsive of allies.

They crossed into India together at the head of hundreds of elephants; together they descended the Indus to the sea. Aristotle had described the two lovers as ''One soul in two bodies.'' This proved to be the case when they both came to Troy, home--thanks to Homer--of the most famous battles in the history of mankind (10). They laid a wreath on the tomb of Achilles and Patroclus and it was at that moment that Alexander declared that his friendship with Hephaestus was in every point identical to the love between Achilles and Patroclus. They then ran a race, naked, in honor of the two heroes. Claudius Aelianus, the Roman author and teacher, states that ''Alexander laid a garland on Achilles' tomb, Hephaestion on Patroclus'.'' Alexander was Hephaestion's lover, friend, king and commander, but would this count in matters sexual? Plutarch tells us that in bed together, they would go through Alexander's correspondence. When there was a letter that Alexander wanted kept secret, he would touch his ring to his lover's lips, a wondrously moving example of love, spanning so many centuries, so incredibly numerous life spans, all thanks to Plutarch, himself homosexual, and certainly as stirred as am I and the reader. And, lastly concerning their intimacy, we have the quote from Diogenes of Sinope who maintains that the only time Alexander was ever vanquished, was by the thighs of Hephaestion.

Alexander and Hephaestion

When Hephaestion died from fever in Ecbatana at age 32, Alexander was prostrated with grief. He sent to the Oracle at Siwa to ask if he could deify his lover. The Oracle allowed him to make Hephaestion a divine hero, which seems to have satisfied him. Funeral games with 3,000 competitors took place. A pyre 180 feet high, with steps, was raised. It was decorated with ships and banners and figures of armed warriors, torches with snakes entwining them, golden wreaths and eagles, lions and bulls and weapons taken from the enemy. Diodorus recounts that Alexander had the sacred flame in the temple extinguished, an honor exclusively reserved for the deaths of the great Persian kings themselves.

As for Alexander, he died a year later, at age 33, also of fever, also typhus. Some say Aristotle was present. Alexander's body was placed in a gold sarcophagus and filled with honey. On its way to Macedon it was stolen by Ptolemy and taken to Memphis. His successor, Ptolemy II, transferred it to Alexandria where the sarcophagus was later replaced by one made of glass. There it lies today, under unknown sands.

CAESAR
100 – 44 B.C.

Caesar is ranked as perhaps the greatest military leader to have lived, an innovative strategist whose men worshipped him, sexually versatile as were most of them, so sexually insatiable that even during official functions he would, when he saw a woman or a man who aroused him, have him/her brought to him by a servant, expulse his lust, adjust his robes, and return to his duties, one of the many perks of his tyrannical hold of Rome. He did everything different from his contemporaries, down to the extra-long sleeves of the robe he took in at the waist, leading Sulla to say of him, before the senate, beware of that belt-girded boy. Catullus accused him of having intercourse with Mamurra, whom Catullus nicknamed Rod, further stating they both suffered from venereal disease, Caesar's picked up in Rome, Mamurra's in his hometown of Formiae. ''Both are equally debauched, like twins, both learned scholars in affairs of the bed, both friendly rivals in pursuit of girls, both lewd lechers.'' When Catullus later apologized to Caesar, Caesar invited him to dinner, for such was the nature of Caesar, a man all could trust, his word as good as gold, yet unpretentious enough to admit that many of his successes were due to blind luck. He was a hero to his people because his victories brought them wealth and all the pleasures of his conquered realms, in food, fine tissues and slaves for their beds.

Part of Rome's imported affluence were slaves bought for multiple reasons, one of which was to pleasure both sexes, Roman women often as free and as licentious as men, the only obligation for both the requirement to gratify their ardor with a non-citizen, while Roman men were obligatorily the swordsmen, slaves and boys the receptors, the best endowed slaves worth their weight in gold, as shown in the above fresco taken from Pompeii. In the baths men with the longest and heaviest assets were applauded as they strode naked through the corridors, blatantly displaying their wares, assured of a dinner invitation and a well-remunerated evening at the palace of one of the wealthy men present.

Caesar was fond of married women more experienced than he--more hours of flight, as the French say--capable of those small things that can bring a man pleasantly up and over. And he knew, too, that they would keep their mouths shut in order not to jeopardize their marriages. So sexually he took full advantage of life and his body, giving of himself while taking in equal measure, the veritable *raison d'être* of our existence.

We learn this from Suetonius: "When sent to raise a fleet in Bithynia Caesar wasted so much time at King Nicomedes' court that a sexual relationship between them was suspected, and even when he left the king to regain his headquarters, he dashed back at the first opportunity." In the senate, when stating that he would destroy his opponents, someone cried out, "A feat difficult for a woman," implying that the woman in question was Caesar, who retorted, "And why not? The Amazons once ruled over vast areas of Asia." Suetonius tells us that Licinius Calvus published this verse:

> The riches of Bithynia's king
> Whom Caesar on his couch amused.

A certain Bibulus called him "The Queen of Bithynia who slept with the monarch and now wants to become one," in response to which Caesar had a bucket of feces emptied on Bibulus' head. Roman guests at one of Nicomedes' banquets stated, shocked, that Caesar had served as his cup bearer, exactly as Ganymede was Zeus's, although Caesar was there as an ambassador representing Rome. Suetonius tells us that his own soldiers mockingly sang that Caesar had conquered the Gauls, but Nicomedes had conquered Caesar, similar to what Diogenes of Sinope said about Alexander who had been vanquished but once, by the thighs of Hephaestion (30). Cicero, in a letter, wrote: "Caesar was led to Nicomedes' bedchamber where, spread out on the king's couch, he lost his virginity." And once, in the senate, when Caesar mentioned how much Nicomedes had done for Rome, Cicero shouted out, "Enough! We know what he gave you and what you gave him in return." Caesar didn't kill Cicero but his friend Marc Antony avenged him by having Cicero's head lopped off, Antony whom Cicero had accused of being the slut of the very wealthy Gaius Scribonius Curio, an added incentive for the murder. And finally, the immortal sentence handed down by the inimitable Cicero, saying Caesar was "every woman's husband and every man's wife," Cicero's life covered in my book *Cicero*.

Caesar was said to have descended from Aeneas himself, Trojan Aeneas who had founded Rome alongside his lover Pallas (23) following the fall of Troy (10). He lost his father young, as Alcibiades had lost his (12), and like the extremely sexually versatile Greek, Caesar had grown up surrounded by men who spoke of laws and government, men who excelled in oratory, many of them the finest speakers in one of the world's most beautiful languages, a language in which one could express oneself in gorgeous versus and, as in the army, the crudest possible idiom. Schooled by the finest tutors, often slaves, introduced to literature and books in his father's and his father's friends' libraries, from childhood he was put on the path to great achievement. As the poet wrote, given his background ''What did Caesar have better to do than to rule the world?'' He ran, he swam in the Tiber, he worked out in the gymnasia, not naked as did the Greeks, and not the prey of sexual predators, or at least none that too overtly made their lust known, unlike the gymnasia of the Greeks (8). He learned to handle weapons, swords and spears, and was an excellent rider, maneuvering a horse with the pressure of his knees. From his statues we see him as being slight of build, well-proportioned and handsome.

All periods of time were harrowing for the Romans who gained wealth through wars and new lands through conquest, and Caesar's own childhood, no exception, was marked by the Social Wars. While the inhabitants of Rome were Roman citizens, the inhabitants of other cities in Italy, outside of Rome, were not. They had to content themselves with furnishing Rome with money and troops, while having no say in government and the other benefits offered Roman citizens. One senator, Livius Drusus, finding this state of affairs unjust, tried to convince the senate to offer Italians, who fought and died from Rome, citizenship. For his troubles he was assassinated, providing the spark that provoked the Italian city-states to revolt. They joined to form an entity they called Italia, with a new capital, Italica (nearly 2,000 years before Garibaldi). As the revolutionaries were former Roman soldiers, they were extremely battle-hardened and numbered 100,000. The senate had a change of heart and citizenship in one form or another was offered to Italian cities, but only up to the Po River.

To gain power Caesar joined forces with Sulla, a general who had marched on Rome, the first time in the history of the city. Pompey, known as the ''teenage butcher'' due to his brutality, also threw in his lot with Sulla, Sulla who gathered 9,000 prisoners and herded them into the Circus Maximus where, in the presence of senators and the general public, he went over the fine points of his assuming ultimate power in Rome, while down below the prisoners, screaming for mercy, had their throats slit or swords thrust into their chests. He was named dictator, a position granted him by the consuls.

Plutarch tells us the rest: ''Sulla began a bloodbath, filling the city with deaths without limit. He immediately proscribed 80 persons, and when this caused displeasure, he followed it the next day with 120, and the day after with another 120. He then declared that he had proscribed all he could think of, but if others came to memory, he would proscribe them too,'' proscriptions lists of people to be illuminated, their property confiscated. To these dead Sulla added 1,500 more from the nobility, mostly senators. In the end, the massacres are thought to have ended the lives of 9,000 citizens, their wealth seized, making Sulla and his supporters wealthy beyond belief. The sons and grandsons of the proscribed were banned from political office, a penalty that was in place for 30 years. Then he doubled the number of senators from 300 to 600, the vast majority his close friends, Sulla the unsung candidate for one of the world's foremost murderers.

Caesar himself was condemned to die and fled, but his mother, well known to Sulla, begged for his life. Sulla caved in, but in his autobiography he states that he regretted the decision, having underrated Caesar's endless ambition. He predicted that those who pleaded for Caesar's head now would lose their own, by Caesar's command, later on. And when Caesar restored proscription in the following years, they did.

Sulla then resigned the dictatorship and had himself elected consul. He dismissed his guards and walked the streets of Rome accompanied only by his friends and supporters (his clients, as they were referred to in Rome).

The byzantine twist to Sulla's equally byzantine personality is that his successful seizure of power is thought to have inspired Caesar, in 49 B.C., to cross the Rubicon.

At age 15 Caesar had exchanged the *toga praetexta* with its purple fringe for the pure white *toga virilis*, which is self-explanatory. He was now a recognized citizen of Rome, responsible, in case of his father's death, for his mother and sisters and younger brothers. In Caesar's case, he had become the paterfamilias. He also put aside his *bulla praetexta*, a charm of gold held in a leather sack that parents put around their boy's neck, at age 9 days (time to see if he lived through the unsanitary conditions of childbirth), aimed at warding off evil spirits. The bulla, along with a lock of the boy's hair or, if the boy could, the first shavings from his chin, were placed on the family altar and dedicated to the Lares, guardian deities of the household. Mothers recuperated the bulla to protect the boy as he grew, to protect him especially from envious people who might wish him harm. The ceremony of the Lares must have been very moving and certainly would be today if it existed. The ceremony took place on the 17th of March. Forty-four years later, nearly to the day, he would be assassinated by men who had worshipped him until then, one of whom could have *conceivably* been his son, as Brutus was born when sexually-randy Caesar was nearly 16, and Brutus' mother was a very long-term mistress of Caesar's, Caesar, as said, who preferred cougars.

In fact, at age 16 he married Cornelia. An extremely telling story about Caesar's courage is that Sulla, who didn't shy away from killing 1,500 nobles and 9,000 young men on a parade ground, each begging for his precious life, ordered Caesar to rid himself of Cornelia in favor of someone from Sulla's own family. Sulla had already ordered the Great Pompey to do likewise and Pompey, despite the fact that his wife was fully pregnant, had done so. But Caesar refused, the only man in Rome to show such immensurable courage. His name was added to the proscription list, but he was saved by his mom, as reported).

At age 19 he was sent as an ambassador to King Nicomedes IV's court in search of warships, but where, as also reported, he dallied a rather long time. Adrian Goldsworthy states that he may have been dazzled by the Hellenic culture that reigned in the East, so different from crude Rome. Goldsworthy adds, ''Perhaps the nineteen-year-old did feel and succumb to an attraction to an older man--'experimenting with his sexuality' would probably be the fashionable modern euphemism.'' The reality was far more prosaic, I would imagine. In Rome men just had sex, often with whatever was closest at hand, be it a boy or a girl. Male-to-male sexuality, although not nearly as open and accepted as in Greece, was nonetheless the norm for *every* boy and man. Of course, an ambassador shacking up with a king while on an official mission was not a situation known to your everyday Roman citizen.

Both Nicomedes and Bithynia deserve a word. Bithynia encircled today's Istanbul, making it a vital crossroads between Turkey and Greece, a fertile land with superb ports and endless trade. It was Hellenized by Thracians and occupied later by Persians. The Bithynians knew how to take advantage of their forests and mountains to remain free, which they did even when attacked by Alexander the Great. Nicomedes sought close ties with Rome, very close concerning his friendship with Caesar, but nonetheless so close that at his death Nicomedes bequeathed his kingdom to Rome!

At age 25 Caesar was captured by pirates while sailing the Aegean, a plague against commerce that Pompey would later take care of. Caesar's reaction is reported as being gutsy, telling the pirates to request a ransom of 50 talents when they had originally requested 20 (he felt he was worth more than just 20), ordering them to shut up when he took a nap or slept at night. He read them poetry, led them in physical exercises, playfully warning them that he would have their heads once he was freed. The pirates supposedly grew found of him and wished him well when his shipmates returned with the money for his liberation. Caesar returned with a small army of his own and crucified them all, after first slitting their throats--saving them from atrocious suffering--in thanks for their comradeship.

Back in Rome he was named to a series of offices--tribune, quaestor, Pontifex Maximus, praetor and others that I won't go into as they do not advance our story and, anyway, they will all lose their importance in a few short years with the coming of the greatest of all emperors, Augustus.

From Rome Caesar was sent to squelch rebellions in Gaul. And from Gaul he went to the Rubicon.

In crossing the Rubicon, Caesar is said to have borrowed the Greek playwright Menander's words, '' let the die be cast,'' leaving no doubt that he knew his act would trigger civil war. Since the cruelty of Sulla, the very thought of civil war, for Romans, was synonymous with annihilation, and the fact that Sulla died peacefully in his bed made clear the inexistence of justice. That so many men followed Caesar in such an apparently insane venture is proof of the incredible bond he was able to forge between them and himself, a far from easy task involving rough men little known for their patience and empathy. Yet Caesar had constantly awarded them, sharing the riches brought forth from his victories. This was not true in Rome where the people cared little for him, and where problems arising between Caesar and Pompey were the affairs of the nobility, concerning the people not at all. They just wanted to live reasonably well, raise their families in peace and die in bed, living on immortally through their sons.

In 50 B.C., at the age of 50, Caesar had been requested to disband his troops in Gaul--where his victories had placed him in the firmament of Roman heroes, just behind the Great Pompey himself--and return home. Gaul had provided Caesar and his men, alone with glory, with immeasurable wealth through plunder and the number of slaves they had amassed. But Caesar hesitated to return to Rome, fearing that he would be prosecuted for a number of events that had taken place in previous years. He had become consul in 59 B.C., after one of the most contested elections in Roman history, where bribery was beyond all limits. He formed an alliance with super-rich Crassus and super-powerful Pompey, even marrying Pompey's daughter, Julia. The three, united, were able to pass a number of bills, one of which provided land for legionnaires, a soldier's wet dream come true. With power had come jealousies and new enemies, all of which were now out to get him. Added to this was suspicion on all sides; as well as stubbornness and pride on all sides; and always the idea that if ever Caesar, at the head of so many troops sacked Rome, perhaps all the nobility would die as so many had under Sulla. The poet Lucan would later add, ''Caesar could not accept a superior, and Pompey could not accept an equal.'' So Caesar came up with the plan to return to Rome accompanied by his legions, and since an army was forbidden to enter the city, he would remain outside until elected consul, after which he would become inviolable, totally untouchable by those out to get him. His plan was not without precedent, as both Pompey and Crassus had done the same thing in 71 B.C.

When this was refused him, he crossed the Rubicon.

Pompey had infinitely more men and money than Caesar. He even boasted that he had only to stamp his feet on the ground for soldiers to spring from the soil, as the great Achilles had done to encourage ants to leave their tunnels, immediately changed into Myrmidons by the sun (10). But Pompey needed time to get both men and wealth together. This, Caesar didn't accord him, proof of his knowledge of events and his military sense. Taken off guard, Pompey fled Rome for Brindisi where he embarked for Greece. Caesar left Rome in the hands of Marc Antony.

At first blush, this seemed a strange choice. Antony's father, Marcus Antonius, had been an incompetent and corrupt lush who had been given power, says Cicero, because by bribing him one could obtain whatever one wished. Marcus (the father) fancied himself a Sulla and behaved with such extravagance (bacchanals and drinking bouts) that he attracted the never-complacent eye of Cicero whom he tried to assassinate as a first step to seizing power in Rome (it was actually reported that he wished to burn down the city). As the Romans were afraid of what he might do next, he was murdered, with the approbation of Cicero. This most probably entered into Marc Antony's decision, later, to put Cicero to death, although Cicero's hatred and vile words concerning Antony would have been more than enough; not only did Antony want Cicero's head, but he also had his hands cut off and sent to him, the hands that had written such vile filth. Antony would have had to have been a saint not to have been influenced by his dad, and the one thing we know for certain about Antony is that he was in no way a saint. Antony was said to have borrowed a huge amount of money from his lover Gaius Scribonius Curio who was deathly afraid of his father finding out. Curio, Antony and their companions soon became notorious in Rome, as Alcibiades had been in Athens (12), for their reckless, drunken behavior, and as was also true with Alcibiades, their families were too well known and too wealthy for Romans to be able to curb their mindless turbulence. Antony eventually became a staff officer in Caesar's armies in Gaul and they became fast friends. Thanks to Gallic plunder, Caesar is said to have loaned great sums of money to Romans for political gain, among whom was Curio whose debts Caesar paid off to the tune of millions.
Later, following the death of Pompey, Caesar would have to relieve Antony of his functions when he stole Pompey's property, after maintaining that he had bought it. Still later, Antony would hear of the planned assassination of Caesar and try to warn him, but too late.
From his youth onwards Antony was a good general, a loyal friend to Caesar, but little else: a gambler, a rent-boy always in deepest debt, a ceaseless womanizer, the lunkhead who killed Cicero.
Before racing to Brindisi to stop Pompey from sailing away from Italy, Caesar made a stopover in Rome where he assured every one of his good

intentions, promised the people that they would not lack for wheat, and awarded each citizen 300 sesterces, a sum easy to raise as he broke into the treasury--literally axing down the door--and made off with 15,000 gold bars, 30,000 silver bars and 30,000,000 sesterces. Leaving Marc Antony in charge of the city, he finally set off for Brindisi but arrived too late to stop Pompey from sailing to Greece. He too embarked for Greece and met up with Pompey and his troops at Dyrrhachium.

Pompey must have been a truly extraordinary man judging from the caliber of those who respected and followed him, beginning with Cicero who was no man's fool. He was also followed by Brutus, whose father Pompey had nonetheless murdered because he had rebelled against his growing authority. Pompey's father had been a noble and a general, known for his greed, greed that was transformed into the wealth that Pompey inherited. As a general Pompey secured Sicily, guaranteeing Rome's supply of wheat. There followed other victories in Africa, thanks to which Sulla hailed Pompey as *Magnus*, the Great. Crassus, the wealthiest man in Italy, was given the task of bringing an end to the revolt led by Spartacus. He did so, lining the Appian Way with their crucified bodies, 6,000. But Pompey, returning to Rome, came upon the remnant of Spartacus' army and captured 5,000 that he led to Rome, thereby winning credit for ending the revolt. (The body of Spartacus, who was thought to have been killed by Crassus' legions, was never found.)

As piracy had become the plague of the Mediterranean, Pompey was called on to end it, a task no one else had been able to accomplish. With a genius for organization, he divided up the area into thirteen zones and sent out a general and a fleet to comb through every nook and corner of the western Mediterranean, bringing piracy to an end in just forty days. (Although some modern observers think that he accomplished far more by bribing the pirates than by really fighting them, and as his victory had taken place with such incredible rapidity, this is not difficult to believe.) Freeing the seas from pirates meant opening them to trade and the assurance that Rome would not lack for food and rich imports, all of which made Pompey wildly popular. He went on to Jerusalem where he discovered vast riches in the Jewish temple, and, against all expectations, he left everything intact. Thanks to such clemency, when he again returned to Rome it was with the entire East in his pocket. The Greeks acknowledged him as a god, something that cost them little but had the potential of reaping great rewards in goodwill and trade. He rode through the streets of his native city triumphantly, with a servant murmuring in his ear, ''Remember, you are a man, not a god.'' Plutarch stated that Pompey's achievements outshone even those of Alexander the Great.

It was at this point in the life of Pompey that he united with both Caesar and Crassus, as mentioned above, in order to pass the laws he wished to be passed, especially those concerning land distribution to his beloved soldiers.

That was Pompey, that was his glory, until he embarked for Greece, followed by Caesar right up to the gates of the city of Dyrrhachium. Along the way there had been problems. Some of the ships carrying Caesar's men from Brindisi to Greece had been waylaid by Pompey's navy and captured. Both ships and men were deliberately torched. The Ninth Legion revolted because of Caesar's decision to be clement to the towns Caesar went through in both Italy and Greece, deciding, for example, to not burn Brindisi to the ground for helping Pompey escape. This clemency deprived the troops of spoils, an integral part of their pay. Caesar decided to apply the traditional punishment, decimation, recounts Appian. One man out of every ten would be beaten to death by his fellow soldiers. When the men begged for forgiveness, Caesar order 120 of the ringleaders to be brought before him. Decimation would apply to them only, meaning 12 would perish. Luckily, before the sentence was carried out Caesar discovered that one of the 12 hadn't even been in camp when the revolt broke out. He had been chosen by a commander who simply wanted to get rid of him. The commander in question took his place. From then on, the Ninth was the most valorous of all of Caesar's legions.

At Dyrrhachium Caesar blocked Pompey's troops inside the city. Pompey refused battle because it was winter and he felt he could starve Caesar's legions into giving up the siege. As Dyrrhachium was on the coast of Albania (Durrës today) and given the fact that Pompey had a quasi-unlimited supply of ships, he could be easily provisioned. But Caesar's men were motivated, stating that they would eat the bark off trees in necessary. His troops were nonetheless confronted by two major problems: the first was the battlefield scourge, diarrhea, humiliating and dehumanizing; the second was an order given by Pompey to shot arrows into the hundreds of campfires, thousands of them, a hit-and-miss attempt to kill Caesar's men, one that worked until the men moved away to sleep in the cold. Finally Caesar gave up and withdrew.

It was said that many of Pompey's men, heartened by the withdrawal of Caesar, sent representatives to Rome to buy up land and houses that would serve as the foundation of their future wealth, as at that moment prices were garage-sale low due to the pessimism concerning the outcome of the war. But such optimism was not the case for Pompey. In fact, Cicero says that after Dyrrhachium Pompey ''ceased being a general.''

Their next encounter was at Pharsalus, a battle in which Pompey was reported to have lost 6,000 men to Caesar's 200, although 20 centurions died, the cream of each legion, each responsible for 1,000 men under their orders. As the centurions were the vanguard of the troops, they were also by far the best paid and the first to die. Brutus, the son of Caesar's mistress, Servilia, (whom many historians, as said, believe to have been *his* son) was captured but spared. In fact, Caesar sent a party out looking for him. Pompey escaped. The other inhabitants of Pharsalus didn't fare as well. His soldiers, furious at having been defeated at Dyrrhachium, took out their anger on the population and Caesar, usually so moderate, gave them their head. Those within the town who did not commit suicide were raped and slaughtered. The next morning the soldiers walked or rode away, their stomachs full of food and drink, their heads cleared and their balls empty for the first time in months. Left behind were men and boys sprawled out in the distorted forms of rigor mortis, their bodies pierced, sliced or dismembered by dagger and sword. Their women folk were spread out too, but they were on their backs naked, their legs push up and thighs open, frozen in the postures that death found them, some knifed while still penetrated by men inured or even aroused by their suffering, achieving release while seeking traction in the brew of blood and semen at their feet. The silence of their leave-taking, after a night of screams, was deafening.

Pompey sailed to Egypt where the young king, Cleopatra's brother and husband, had him beheaded the moment his feet touched the beach of Alexandria.

So ended the life of this extraordinary man, harbinger of Caesar's own death just four years in the future.

Caesar had the leader of Ptolemy's army and Ptolemy's regent, a eunuch, put to the sword. Plutarch says that the body of Pompey was cremated by Pompey's freed slave, using planks from a rotting fishing boat. Caesar had the ashes sent to his wife for burial. His head was interred at Alexandria. Ptolemy drowned in the Nile while fleeing.

Those of us born on the planet Earth know about the ups and downs of Caesar's relationship with Cleopatra, which will therefore be bypassed here. Even if he had married her, a marriage was recognized only when taking place between Roman citizens, but their association did last fourteen years and a boy was born, Caesarion. Cleopatra is thought to have visited Rome several times.

Caesar named his grandnephew, Gaius Octavius, the future Augustus, as his adopted son and heir, stating that should he die Brutus would be his second choice. There was curiously nothing in his will about his son Caesarion.

After avenging Pompey, Caesar returned to Rome where he received four Triumphs, for his exploits in Gaul, Egypt, Asia and Africa. Triumphs were fabulous affairs, granted by the senate. The person so honored rode through Rome on a chariot pulled by four horses, wearing a crown of laurels (something Caesar adored doing, as it covered his baldness) and a purple toga. Prisoners captured during the wars, as well as the victory spoils--armor, gold, silver, even paintings--led the march through the city. The most famous prisoner now was the Gaul Vercingetorix who would be publically throttled to death. He was just one of what Pliny said made up the 1,200,000 enemies Caesar had killed during the aforementioned campaigns. Even Cleopatra's sister Arsinoe was a captive, but thanks to the crowd's pleading, she was not put to death. Following the spoils came the senators and other nobles on foot, while his officers rode horseback nearby. Then came his soldiers, singing ribald songs, especially those concerning Caesar's sexual prowess, including his adventures with Nicomedes. They had the right to do so, and used it to the hilt, even though Caesar was visibly pained by the insults which inferred, of course, that he had been penetrated. He didn't seem to mind, however, the soldiers' warning to Romans to lock up their wives and daughters as protection against the bald fucker. In addition to the soldiers' songs, there were clouds of incense and maidens who dispersed flowers.

As the cast was composed of thousands, prisoners included, there were incredible logistic problems, the least of which was housing and feeding of the masses. At night feasts were provided for the populace, 22,000 tables laden with the best food and wines. Then came the entertainment, days of more feasts, games, sporting events, gladiatorial fights, chariot races, as well as the killing of giraffes, seen for the first time in Rome, and 400 lions. Caesar worked during the gladiatorial fights, reading and signing petitions and laws that an endless stream of functionaries brought him, to the displeasure of the people, something that Augustus, who was there and observed the reaction of the spectators, would be careful to never do when he became emperor. But in Caesar's case it was proof that he simply never stopped working for his country (as Augustus would also work unceasingly for Rome, later on). A naval battle took place thanks to a lake dug next to the Tiber. The soldiers, despite their filthy ditties, received 5,000 denarii, more than they would have earned, Goldsworthy tells us, in 16 years of service! Their leaders, the centurions, got 10,000 each. Notables were tipped 20,000 and each Roman 100 denarii, plus wheat and olive oil.

Later, during another ceremony, Marc Antony approached Caesar, sitting on his gilded chair of office, and offered him, in front of a huge crowd, a crown, begging him to become king. Caesar refused and the crowd cheered. Antony offered the crown a second time and again it was refused, to even louder cheers. Some say that Caesar was secretly disappointed, and that had the crowd showed enthusiasm for his kingship, he would have accepted it. He did not become a king but he would become a god at his death, a phenomenon that would become so automatic that when Vespasian was on his own deathbed, he joked, ''Oh, I think I'm becoming a god!''

The reasons for the conspiracy to murder him were as varied as the participants. Some thought that he had not accorded them sufficient honors, others hated his dictatorship, and although Sulla had been far more destructive, he had at least given up his dictatorship and returned home. Brutus seems to have been sincerely motivated by philosophical reasons, based on the reestablishment of the Republic. Cassius was thought to have been bitter because Brutus received so many honors from Caesar, and this due only to the fact that the boy was the son of Caesar's former mistress. Wall graffiti accused Brutus of doing nothing against the dictatorship, he who spoke so often about the joys of freedom. Goldsworthy states that once Brutus had decided to join the conspiracy his mind was made up, as it was in his character to be unshakeable. Even Caesar had said about him, ''Whatever Brutus wants, he wants badly.''

The Ides of March, the 15th, came and we have the Shakespearean warning as he made his way to the senate, ''Beware of the Ides of March Caesar!'' ''The Ides of March have come,'' was Caesar's answer. ''Yes,'' said the soothsayer, ''but have not gone!'' The night before, Caesar had dined with his purported son, Brutus, and the topic of the best possible death was raised. Caesar had replied, ''For me, a sudden, unexpected death!''

His end was certainly unexpected and given other lingering forms of dying, one can say that it was sudden too. This man, who had worked as constantly as the ever-moving ocean for his country, was surrounded by the men he had raised to prominence, one perhaps his own boy or, at the very least, a boy he loved as his own, struck with hidden daggers, twenty-three thrusts and but four words, ''You too my son...''

EMPERORS TRAJAN AND HADRIAN

Two Roman emperors were exclusively homosexual, Trajan and Hadrian, the impassioned homoerotic love of one of whom has spanned millenniums. Known as one of the Five Good Emperors, Trajan expanded the Roman Empire to its historically maximum limit, while catering to Roman citizens' needs, providing them with abundance and security, reshaping Rome thanks to his building projects, deified at his death, his ashes laid to rest under his column.

Gibbons wrote: ''If a man were called to fix the period in the history of the world during which the condition of the human race was most happy and prosperous, he would, without hesitation, name that which elapsed from the death of Domitian to the accession of Commodus.'' This was the period shared by Trajan and Hadrian, Trajan who raised Hadrian after the death of his father, both of whom preferred men and boys, Hadrian's love for Antinous placing him in the godhead of man/boy love. Trajan and Hadrian are heroes for having created, as Gibbon wrote, this unique, happy and prosperous time in human history.

Trajan rose through the ranks of the army and married Pompeia Plotina, a childless marriage for the reason that Trajan may have left her, according to the busy-bodies of the time, as untouched as the Vestal Virgins. Indeed, Trajan's homosexuality was so blatant that chroniclers and authors remarked on it, among them Cassius Dio and Julian, stating that actors and dancers were common bedmates, that the sons of his intimate friends were prime targets, that not only had he participated in his predecessor Emperor Nerva's debauches, but was perhaps the first to relieve the cousin he raised, young Hadrian, of his noisome virginity, Hadrian whom he adopted as his son prior to his death, although his favorites were, by far, the legions of pages who entered his service, boys he shared with his friends and with Hadrian himself.

Publius Aelius Hadranus Afer, called Hadrian, was born in 76 A.D. in either Rome or Italica, near Seville. The lack of exactitude signifies that his family was part of what the ancient aristocrats called ''new men'', rich thanks to Spanish lands but relatively unknown, and certainly not marked for future emperorship. For the ''new men'', being born in Rome was far more advantageous for their careers than being born in a hicksville such as Italica, and so Rome was often substituted for their veritable birthplace. As with all the gentry who shunned the strong possibility of having their child taken from them by dysentery or other maladies, Hadrian's mother, Domitia Paulina, farmed him out to a wet nurse, in Hadrian's case a healthy peasant who would outlive her charge. At age ten his father died, always a traumatic experience for a boy, leaving him a very wealthy lad. He became ward of a cousin, Trajan, a native too of Italica.

In the ancient world puberty set in later than today, around ages 14 to 16. Boys had facial down around age 16, not 14 as today, and shaved around age 18, far from today's 15/16. Hadrian exchanged the purple-edged toga of a boy for the pure-white *toga virilis* of a man, an immensely important ceremony described in the life of Julius Caesar. Although young, Hadrian was far from the purity of a Vestal Virgin. In addition to the sexual stimulation within his uncle's palace, he knew furtive caresses as he passed through the streets and through the corridors of the baths, looks and gestures of admirers who often paid boys' tutors for surreptitious introductions, down to the classroom itself where, as the poet Juvenal wrote,

Boys played dirty games,
Taking turns with one another,
Trying not to be caught,

While hands feverishly jerked,
Until they came.

At home Hadrian had the continual spectacle of Trajan, his guardian, in delightful and casual interplay with the household youths, especially, as mentioned, the handsome pages he was said to be infatuated with. Later, when Trajan became emperor, Hadrian knew instinctively that he could gain influence through the men important to Trajan by servicing them sexually, plowing through their bellies.

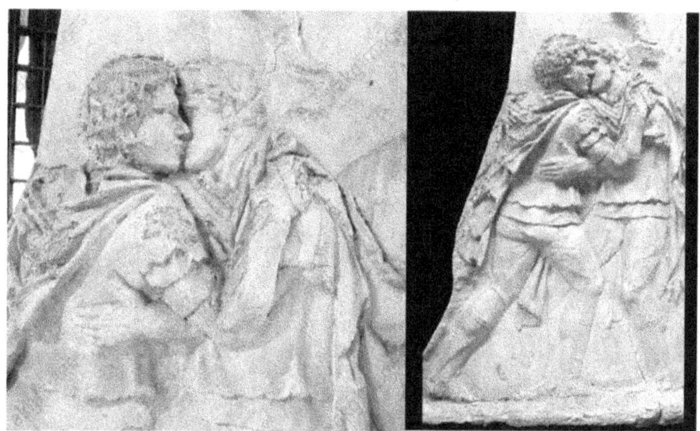

Trajan's Column was built in celebration of his proclaimed victory over the Dacians (today's Romanians), 101/102 AD, where he was joined by Hadrian. It was basically a self-declared win, Trajan simply proclaiming his triumph as his troops withdrew back to Rome. One can read what one wishes into the kiss depicted on the Column, from two soldiers in love to two men embracing on being reunited, more a bromance than a love affair.

When Hadrian became emperor he traveled a great deal in the belief that, like Emperor Augustus, a ruler could only know what was going on in the empire by going into the provinces himself. He went through Gaul to Britannia where his famous wall was already under construction. He went through Spain to Mauretania in the north of Africa, then east to Libya and on to the Euphrates and the Black Sea, Anatolia and Pontus. From Pontus Hadrian went on to Bithynia where he met the love of his life.

Hadrian and Antinous.
**Hadrian was called the Little Greek thanks to his love of Hellas and
the Greek language, and he initiated the growth of beards, which became
the rage at the time, as it is today in 2022.**

We don't know where and how they met, but most probably it was in Antinous' hometown, Claudiopolis, a citadel surrounded by mountains and known for its cows, milk and cheese. It was probably at a banquet of some kind, as emperors do not normally pick up boys off the streets. No one knows what went on, physically, between the man and the boy, but we can hope that it took place often and lustily, that Hadrian showed tender affection and rough vigor when the moment demanded it, that they were clean in body and dirty in the way that only the human animal can be. I'm not going to invent the lascivious scene when, for the first time, they found themselves alone and randy (is there another word?). But I do hope the experience included tears as well as laughter, because nothing in nature can be more exquisite and inspiring than love in general, love between youths in particular.

Antinous, a beauty that only an emperor could offer himself.

Upon his return to Rome, Hadrian found the Pantheon he had commissioned completed. At first built by Augustus' great and faithful friend Agrippa, it had burned to the ground. Now it had risen from its ashes, one of the few great monuments from the period that has come down to us. The inside is magnificent, and at the time of Hadrian the roof had been covered with gold leaf. Hadrian then withdrew to the enormous complex of buildings still under construction at Tibur, a complex big enough to house government officials; conference rooms that accommodated his council, often senators who advised him on policy; lodging for his friends, men he had known for years and whose advice he sought; cooks, cleaners, gardeners, builders, slaves, servants and his boys; as well as pools, lakes and cascades.

Hadrian designed and named sections of the Tibur complex after the sites that had most impressed him in his travels. He had works of art shipped in from all corners of the Empire, mostly Greek masterpieces. A unique hydraulic system was installed for his lakes, pools, waterways, fountains and canals, the whole contributing to a Paradise on earth.

Another view.

Hadrian was absorbed by mysticism, the occult and fortune telling, which could not only cast the spells that could bring one a lover or assure the death of an enemy, but could also help in one's sexual performance-- supernatural aphrodisiacs. Pornography was an aid and walls were often covered with erotic frescos. Males were naturally attracted to boys as well as girls, and it must not be forgotten that words for homosexual or heterosexual didn't exist in any form, although there were words for effeminacy (25). Prostitution gave a boy a chance to gain life experience and put money in his pocket, and it allowed a married man needed release from a wife he knew all too well, thusly helping to preserve the couple.

Horoscopes were forbidden by Hadrian, except those he himself ordered or carried out, as he became an accomplished astrologist. But horoscopes done by others could give the date of an emperor's death, an encouragement to his enemies who felt safe in rising up against him--they were therefore banned and those who cast them put to death.

Hadrian was deeply influenced by the story of Osiris and Isis, an ancient Egyptian myth of huge importance because thanks to it the dead could reach a pleasant afterlife. It was his interest in Isis and Osiris that brought him to Egypt, he and Antinous heading the imperial fleet that sailed to Heliopolis, home of the phoenix, a bird reborn from its own ashes, the ultimate representative of transformation and resurrection. Here Hadrian consulted with Pachrates, a sorcerer and caster of spells cum priest who had built his reputation for having magical powers on his Egyptian heritage. From Heliopolis, on their way to Hermopolis, the man and boy visited Memphis, the pyramids and the Sphinx. At Hermopolis its yearly festival--celebrating the death and resurrection of Osiris, a celebration concomitant with the flooding of the Nile, the source of all wealth to ancient Egypt--was in full swing. The Nile had mysteriously failed to overflow its banks for two years running, and the people were threatened with starvation. The ceremony had thusly taken on a gravitas unknown in earlier years. Hadrian had always been a fervent believer in the occult, the mysteries, the forecasts of soothsayers and fortunetellers--an interest that he had manifested even years before it had been predicted that he, the son of a simple senator, would one day lead the Roman world. The story of Osiris and Isis was of special importance, as stated, because Osiris, after his death by drowning in the Nile, had been resurrected. Hadrian knew that in ancient times boys of great beauty were thrown into the Nile to drown, a human sacrifice in memory of Osiris' martyrdom. The boys went willingly as they were led to believe that they too would be resurrected, and as Osiris, they too would become gods.

It is believed that Hadrian had cast his own horoscope and found nothing but impending disaster, a far cry from the horoscope predicting he would become emperor. His travels had tired him; he was becoming old; he suffered from bodily aches, especially his legs that were not only racked with pain but seemed cast in iron; and from every corner of the empire unrest, revolts and other never-ending problems assaulted him. The Nile itself was suffering, as were the people scratching a living on its banks. Everything combined to bring out the morbid aspects of his personality. He knew he was dying, that he was losing his grip on the Roman world ... and on the boy at his side. He could see in his belovèd's eyes that he was not the virile man who had fought his way to power, had led armies, had governed wisely and generously: he saw instead the ageing head that could no longer inspire love--and it was unacceptable. Yet he chose not to destroy himself, he chose--perhaps--to destroy the vital living beauty he contemplated, unquenchingly, at his side.

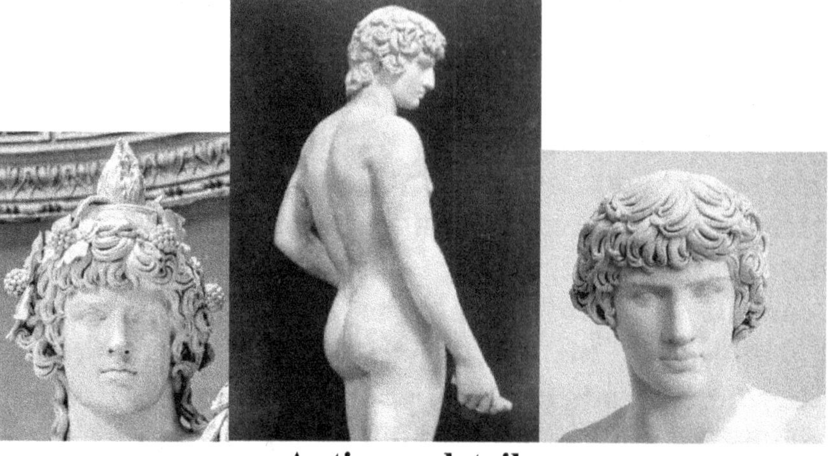

Antinous details

For this kind of spell to work Antinous had to be in agreement, he had to go to his death willingly. Free will was essential, and even the Devil himself has no control over a man until he is accorded such control, through free will, which, in the case of a man's soul, demands that he sign it over to the Prince of Darkness. Had Hadrian's years of experience convinced the boy that he, Hadrian, was at the end of his tether, and that without him the Roman empire, assaulted from all parts, would flounder, bringing misery to countless millions? Did Hadrian believe that the boy's sacrifice would cure his ailments and perhaps even prolong his life? Had Antinous undertaken the voyage to the oracle of Siwa to ask for confirmation from the gods?

We know that the body, as beautiful as ever even in death (as the ancients claim), was brought to the surface of the Nile in a fish net. The emperor was informed that the boy had certainly fallen from a bark while fishing. There was no mention of suicide, none concerning human sacrifice. The local priests maintained that traditionally all beautiful boys drowned in the Nile became gods, and indeed on the night of Antinous' disappearance the emperor had seen a star rise up from the river and ensconce itself in the heavens where it was embraced by the other stars. The priests begged for the honor of establishing a city in memory of the new god, a city called Antinopolis, that exists to this very day. Hadrian had it populated by Greek families and army veterans, offering the new inhabitants tax breaks, an assured food supply and other privileges. A new festival, the Antinoeia, was founded in his lover's memory. It included footraces, wrestling, boxing, chariot races, swimming and rowing, all performed by local ephebes. The prize was a garland of red lotus flowers.

The final question is this: In the secret of the alcove, in his belovèd's arms, had Hadrian convinced the young and grateful Antinous to sacrifice his beauty and the years left to him so that he, emperor of the civilized world, could live on to do good … or, more prosaic, so he could simply live on? (13)

Hadrian's Roman mausoleum.

RICHARD COEUR DE LION
1157 - 1199

When William the Conqueror died, his son Henry became Henry I, King of England. He defeated and imprisoned his brother who had been Duke of Normandy, lands Henry took as his own, bringing him into conflict with Louis VI, King of France. Henry named his daughter, Matilda, as his successor. She married Geoffrey Count d'Anjou and produced Henry II, the future father of Richard Coeur de Lion. Henry II was one of the most outstanding kings in world history, as was his future wife outstanding, Eleanor d'Aquitaine (31). Henry I's sister's son Stephen usurped the throne and kept hold of it until old age forced him to turn it over to the boy who would become Henry II at age 20. At age 18 the future Henry II met and apparently fell in love with Louis VII's wife Eleanor, the then richest woman in the world, possessor of French Aquitaine. As she had not produced a son and was noted for her infidelities, Louis had the marriage annulled and Eleanor immediately married Henry. When Henry entered London two years later Eleanor, former Queen of France, became Queen of England, the only woman ever to hold both titles.

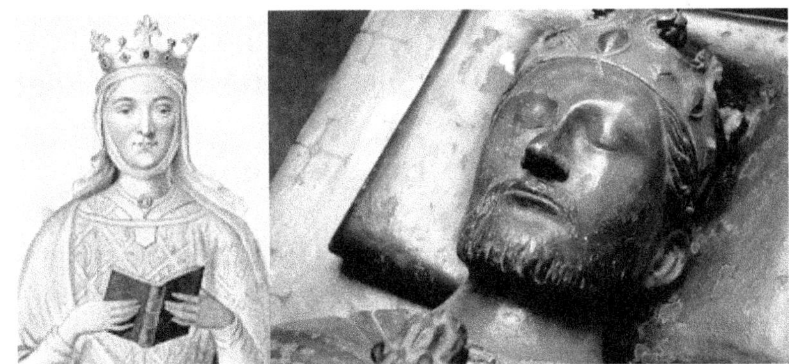

Eleanor of Aquitaine and Henry II, two historical giants.

Eleanor had accompanied Louis on the second Crusade. In Antioch she fell for the reigning prince, Raymond de Poitiers, her uncle, and had to be pulled away from him after she told Louis she wanted a divorce in order to stay at Raymond's side. She had the self-assurance of a woman far richer than her husband, and a character that made her, in my eyes, perhaps the most significant woman to have ever lived (among, nonetheless, four others, covered in my book *Five Renaissance Wonders*).

The match was made in Heaven or, as chroniclers hinted then, perhaps more likely in Hell: An ancestor of Henry's was said to have been the daughter of Satan and her issue was therefore tainted with diabolism. It's true that Henry had an other-worldly way of judging men, seeing into their hearts, clearly reading their wants and aspirations. His libido was without limit, and it was said that he forced himself to hunt and to keep on the move, from castle to castle, in order to not fuck himself to death. Every woman was his target, and his gift for reading men, and his limitless power--and his generosity--helped him to assuage the disgruntled husbands and fathers of the countless bellies he ploughed, even if most gentlemen at court threw wife and daughter in his direction, reaping the awards should he bed them. Bastards without number were the result, one of whom, Geoffrey, he recognized, giving Geoffrey full princely rights.

Sexually attuned to Eleanor, she--who couldn't produce sons under Louis--gave him five boys in rapid succession. As adultery committed by a woman was punishable by death, she is thought to have limited herself to her husband. Henry was literally at her side the time needed to make her pregnant, before going off to inseminate the four winds, as the French say, Henry's preferred language.

His activities kept him svelte and Eleanor too remained curvaceous all her life. But time was against her, as Henry had been 18 when they married, Eleanor 29. By the time she lost her power to reproduce, he was in his thirties, humping less than at age 16, but still fully operational. He had known about his wife's tastes for boys and men, he knew that his own father, Henry I, had had her because he had revealed as much to his son in the hope of poisoning the marriage. But whether through love or the desire to possess the world's richest woman--or both--Henry did what he desired. In fact, the one thing Henry could not tolerate was the slightest opposition to his will. He was said to have been courteous, charming and charismatic, but because Satan's own blood circulated in his veins, he was also deceitful, cynical and murderous.

He controlled his weight through judicious eating, he kept his temper in check by abstemious drinking, and controlled his loins through perpetual movement. Yet movement was important too because wherever he went the receiving castle had to provide food and somehow dispose of the tons of human excrement his entourage left behind. To have remained in one place would have meant financial ruin to the host and a mountain of filth, while the total lack of sanitation favored dirty, lice-strewn bodies. When the corpse of King Ferrante of Naples was recently disinterred and examined, doctors found the remains of two types of lice, one pubic, the other in his hair (4).

Henry didn't care for a French-style court with pomp and ceremony and elegant clothes. He wore the commonest of tissues and was seen mending his breeches himself with needle and thread. He was the kind of man who would break the ice over a basin of water in winter so he could splash the dirt from his face, and he would put his hands inside his trousers, cupping the cheeks of his ass, while he warmed his backside in front of the raging fire in a monumental fireplace. He was intellectually curious and it was said that for him and those that accompanied him, it was everyday a school day. Physically his complexion was ruddy, his hair short, his height average. His arms were massive and his face so magnetic that one couldn't take one's eyes off it. He established hegemony over Wales, took Brittany and Toulouse from Louis VII, made his might felt in every land he possessed, Henry as much a hero as his son Richard, and although his homosexuality was far less ostentatious than Richard's, it's known that he appreciated boys and boyish buttocks.

Eleanor was always described as a genuine beauty, but it must have been difficult for her never knowing to what point she was loved for herself or for her immense lands, since the Aquitaine at the time covered a good fourth of France. As intelligent as Henry, she would eventually rule England and huge parts of France once Henry was dead and her beloved boy Richard reigned.

Eleanor's Acquitaine in the south-west of France.

Richard was born on the 8th of September 1157. He was a Virgin and it's not inconceivable that he remained one, heterosexually speaking, all his life--although improbable. Born in England, Richard spent most of his life in the southwestern part of France, in the Aquitaine he grew to cherish, as did his mother, until his death (and where I am now writing this, as it is my homeland too). Richard was brought up by a wet-nurse he adored, on whom he showered riches until his death (Hadrian who had also been born in September, may also have died heterosexually virgin and had, as well, been raised by a nurse he adored and who outlived him). Eleanor loved the boy, perhaps influenced by the prophesy of Merlin that a great king would arise from the 3rd nesting of the eagle of the broken covenant. The eagle was Eleanor, the broken covenant was her divorce from Louis, and the 3rd nesting was the birth of Richard. (He was actually the fourth of her children, but one had been a girl.) Eleanor has *always* been attributed with having ulterior motives for her actions, as, for example, the accusation that she placed her love of Aquitaine above that for Henry, when perhaps Henry, by his daily--nearly hourly--dalliances, pushed her into finding consolation in the home of her birth and heritage. Henry himself probably cared little for them all, certainly too busy governing his kingdom, certainly too occupied with himself and his own creature comforts, certainly, too, due to the fact that the death rate for children was so high it was best to ignore them until their seventh year, a practice dating back to the earliest Greeks, Sparta included, as well as in Rome, and during the Renaissance, right up to near-modern times in France, when children were farmed out to governesses until they reached the age of schooling. Eleanor and Richard spoke a dialect of French, and Richard himself spoke French, and indeed lived only a few months of his life in the cold land of ugly barbarians. He was as rough and unpolished as his father, but appreciated the elegant French boys of the French court as well as lusty Basques and Gascons, the latter known for their promiscuity. Troubadours were common to the area and they may have played an unsuspectingly large role in the events to follow, as they flattered young seigneurs, Richard's brother Henry among them, into thinking that they were far more important than they were in the eyes of their parents, thereby sowing the seeds of revolt. They also placed women on unapproachably high pedestals, exactly where Richard wanted them.

Richard was tall, even for our modern times. His hair was light in color and his eyes as blue as his father's, his speech said to have been eloquent. He preferred the company of unpretentious virile males but his first sexual experiences are naturally unknown, at least until his time with Philippe, the future Philippe II of France, whose loves were related by court raconteurs, plainly sensual as we shall see, but distorted by modern historians, from the 18th century to our own days, who saw their union as a form of passing experimentation, or short-lived bisexuality, or nothing more than the customs of the times, when men regularly shared the same bed.

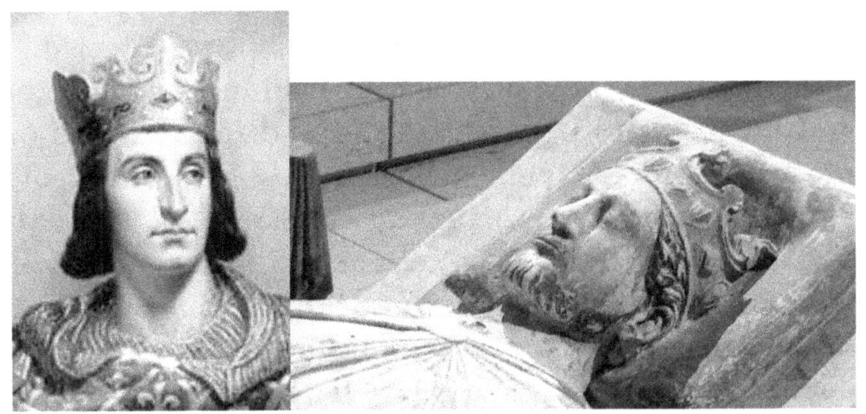

Philippe II of France and Richard I

Eleanor gave birth to Geoffrey. Of them all, it was he who inherited most of Satan's blood. Like Lorenzo *Il Magnifico* de' Medici, he could charm the birds out of the trees (4), both of whose eloquence rivaled Orpheus's lyre. For Geoffrey promises were made to be broken, and deceit, hypocrisy, corruption and cunning were the tools of his trade, the purpose of which was gaining influence and power through dissimilation, a boy far too complicated to interest his father or his brother Richard, far too serpentine for his mother who, even so, possessed an equally brimming bag of tricks. Too young for Henry's son Henry, too old for the brother soon to arrive, John, Geoffrey somehow survived by himself, so certain of his gifts that he could allow himself to hang back, survey the others, smile at their quirks, judge and place them on the chessboard of life, a twinkle in his eye, so beautiful that Philippe of France--the same who would love and lose Richard--hysterical with grief, threw himself into Geoffrey's grave when the lad was buried in the Cathedral of Notre Dame, killed during a tournament at age 27.

Eleanor had two more daughters and perhaps even another son, lost in time due to an early death, before ending with John. She went through menopause, one that stilled her sexual ardor but freed her mind for breathtaking exploits, making Eleanor of Aquitaine one of the most vital forces since Sappho, proof that women need not beg men for anything in our times where intellect rules supreme (31).

The story of John is a tragedy because his priceless youth was wasted in feuds with his parents and brothers. It is true that he was closer to his father Henry than were any of his brothers, especially after the deaths of Henry's first heirs, William and Henry. John was carted around like a piece of luggage, without even the warming presence of a wet-nurse as had been Richard's luck, perhaps the only woman Richard truly ever loved. John seems to have been a lad who whined, and his father's resolve to make him a man overlooked the small detail that John was a boy, and boys need guidance, they need their father's presence, stern perhaps but with the underlying certainty of love, even if only expressed by the tousling of his hair. But Henry had him beaten when he sniveled, and John's compensating arrogance was such that he couldn't make friends of the lads his age, and his brothers were all too old and too centered on themselves. For unknown reasons Eleanor shirked him as she did Geoffrey, perhaps because John was Henry's favorite and she had grown to hate his favorite in girls, sons and an occasional boy. Deprived of stability, John's tantrums saw him literally frothing at the mouth, his eyes blood-red, exactly as his father's when Henry too was seen pulling the stuffing from a mattress with his bare teeth, in rage when thwarted. Of Henry, John had his height and blue eyes, but these were hooded, without either the intelligence of Henry or Henry's burning need to learn, and also, John was the least handsome of them all, although his brooding was such that it may have erased softer, warmer physical traits. The lad was a distant cold planet, and such he would remain, unloved, until the even colder earth finally claimed his remains.

As Geoffrey was a chameleon, a master at dissimulation, we'll never know the extent of his love for Philippe, meaning his degree of homosexuality. Richard on the other hand was the perfect storm: a wet-nurse and mother that cocooned him, and a father who was invariably absent. The direction that his sexuality took surprises no one, other than writers who move heaven and earth to put him on a heterosexual track. The formula for creating boys who appreciated other boys worked wonders for Greeks and Roman households, where boys were raised by women and grew to desire what women desired (compounded in England by the English custom of sending their boys to boarding schools at age 8, hotbeds for every form of homosexuality, covered in my book *Boarding School Homosexuality*).

Here we need a brief flashback. Henry's first son William died at age 3. To ensure the stability of his reign, Henry had his second son, Henry, crowned at age 15, who was thereafter known as the Young King. He was the only co-king in English history. The Young King died of dysentery at age 28 while fighting his father and his brother Richard, thusly leaving the way open for Richard's ascension, although Henry II, no fool, refused to give Richard major responsibilities. This infuriated the boy who, accompanied by his dissatisfied mother and brothers, fled to Paris to place themselves under Louis VII, the occasion for both Richard and Geoffrey to meet and mate with Louis' handsome son Philippe, and for Geoffrey to perfect his art in treason.

That a king's wife would not only betray her royal husband but would also, in Eleanor's case, return to the former husband whom she had treated so shabbily, was a historical first. That Henry had mistresses was routine for the times and Eleanor accepted it, but that he treated one of them in kingly fashion, a certain Rosamund, was intolerable. Yet worse was still to come. He had welcomed into his hearth ten-year-old Alys, Louis' daughter and Richard's promised wife, whom he bedded as soon as she was of age to be deflowered--something left entirely to his discretion. It was Eleanor who headed the conspiracy against Henry, especially since Richard was just 15, Geoffrey 14, and Young Henry, the empty-headed co-king, 18.

In Paris Louis threw his support behind the Young King and Eleanor, and Eleanor's young Devil's brood vowed allegiance to Louis. The treason of his family provided the occasion for treason among all those--counts, dukes and what-have-you that governed Henry's lands--who were tired of submitting to Henry's iron fist, leaving Henry genuinely alone. They rose against him, but there was no one to unite them into a coherent force, as Young Henry lacked the brains and Eleanor was a woman in a world held by men. Henry II had funds that he used to raise an army of mercenaries, which was of upmost importance in times when there were no standing armies. Mercenaries were the scum of the earth, living for war, wages, ransacking and rape. They were excommunicated by the church, not for their evil ways but because their occupation was tantamount to suicide, an unforgivable sin. They were also the world's finest warriors.

Louis lacked both the decisiveness and the knowhow for military victory, and during the battles that followed there was a major and decisive *coup de théâtre*: Eleanor was captured while on the road to encourage the Young King in the field, at the head of his troops. Dressed as a man, she was betrayed by one of her entourage and hauled away to prison where she would remain until freed, after Henry's death, by her beloved Richard.

Richard, by now 16, incensed by his mother's capture, turned against his father in such majestic style that it was Richard who became the target of all of Henry's major attacks, Richard who would gain his father's respect, although never, ever, his love, to Richard's profound sorrow. But as there was no way Richard could defeat his father's endless number of troops and limitless wealth, the two made peace. Henry now employed his boy as his spearhead against those throughout Henry's territories who had used the revolt of his sons as an excuse to seize Henry's lands in their own names, disavowing their former pledges of loyalty to Henry. Richard defeated them all, and although in most cases he left them their lives, he also ordered the destruction of their major fortifications--a show of steel at the astonishingly young age, by then 18. Not only did these former rulers go to Henry on bended knee, Richard himself kneeled before him and kissed his hand, certainly proud to be respected by this man among men, his invincible father.

Louis was seen for the second-rate king he was, Henry and England as the age's greatest powers, and Richard as a rising star who loved war, who loved the exhilaration of war, the virile ambiance of war. Richard had found his path and his name from hereon would be placed alongside that of the Great Alexander himself.

Other revolts followed, especially that of 1183 involving Young Henry and his brother Geoffrey against Henry II and his ally, his son Richard, but that came to an end with Young Henry's death. King Henry's sad, tender words when brought the news, ''He cost me much but I wish he were here to cost me more,'' should have encouraged him to better understand his son Richard, which was not the case. The misunderstanding between fathers and sons is one of the true tragedies in a life. Few boys seemed to have had the happiness of Cellini and his father Giovanni, each of whom adored the other (27), while Michelangelo's father said, ''I have had sons, and none of them would offer me a drink of water.'' So it was, too, between Henry and Richard, Richard who most resembled his father in fearlessness, intelligence and physical comeliness. It was said that Henry was hurt when he learned of his son's preference for boys, not necessarily because of the boys, but because, on the most basic level, a lad was destined to sire sons. How else could a man know immortality--the very building blocks of humanity, as Plato made clear in his *Symposium*? (12)

As Henry held dear none of his territories, other than perhaps Le Mans, his birthplace, he never understood Eleanor and Richard's love of Aquitaine. He surely thought, as did everyone then, as most historians today, that Eleanor's refusal to surrender Aquitaine was a simple question of maintaining her source of power. In Medieval times a woman was nothing, yet her lands were hers, a paradox, yet, at the same time, if she lost a husband, literally anyone could seize her and claim her possessions, as Henry II's own brother tried to capture Eleanor following her divorce from Louis VII, actually attempting to waylay her as she desperately rode to the site of her wedding to Henry. Women could rule in England, but it was forbidden in France. A man, like a bee, could and should go from flower to flower, but let a woman try, she would be decapitated at the stalk. Yet so many women got away with it--starting with Eleanor--that chastity belts were really in use, belts that also kept women from pleasuring themselves, heightening their lust for their husbands' attentions.

It was because Richard kept an invincible hold over Aquitaine, rebuffing his father's every move in that direction, that Henry came to hate him. Richard was Eleanor's boy not his, Eleanor the traitor now safely locked away, Richard on the loose thumbing his nose at his father. But Henry did seem to genuinely love John, a boy who dissipated himself in drink, debauchery and hunting; lazy and demanding instant gratification. Perhaps Henry saw something there that others didn't; perhaps he needed the solace of an obedient and grateful puppy, although John was known for being grateful for nothing. Yet he loved the boy--only all-seeing God knew why.

But what God saw or didn't see was of no interest to John. He hated the church, a reason he was drawn towards his brother Geoffrey, who was equally anticlerical. Such free thinking during the Middle Ages was highly exceptional, and one could be burned at the Catholic stake as one can be beheaded in our more enlightened times by Islamic fanatics.

The reader may remember that I referred to another Geoffrey, a son born on the other side of the blanket, as the expression goes, whom Henry recognized and brought up with his own children. This son was destined for the orders but held out the hope that Henry would disinherit the ungrateful legitimate wretches he had engendered and name him as his heir to the throne. It was true that this Geoffrey was so loyal that Henry said of him, ''You are my only true son; the others are the bastards.'' This Geoffrey eventually became archbishop of York and exited the pages of history.

The other, legitimate Geoffrey, was trampled by a horse in Paris during a joust and died from the resulting infection. As stated, he left his lover Philippe, King of France, on the edge of the grave, physically restrained from throwing himself onto the casket.

It was at this point that Richard joined Philippe in Paris and chroniclers reported their eating from the same plate and sleeping in the same bed, although their liaison may have begun well before then. Today's historians, influenced perhaps by our present-day division of sexuality into three distinct categories, homosexual, heterosexual and bisexual, seem unable to accept the fact that since the early Greeks men have had a sexuality that was omnisexual (25), in which their wives were but one alternative among many, self-pleasuring included.

The two men were together and inseparable. Philippe used the time to convince Richard that Henry was set on marrying his beloved John to Philippe's sister Alys (King Henry's very young mistress), with Aquitaine as their wedding gift. War would certainly have followed had there not been a second *coup de théâtre*: Jerusalem fell to the Turk Saladin, Christians were being massacred, and Christianity itself was on the verge of extinction. Richard decided to stop the immensely powerful Saladin, a decision that sent both his father and his lover into a state of shock.

Jerusalem had been won in 1099 during the First Crusade. The crusaders built 50 fortifications, the most stunning and impregnable of which was Krak des Chevaliers. Two Christian organizations, the Templars (11) and the Hospitalers, formed to help the crusaders, added military might to their function and became the backbone of the defense of Christian territories, centered around Acra, Jaffa, Tyre and Ascalon.

Krak des Chevaliers

Saladin spent years in wars against fellow Muslims in the hope of uniting Syria and Egypt into an all-encompassing caliphate. Two major obstacles were Aleppo and Mosel. The Aleppo ruler turned to the Assassins for help. The Assassins was an organization capable of doing, in real life, what the godfather had done in film-fiction with the horse's head placed stealthily between the director's legs while asleep in bed. Both Richard Coeur de Lion and Saladin, the finest warriors the world had to offer at the time, were so terrified of the man responsible for the Assassins, Sinan, that they did everything in their power to placate him--bowing to his every wish and ultimatum. Boys were accepted into the Assassins cult very young, and when the moment came for them to be used as killers they were drugged (*assassin* comes from the Arabic word for *hashish*) and carried into a garden where they found, upon awaking, fountains, wonderful food and all the girls their young bodies could accommodate. They were told that this was Paradise, and that if they were lucky enough to be killed during their mission, this is what awaited them in recompense. Sinan then sent them to perform various tasks, aimed at securing power and wealth for Sinan himself. Saladin must have paid Sinan better than the ruler of Aleppo because the ruler was assassinated and Aleppo fell to him.

In Jerusalem King Baldwin died of leprosy, leaving the city to his son-in-law Guy de Lusignan. Guy was from Poitevin in France, held by none other than Richard. Guy's wife was Henry II's cousin. Another crusader was Reginald de Châtillon. Reginald had been a prisoner of the Saracens for a mindboggling 14 years before being ransomed for an equally mindboggling 120,000 gold dinars (Saracens was the name for Muslims used by the crusaders). Immediately on release he set out to destroy Mecca where he planned to steal the sacred black stone. Saladin defeated his army but Reginald escaped. Until then Saladin had sought peace by entering into peace treaties with Guy de Lusignan and his predecessors, but then Reginald de Châtillon attacked a group of Muslim pilgrims, taking Saladin's sister prisoner and killing the rest. Saladin requested her return and an apology from Guy, who was set on consenting until Reginald came before him with a group of like-minded hawks and demanded that Guy raise an army to fight Saladin. When Guy was treated as a coward for hesitating, he caved in. A huge force, over 20,000 men, mostly Hospitallers and Templars, was formed. The leadership, apparently inept compared to Saladin's, allowed themselves to be stranded in a desert region and rendered powerless when Saladin ordered his men to aim their arrows at the crusaders' horses, killing most. Reduced to animals by horrifying thirst, Saladin massacred them all, taking only the leaders as prisoners, Guy and Reginald among them. He offered Reginald his life if he would convert to Islam, and then, sword in hand, ended it himself when Reginald refused. Guy acquiesced and was freed. Saladin then captured what remained of the crusader towns, with the exception of the valiantly defended Tyre, a tiny island held by the indomitable Conrad de Montferral. Tyre had twelve towers, 15-foot thick walls, and was connected to the mainland by a causeway. Saladin crowned his victories by taking Jerusalem. He didn't massacre the entire population of 40,000 as the Christians had massacred the Muslims in 1099. Those who could pay were freed, those who couldn't were enslaved, mostly children and women, the women immediately raped, their wombs the source of future Islamic warriors.

In France both Richard and Philippe knew that the crusades had become a bottomless pit for both money and men, but the population, brought to the boiling point by the claims of death, destruction, child slavery and rape, conveyed by the archbishop of Tyre, forced both kings to comply. Richard was always ready to wage war and now saw himself riding to the succor of Jerusalem on a white charger, his chance to be seen as more valiant than his father.

But before leaving Aquitaine Richard had to be assured of having something to return to: Henry had to publically promise that Richard would follow him as king. But Henry refused to do so, perhaps because he really did intend to install John in his place. Revolt again broke out, with Philippe on Richard's side. In gratitude, Richard knelt before Philippe in sign of fealty. Henry lost battle after battle against both, and indeed was even obliged to flee from his birthplace, Le Mans, that was burned to the ground. Finally forced to surrender to Richard, he told his son to his face that he had given up on God, and hoped only to live long enough to destroy the boy of his loins. Richard supposedly recounted the story of his father's caving in that night over dinner, enjoying the mirth it occasioned. When Henry's beloved John kneeled before Philippe in homage, Henry was said to have lost all will to live.

He died refusing last rights. Richard came to view the body, behaving, said the chroniclers, in kingly fashion.

Richard was now king and lord over England and nearly 2/3rds of today's France, while Philippe, France's king, ruled over an area barely the size of a pustule on a donkey's ass, stated a chronicler.

Nothing facilitates the union of a same-sex couple. Financially independent, constrained by no written accords or palimony laws, their natural bent is to seek excitement in outside couplings. If one adds to this the dispute over lands and vassals, as was the case for Henry and Philippe, it was not surprising that they left to crusade on separate vessels.

One of life's most astonishing quirks is that Henry II was followed by someone nearly as great, his own wife Eleanor, that Richard freed from captivity. It was she, far more intelligent than them all, unhandicapped by the testosterone that push men to often unreasonable extremes, who would take Richard's place during his absence. She was the only soul in the world Richard could count on with absolute certainty, the one person equipped to hold together the wealthiest and most far-flung empire then in existence, England and Aquitaine. Listening to her advice, Richard showed incredible restraint towards his former enemies, giving lands to some, lordships to others, as well as marrying them to wives with rich dowries. He brought John, his last remaining brother, into the fold and granted Philippe nearly all of his wishes. How much was truly due to his mother's counsel is unknown, but with Eleanor at his side, Richard was a formidable figure, militarily and intellectually.

He went to Genoa where he had a spat with Philippe over boats, and then to Sicily where Eleanor in person met him with his future bride. Eleanor then returned to England and the bride sailed on to Cyprus where its leader Isaac Comnenus--who had made a pact with Saladin by drinking each other's blood--tried to lure Richard's fiancée ashore with the intention of kidnapping her. Richard arrived in time, stormed the island, married his bride and captured Comnenus. (Comnenus had robbed and killed Cyprians from the moment he was crowned, his specialty the deflowering of virgins, all of which led to his later poisoning).

The bride was sent back home after their marriage and Richard sailed to Acra, held by Saladin but besieged by Guy de Lusignan. Guy had been released by Saladin when he gave up a few remaining possessions and also vowed to never again raise arms against Saladin. He broke his word, not because he had agreed under constraint, but because no vow, he said, was greater than the defense of holy Jerusalem. At Acra the usual crimes followed day after day, prisoners on both sides decapitated and their heads returned, shot through cannons. There was even a miracle: a Muslim was killed by an arrow from an impossibly long distance while he was in the midst of pissing on a picture of the Virgin. Philippe arrived with a small fleet, followed by Richard with one much larger.

Richard's military genius saw the fall of Acra and the imprisonment of it defenders. His use of siege engines was considered magisterial, down to his importation of special stones from Cyprus that didn't shatter when they hit the fortified walls, stones that he paid out four gold pieces to whoever would recuperate them. Diplomatically he had his way too, imposing Guy de Lusignan as King of Jerusalem--which was still to be conquered. When Philippe's candidate for King of Jerusalem was rebuffed, Philippe returned to France in a huff. Richard then entered into negotiations with Saladin for the release of the Acra prisoners in exchange for Christian captives, plus part of the true cross Saladin had in his possession, as well as a substantial amount of money Saladin was to fork over. When negotiations dragged into weeks of indecision, Richard ordered his men to gather the captives together in a field in plain view of Saladin's army, and then hack them all to death, 2,700, an act that would tarnish Richard's reputation to our own days. Some claim the Saracens were disemboweled in search of jewels they had swallowed or hidden in the anus. Saladin had his Christian prisoners put to the sword as a result, and all hope of conciliation between the two forces came to an end.

From Acra Richard then gave orders for the assembly of his troops, 29,000, to take back the lost coastal towns. The men were unhappy as they were obliged to leave whorehouses that had welcomed men in Acra with oriental sensuality, and that since the early Greeks. The army was followed by Saladin's troops, estimated at 25,000, who had orders to harass the trailers, especially the baggage train. The harassment was so terrible and inflicted such damage that the troops defending them had to proceed by making the horses march backwards, so that the soldiers would be on maximum alert (or so sources at the time reported). Finally, tired of being picked off one by one, the troops attacked their attackers, despite Richard's order that this was not yet the right moment. But obliged to come to his men's aid, he engaged Saladin in battle, one that he won decisively, killing 7,000 Saracens to his loss of 700.

The victory was proof that Richard was at the height of his powers, the greatest leader in the world at that time, and for decades to come. He nonetheless harbored the fear that he might win but not hold on to Jerusalem, the proof being his dire request to the pope to send thousands of pilgrims to the Holy Land--how else, he knew, would he ever be able to preserve it, once freed? And, of course, everything that Europeans needed for their survival in what they called Outremer--Over the Seas--had to come in by boat or across thousands of dangerous miles of land, while everything the Saracens required was within the reach of their hands. So Richard came up with some ridiculous ideas, the aim being to free him so he could return to his increasingly pressing affairs in France and England, all the while restoring Jerusalem to Christians. He suggested that Saladin's brother Safadin marry his own sister Joan. Saladin and Safadin would then have rule over most of Outremer, in exchange for the return of the true cross in Saladin's possession. Jerusalem would be under some sort of Christian rule, the exact nature of which would be decided through honorable negotiation. The chimera was staggering.

Richard also felt pressure to come to terms with Saladin because back home John had aligned himself with Philippe, despite Eleanor's attempts to keep him in check.

Then Conrade de Montferrat was murdered by Sinan's Assassins, supposedly under orders from Saladin, although this is highly disputed. Guy de Lusignan, perhaps because Richard realized he would never become King of Jerusalem, was sold Cyprus as a consolation, over which his family would rule for the next 300 years. Skirmishes continued between Richard's forces and those of Saladin, one of which apparently brought Richard in sight of Jerusalem, causing him to shed bitter tears over the city he would never possess. Relations between Richard and his enemies were of the strangest kind: After one heavily-fought English victory Saladin's brother Safadin sent Richard two white Arabian horses in admiration, and during two illnesses, Saladin sent him chickens for his soup during the first, fresh fruit in snow to see him through a second. Saladin could afford to be generous because he knew the end was coming for Richard, Richard who would sooner or later be obliged to return home to care for urgent business there, and that he, Saladin, had only to be patient.

Eventually a peace was arranged: Christian pilgrims would be allowed in Jerusalem and trade resumed, which would enrich Christians and Saracens alike. Part of the coast would remain in Christian hands, the interior in those of Saladin. The treaty signed, Richard and Saladin separated, having never met in person. Saladin would soon be dead, his task of defending his rightful homeland accomplished. And so we now leave this enigmatic, forceful, entirely worthy personage to the judgment of History and his One God.

Richard returned to a hero's welcome, for he had carried the torch high for his God too, and although he had not succeeded, no other man of woman could have done more or better. Trials awaited him in the form of John and Philippe and petty vassals who were in eternal revolt, all pissants in comparison to the land of men he sailed from.

Richard sailed to Cyprus and a final goodbye to Guy de Lusignan, then to Rhodes, Crete and Corfu--a single sentence on paper which masks the insanity of attempting any movement over the Mediterranean in winter, sudden winds that could snap fully furrowed masts in seconds, strong and unchartered currents, cold that bit into the bones, and inexistent hygiene, the cause of demeaning dysentery. In Corfu Richard learned that literally everyone except his mother and his new father-in-law, the King of Navarre, was against him. In Aquitaine his brother John had tried to stir up revolt. When Philippe returned to France he badmouthed Richard to both the pope and the Holy Roman Emperor Henry VI, making two allies for himself, two enemies for Richard. Revolt in the south of France and Henry VI's influence over Italy made landing there extremely dangerous, and Richard couldn't go to Spain because of feuds between his father-in-law in Navarre and various Spanish powers. He thusly was blown from island to island, nearly losing his life to storms or brigands. He was finally obliged to make landfall on a shore of woods and marshes near Venice. From there he preceded north, through towns that obliged strangers to state their names and business before being allowed entrance. Richard and a German-speaking boy traveled through forests, across mountain torrents, in the dead of winter (December), through snow, sleet and hail, over paths untended since Roman times. Little wonder that Richard fell ill and he and the boy took a room in a lodging. Richard sent the boy out for food and the lad, flushed with money, wearing Richard's beautiful gloves and arrogant because of the rich stranger he was accompanying, was noticed and arrested, as was Richard.

He was taken to Leopold of Austria. Here we need a flashback to the siege of Acra. Leopold and his Germans had been at work attacking the fortification for years before Richard and Philippe showed up. So when Acra fell Leopold thought it natural that his standards be placed on the crenellated tower along with those of the two kings. But Richard and Philippe, fearful they would be obliged to give Leopold 1/3rd of the loot taken from Acra, tore down his standards, leaving them to be trampled in the dirt. Leopold returned to Austria, vowing hatred for them both. When Philippe returned to France he was able to not only win over the Holy Roman Emperor Henry VI, but he eventually charmed Leopold into forgiving him.

Leopold and the Emperor now entered into an agreement: They would hold Richard for a ransom of 100,000 marks, a colossal sum that would impoverish England. This was accompanied by the direst draconian measures to ensure payment, among them 200 royal English nobles put in Henry's hands until every mark had been handed over. Philippe entered the dance by offering to pay both Leopold and Henry more money still if they would keep Richard prisoner for life. This was refused, especially as Richard had the protection of the pope, as did every man going on a crusade. In fact, the pope threatened to excommunicate all three, Philippe, Henry and Leopold, if Richard were not immediately freed. Leopold had a mortal fear of excommunication, but nonetheless decided to hold out until enriched by Richard's ransom. In England Richard's brother John assured the entire world that he had proof of Richard's death, and forthwith declared himself King of England. Richard was no saint, but with the exception of his mother, the pope and his brother-in-law, the King of Navarre, Richard was indeed alone.

It was finally agreed that Henry would be paid the 100,000 marks,

Leopold would receive 50,000 more, bringing the total to 150,000; the cream of England's nobility would be handed over as hostages to Henry, including the King of Navarre's own son; and, incredibly, Henry would be recognized by Richard as Lord over England, receiving a yearly homage from Richard of £5,000. Richard was freed and Englishmen financially enslaved for generations. Yet the tide turned: Leopold was excommunicated for having imprisoned a crusader, Richard. In revenge he decided to kill his hostages, but fell from his horse, injuring his leg so badly it had to be amputated by axe, precision surgery that gangrened, bringing death, before which Leopold begged God's forgiveness by repudiating the ransom and freeing the hostages in his possession.

It was during this time that the legend of Robin Hood took root, Robin who strove for the release of Richard whom all wanted to return to England and depose Richard's evil brother John.

Richard received a hero's welcome in England, and after putting his affairs in order there, he returned to his cherished Aquitaine, never to see the country of his birth again. The task before him now was enormous. What territories Philippe had not taken, Richard's former vassals had. He had to begin his conquests again. His weapons were his military genius, a professional army, and limitless funds, for it seems that his subjects were cash cows impossible to milk completely dry. After fighting years in the Holy Land Richard was equipped to siege and seize every fortification that had treasonously turned against him. His brother John came before him on bended knee, as he had with Philippe. Richard forgave him and John, happy at the reprieve, ran off to slaughter the towns that had recognized John as their sovereign, all to show Richard what a faithful boy he had become. Philippe skirted direct battle, although he did finally find a husband for his well-used sister Alys, paying the lucky man off with towns that offered vast revenues. The inhabitants of the villages and fortifications that Richard captured during the fighting were raped and massacred, often down to the children, while the nobles were ransomed--accepted consequences and behavior for the Middle Ages. Richard had a castle, his Camelot, built at the incredible cost of £12,000. It is, today, alas, in ruins. All the while Richard was seconded by his father-in-law, Sancho of Navarre, while, apparently, leaving Sancho's daughter, Richard's wife, in virginal peace; there was nothing to indicate that he had ever ''honored'' her, and nothing to indicate the contrary either, other than the fact she was never pregnant, while his father Henry had left Eleanor pregnant every year, despite his frequent absences. The Holy Roman Emperor Henry VI died of fever at age 34, in heavenly punishment for his having sequestered a crusader, Richard.

Richard's Château-Gaillard Camelot and Châlus-Chabrol where he met his death.

Richard besieged still another castle, Châlus-Chabrol. One boy on the top of the tower shot arrows at Richard's troops, usually with no hope of attaining any of them, a gesture motivated perhaps by bravado, perhaps by anger. Richard liked to wander out on the grassy plain to observe the boy. Sure of himself, his reflexes and the distance separating the two, he ventured forth totally unarmed, dressed in royal red, having for unique defense a small shield. It is not impossible that Richard saw the arrow aimed at him, certain it would fall short. It hit him in the shoulder instead. Taken to his tent, the removal was messy as the doctors dug into the flesh to find the metal point. Gangrene set in. The castle had been taken in the meantime and the boy was brought before the king who knew he was dying. He asked the lad why he had shot at him, as the lad knew, from his red clothing, that the target was Richard himself. The boy declared that Richard had caused the death of his father and brother. Richard thanked him for telling the truth and gave orders for him to be released with a pouch of gold. Taken beyond hearing distance, the boy was skinned alive. Richard's body was sent to Fontevraud to lie at the feet of Henry. Eleanor would soon join both.

Richard I at Fontevraud Abbey

JOHN (JACK) NICHOLSON AND HERBERT EDWARDES
Hero of the Indian Mutiny of 1857

As John Nicholson's destiny was intertwined with the Indian Mutiny of

1857, that's where we will begin our story of this unique man, and the story of one of the most horrid massacres in world history.

John (Jack) Nicholson

The standard of living was immeasurably higher for a British soldier in India, because he had far greater buying power than being stationed in England. An officer had around 13 servants and even an enlisted man could count on being shaved in the morning while still in bed, he could depend on his shirts and trousers being as white as snow, his shoes polished, his clothes tailored to his body. The barracks were airy, with rows of beds and ceiling fans, saddles and bridles hanging from the rafters. There was a veranda and piss tubes emptied regularly, but men being what they are, the lack of aim made them smelly, as were the surrounding open latrines. There were coffee rooms where one played chess and checkers, billiard rooms, a theater, and libraries. When the climate allowed it, they played polo, football and cricket, and they hunted. The major inconvenience was the heat, soaring daily to 115, leaving them prostrate. Breakfast at eight consisted of beef steaks and curry. They then retired to bed where they literally gasped for breath. At one in the afternoon they lunched on curried meat, potatoes and rice, and returned to their rooms as listlessly as during the morning. At four there was a beginning of movement as they prepared for dinner, augmented by as much beer as they could drink, after which they staggered back to their barracks. Alcoholism was the greatest source of death, claiming several men every week. Most carried rum back to the barracks in whatever they could hide in their shirts and down their trousers, for its possession was illegal.

The Indian soldiers were called sepoys. They were in far better physical condition than the British because so many wanted to enter the British army that selection was draconian. Over 5' 8'', they were invariably strong, intelligent and valiant. Their living conditions were infinitely better than those of the Brits. They received a plot of land on which they could build a home, they were married and accompanied by parents and relatives, and although they received 7 rupees compared to the 20 given an English officer, this was far more than they could have earned otherwise. In addition, their employment by the British conferred on them immense stature. Three-fourths were Hindus, the rest mostly Muslims. Good natured, they looked on their English officers with what was described as tender love, and English women would not hesitate a second to put their children in their care. They wore a uniform--white shirt and trousers and red jackets--but at home reverted immediately to the dhoti, a simple loincloth. Instead of drinking, they spent their time playing with their children and in endless gossip with their neighbors, while smoking opium and hashish.

There was a bazaar especially for the use of British soldiers where they could buy whatever they needed, as well as being entertained by jugglers, sword swallowers, snake charmers and acrobats. There were girls to be bought in whorehouses, but due to rampant syphilis the government offered clean girls too at the cost of a quarter of a rupee for enlisted men. There was no real reason why a man should marry but white women were nearly as prized as rum. One story told by Christopher Hibbert in his wonderful *The Great Mutiny* related the case of a woman married and widowed several times due to her husbands' deaths by alcohol, dysentery, fever and cholera. While returning from her latest husband's funeral her hand was asked in marriage. When she broke down in tears, the officer apologized for not giving her time to get over her loss. ''It's not that,'' she replied. It was because at graveside she had agreed to marry a simple soldier, one who wasn't an officer. It must be added that because a widow's benefits were limited in time, she had either to remarry or become penniless.

The forces that would soon be in opposition were these: an army of 300,000 of which only 14,000 were British, this in a country of 150,000,000. There were an additional 23,000 men stationed in the Punjab, but not only had the Punjab just been annexed into the British Empire, its people were warlike, comparable to Afghans, meaning forces as ferocious as the ancient Scythes.

Two immediate catalysts were responsible for the mutiny, but the underlying problem was that no nation will ever stand the tyranny of another, especially when kicked and treated as niggers and pigs, the latter an abomination to the Muslims. The two catalysts were the certainty that Britain would force Christianity on India as Henry VIII, through the slaughter of countless children, along with that of women and men, imposed Anglicism on the English themselves. The most immediate catalyst was the introduction of new cartridges. They were ''modern,'' although of a conception medieval to our eyes. The cartridges consisted of a glazed paper surface that had to be bitten through before being introduced into the gun muzzle. They also had to be greased so they could slide down the barrel. The grease was rumored to be of pig and cow fat, the first forbidden to Muslims, the second to Hindus. When the sepoys refused to bite through them, the British suggested they visit the places in India where they were made so they could see for themselves the fat used. The sepoys answered that this was not assurance as some cartridges came directly from England where their fabrication could not be inspected. The British then said that the sepoys could tear the end of the cartridges with their fingers and not their teeth. The answer to this was that since they had been used to the old ways for so long, perhaps in the heat of battle they would forget and bite into the cartridges, breaking their caste. One man ordered to shoot a round preferred to place the rifle against his chest and discharge it with his toe, killing himself. Another man who refused in another part of India was summarily hanged. In still another part of the country two whole battalions had to be disbanded when some of the men refused to load their rifles. In one place several sepoys were hauled away to prison in chains, a humiliation that had their comrades weeping. Many of the officers genuinely loved their men, while others knew that the sepoys were in their presence just two hours a day, so in reality the officers had no idea of what they were doing in their free time, nor what they were thinking.

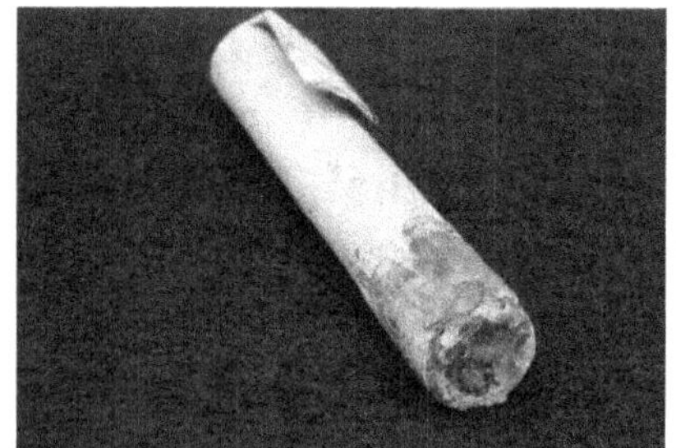

Enfield cartridge

The Enfield rifles that used the new cartridges arrived in Meerut in January 1857. The station there was commanded by Brigadier Wilson, the thirteenth son of a parson. There, too, sepoys had refused to load their rifles and 85 of them were marched to prison in shackles, some weeping. Others took off their boots and threw them at their commanders watching the scene. The other sepoys promised, under their breath, to free the prisoners and kill their jailers.

For months headquarters had been warned of brewing unrest by Indian friends. Now revolt broke out everywhere. In one barracks the sepoys refused to obey when given an order, and actually struck the loaded rifles pointed at them out of the unbelieving officers' hands. A sepoy was put to death for disobedience and his name became a rallying point for dissidents, Mangal Pande. In another location an English woman and her children, returning from church, were attacked and killed. In a nearby bazaar troops out for a good time were set upon by local toughs and sent scampering. Peasants hearing of the revolt came in from the countryside to help the sepoys and to plunder. Soon 50 children, women and men around Meerut were killed.

A large number of sepoy cavalry and sepoys running alongside them made it to Delhi and the palace of King Bahadur Shah II, a former athlete, now, at 82, a devoted painter. He had been stripped of power, but as the leader of millions, he was honored by the British who paid him a salary. A Muslim, he genuinely cared for the Hindus. The arriving sepoys (I'll use the word sepoy, the name for troops, to cover also native cavalry, the exact name of which was sowars) asked for entrance to the palace, and when refused, killed the gate guards. They entered, shooting every British officer who came their way. Fifty children and women were rounded up and made prisoner. Later they were brought into a court where a rope encircled them all. The Hindus gave them to the king's Muslim servants, who massacred them, thusly guaranteeing their entry into paradise, the reason the Hindus had offered them the prisoners.

Bahadur Shah II

Two miles north of Delhi a garrison became aware of what was happening and sent several regiments to Delhi, sepoy troops in which the commanders not only had total faith, but were proud that none had backed mutineers. Arriving in Delhi they stormed the palace. Once inside they were attacked by the rebel forces. Ordering their sepoys to shoot, the sepoys at first shot into the air before turning their guns on their commanders. The man who had said, ''We're with them two hours a day. How can we possibly know how they spend the rest of their time and what they're really thinking?'' was proved right.

The courage of the British was incontestable. But advancement through the ranks due to seniority meant that only some men of intelligence made it to the top. Others were fools out to protect their own old carcasses. The outcome would have been tragic even if only able-bodied men had been involved. But there were hundreds of children and women concerned, which would make the mutiny of 1857 one of history's most dramatic scenes of horror. As for the Indians, those caught and hanged after the

Delhi slaughter of children and women went to their deaths with perfect indifference. There was no struggle, just stoicism. Most went in silence, while a few said they were content to die after seeing British women ''molested and torn to pieces.'' Others said goodbye to the crowd of Indians observing the executions, some even gave a sad farewell to their British officers. They truly took heart in the belief that they were off to a better place, and given how some had been treated, even black nothingness would have been an improvement.

John Nicholson enters the story for the first time. He was the deputy of Herbert Edwardes, both men under Brigadier-General John Lawrence, the Judicial Commissioner. Edwardes had been wounded during what was called the First Sikh War and was taken in by Henry Lawrence, John Lawrence's brother, becoming one of Henry's--and later John's--Young Men. Edwardes took part in the Second Sikh War, permanently wounding his hand in a pistol accident. He was hardworking and intellectually ready for any position offered him, light-years away from Nicholson's impulsiveness. For John Lawrence, as well as Edwardes, work in India was a labor of love, and why not? Despite the incessant feuds between sects, clans and individuals, the Indians of India were a warm hearted, intelligent and supremely beautiful people.

Both of Edwardes' parents were dead by age 4 and Edwardes was raised by a deeply religious Protestant aunt who placed him in a boarding school from age 10 (6). Later he studied Classics and Mathematics at King's College, London, a constituent of the University of London. He was fond of debating, drawing and poetry. He received a cadetship in the Bengal Infantry, as had Nicholson, thanks to a family friend. He arrived at age 22 (Nicholson had been 17) and served in Karnal for 5 years after passing language exams in Hindustani and Persian (Nicholson had passed his exam in Urdu, basically the same as Hindustani) at age 26. He wrote about military matters, which brought him to the attention of Commander-in-Chief Hugh Gough who named Edwardes to his staff.

Nicholson and Edwardes were intellectually made for each other, and Edwardes' calm was the soothing influence that made life worth living for Nicholson. There is no painting of Edwardes during his years of beauty, years so important yet so limited in time. Both men's love was confirmed by Edwardes' wife, who could not have known the entire depth of its intensity--although she did destroy a number of Edwardes' letters, an outrage (to us) common to Victorian times when wives and best friends protected the reputations of those they loved by a full use of the fireplace--often asked to do so by the writer himself, in a mutual promise between friends of self-preservation.

Nicholson and Edwardes took their furloughs at the same time, travelling to England together by a long voyage that began by sailing down the Sutlej and then the Indus rivers to Karachi, on to Bombay and then a streamer to Suez. They sailed down the Satlej on an Indian houseboat that tied up at night so dinner could be prepared for them. During the day and the long nights they were alone to talk and to share the beauty of the night lighted only by the Milky Way, as they lay out together over the sands, the boat gently bobbing anchored nearby, in conversation and in silence, and perhaps, just perhaps, in blessed love. The setting was ensorcelling, and for the first time in his life Nicholson knew real calm and peace, as would always be the case next to Edwardes.

From then on, as Edwardes wife wrote, they were ''more than brothers in the tenderness of their whole lives henceforth, and the fame and interests of each other were dearer to them both than their own.'' They briefly parted company in Cairo, but met again in London where they were seen walking arm-in-arm along Piccadilly and Hyde Park. They dined at the Mansion House as guests of the Lord Mayor, at the same table as the Duke of Wellington. Edwardes rose and toasted Nicholson, saying, ''Here, gentlemen, is the real author of half the exploits which you have been kind enough to attribute to me.''

Back in India their posts were separated by 60 miles. Nicholson nonetheless rode out to spend his weekends with Edwardes, riding from Bannu to Peshawar, changing horses at mid-distance thanks to a fresh mount Edwardes sent out with a servant.

Stationed in the newly annexed Punjab, they were decided on securing the region the moment they heard of the mutiny. Suspected sepoy regiments were disbanded. Some of their officers, certain the sepoys were good men, threw their own swords onto the pile of those of the suspects. One officer even committed suicide, another burst into tears. Sepoy ringleaders were blown from the muzzle of the cannons, a Mongol custom adopted by the British. Most officers ate and prayed with their weapons never leaving their sides. In one regiment 192 sepoys bolted. An offer of 30 rupees was made for each caught by the local villagers. Those brought in were shot, eventually all 192. To which were added 200 suspects. The sepoys had marched up to their extinction in perfect rows and waited passionlessly to be mowed down, the Sikhs doing much of the executing. The Sikhs were believers in one god, the term coming from a Sanskrit word meaning student, and originated around 1400 A.D. in the Punjub. The bodies of the dead were thrown down dry wells.

Cawnpore

The culmination of horror took place at Cawnpore, on the banks of the Ganges, a post between Delhi and Benares. Fear of an uprising saw women and children take refuge in the local barracks, which inspired local toughs to greater disobedience. General Wheeler, in charge of the Cawnpore garrison, decided not to do more for the protection of his compatriots for fear of setting a bad example in front of the sepoys and, anyway, he felt that he could count on the local maharajah, Nana Sahib. Sahib was the adopted son the last monarch, who had been pensioned off by the British for £80,000 a year, making a lifetime total of £2,500,000, in exchange for his lands once he died. Nana Sahib was fabulously rich in lands of his own, in pearls, diamonds, and he possessed an unrivalled collection of pornographic paintings. The British refused to extend the pension to cover him, even when he sent a handsome, clever boy, Azimullah, his representative, to London to plead his case. Nana Sahib had taken the boy, starving, off the streets and had seen to his education. Although the lad failed in having the pension extended, letters later found testified to the success of his beauty and charm among London's better ladies. Nana Sahib therefore backed the revolt when it broke out, sending men to take the British Magazine with its munitions and guns, and the Treasury. He then decided to lead troops to Delhi, but was convinced by the handsome Azimullah to remain where he was, destroy the English, and claim the lands of his father.

Nana Sahib

Wheeler, his troops and the women and children, were attacked in the barracks by sepoys and anyone else who was now armed thanks to the taking of the Magazine. The wounds the English endured were horrifying, recounts Christopher Hibbert in his book. A bullet that killed a soldier, first passed through the arm of his wife and wounded one of the twin babies she was carrying. Another woman lay on her back, a child suckling from each breast, unable to move. General Wheeler's own son, "his darling" boy, had been wounded and was being fanned by two of his sisters when a bullet pierced the wall and shot his head off. The misery went on and on, sparing no one. The temperature rose to 130. Soon 250 were dead.

Finally Azimullah wrote a letter to General Wheeler offering safe passage to Allahabad, a huge British garrison. The surviving men gathered up the women and children and babies and made for waiting boats that would take them to safety. Once on board, machine guns, hidden till then, were uncovered and, accompanied by armed sepoys, the slaughter began. Those still near the shore were clubbed to death, children were bayoneted or stabbed. A boat caught fire and the children went up in flames. Some men did get away, and it was they who would later tell the story that would bring the worst exactions on Indians since the invasion of the Mongols.

Azimullah

There were nonetheless 125 women and children who, along with a few men, survived. Rounded up, they were herded to a small house. The women's earrings were torn from their ears, rings that would not budge were cut free. Two girls were known to have been saved by sepoys who converted and married to them. One later confessed to a Catholic priest, on her deathbed, that she was the daughter was General Wheeler.

Nana Sahib was installed on his father's throne. He distributed 150,000 rupees to his troops, a fraction of what he had stolen from the Treasury. In the prisoners' house they began dying off from hunger, thirst, heat, dysentery and cholera.

The British army knew about the attack on Cawnpore but as yet ignored its fall. Brigadier-General Henry Havelock was chosen to bring aid, seconded by Colonel James Neill. Havelock had received a commission thanks to his brother, so great a hero at Waterloo that General von Alten promised to engage any Havelock whatsoever. Henry Havelock was five feet tall, and only due to incessant study in military tactics did he make his way through the ranks. He learned Persian and Hindustani (Hindustani is the literary version of Hindi), and was so religious he taught bible classes. In Benares Neill had all suspects of rebellion hanged, even boys who dared show the rebel flag. In Allahabad there was confusion due to Sikhs breaking into liquor supplies and causing havoc. The Sikhs were not harmed but everyone else the British came across was dispatched. One soldier wrote to his mother that they were hanging a dozen niggers a day. The troops then went on to Cawnpore, 1,000 British, 10 Sikhs, 20 cavalry, and anyone else, down to shopkeepers, who wanted to come along, ostensibly to lend a hand. On the way they learned that Cawnpore had fallen.

In Cawnpore the death of the prisoners was decided, first because they would be witnesses to the massacres that had already occurred, and second, incredibly, because Azimullah thought that once the prisoners were dead the British would no longer have a reason to liberate them, and would thusly go away. When the sepoys surrounding them refused to do the killing, two Muslims and two Hindus where found. They first brought out what men remained and a boy of fourteen, and slaughtered them. They then entered the house, coming out only when broken swords had to be replaced. The dead and wounded children, babies and women, were dropped down a well, and once full, the remainder was thrown into the Ganges.

Havelock arrived as Nana Sahib was leaving. Greatly outnumbered, the British nonetheless fought with such wild courage that they won the day. Havelock, accompanied by his soldier son, moved on, leaving Neill in control of Cawnpore. Neill, who went through every room of the martyrs' house, studied the floor and walls caked with clotted blood, and decided to exact the ultimate in justifiable cruelty. But first he obliged his officers and his men to be paraded through every room too.

The punishment was heinous, and had Havelock remained it would, without doubt, never have taken place. The prisoners were led to the house one by one. A square foot of flooring was wetted and the man obliged, under a whip, to lick it clean. If he were of great importance, his caste would be broken by forcing him to eat beef and pig. He was then taken to gallows where, to the fury of the officers, many bowed to the waiting nooses. Other sepoys were already at work digging the graves in sight of the men who would soon fill them, including the diggers. The executions went on for months, but very few of those hanged had taken part in the murders. So the soldiers promised that for every man, woman and child killed, he personally would account for the deaths of a hundred. Rumors came to the men that elsewhere in India children were being bayoneted to the walls and English women raped in public. Children were also said to be forced to eat the flesh of their murdered fathers. Even today no one knows how much of this was founded in truth.

The King of Delhi, the 82-year-old former athlete we met at the beginning of our story, decided that he had been chosen by God to defend his religion. He named his preferred son commander of the mutineers. The problem was that now each sepoy felt he was a king, giving him the right to kill whoever offered resistance, from bakers to shopkeepers who refused or hesitated in obeying a sepoy order. Chaos reigned and those who feared anarchy slipped out of the city to tell the British--who commanded a high area looking down on Delhi called the Ridge--everything that was going on within the walls. They exaggerated the extent to which the people sorely missed their former British rulers, but the Brits were not taken in by the optimism.

When the British shelled the city, the men within began to slip out and return home. Some on the Ridge wanted to storm Delhi before the city received reinforcements and while disorder within kept the inhabitants from mounting a viable defense. But better heads on the Ridge cautioned restraint until they themselves were reinforced. In the meantime, bombardments sapped the will of the sepoys. There was dissention between the British, and behind the twenty-five foot walls of the city there was dissention too, the difference being that the British were disciplined. A battalion of Gurkhas, soldiers from Nepal, arrived to help the British and no troops were to prove themselves better than they. The Sikhs too were highly popular among the Brits. The comradeship between the English and Gurkhas and Sikhs was total, there were no niggers here.

Nicholson

All arguments became moot when from the Punjab new troops arrived under the command of Brigadier-General John Nicholson. Tall, bearded and deadly serious, he inspired fear and dislike the moment his peers were introduced to him. Arrogant, sneering even, he was immediately hated by most yet worshipped by his sepoys, sepoys whom Nicholson himself detested. They would be admitted ten at a time into his tent in the Punjab to admire their hero, a few going as far as to stretch out in reverence, a crime they all knew was invariably punished by the whip. At times, on Nicholson's desk, he displayed the decapitated heads of the mutineers, the killing of which had brought the Punjab to heel. He stated that he wanted the captives to be impaled and skinned alive, and he meant it. It was said that to know him was to like him, and some did see beneath the shroud of haughty aloofness a man shy, one ill at ease at the unacceptable attraction he felt for the boys he commanded. As with many homosexuals, he had been born, like Richard Coeur de Lion, into the perfect storm: a father absent due to death just after Nicholson's birth, and a mother he worshipped. At age 15 a rich uncle who had directed the East India Company had him offered a cadetship into the Bengal Infantry, from whence he went on to duty in the Afghan War before being sent to the Punjab and duty under his mentor John Lawrence.

At age 34, he arrived on the Ridge where he immediately earned the disgust of the other officers by his overbearing manners, his disrespect for the competency of the Ridge's commander, Archdale Wilson, and for Nicholson's habit of eating with a huge Pathan orderly covering his back, a cocked pistol in one hand while he served Nicholson with the other. Physically Nicholson too was impressive, muscular and powerful, his eyes intense, his bearing ramrod, his voice deep and grave, his face of flawless beauty.

Under the impulsion of Nicholson a team was organized to capture Delhi, 8,000 men would strike from various sides, escalate the walls and bring the war into the city. That night commanders met in Nicholson's tent and were instructed as to what was expected of them. They then went outside and Nicholson, with Delhi in view, reinforced his exposé.

The commanders returned to their men and gave orders that their wounded comrades would be left unattended where they fell, but would be taken care of after the siege. No prisoners were to be taken but women and children were to be left unharmed. The men were also told not to plunder, and that all wealth within the city would be gathered up later and distributed, equally, to them all. The batteries then opened up to further weaken the walls already greatly damaged during previous bombardments. At sunrise the troops saw an enormous breach that they ran for. Indians were already there trying to fill it in when they saw the troops coming. Taken by surprise, they nonetheless put up such severe resistance that ladders raised by the British to scale the breach were thrown down. The ladders were taken from the dead and dying Brits and thrown up again against the wall. This was done three times before the troops managed to gain entrance. At three other sites the same scenario repeated itself.

The unlucky men were those downed by the walls. Writhing in agony, they moaned their displeasure at not being able to bring the war into the walls. Those who entered the city were heroes of immense bravery, fighting hand to hand with the mutineers. The wounded Brits fell aside, the others continued courageously on, showing no hesitation in front of their peers, as unafraid of dying as were the defenders of Delhi.

Nicholson led the attack on the Kashiri Gate but it had not been sufficiently weakened by the bombardment. He was at the front of two attacks against it, the only result being the death of most of his officers and men. Mad with desire to accomplish his mission, he led a third attack, but was felled by a bullet. The number of dead and wounded was fearful. A field hospital had been set up and literally hundreds of wounded were brought in for care and amputations. The horror was indescribable.

When the Union Jack was finally raised over the walls there were cheers, laughter and dancing. There were also sixty officers and a thousand men dead and wounded. A stock of liquor was found, and although Wilson ordered gallons destroyed, enough remained to fuel the hatred that would see every visible Indian shot or hacked to death. As the bodies of their own comrades were strewn everywhere, no additional encouragement was needed to feed the massacre. Even camp followers, British merchants and civil servants entered into the killing spree, many of whom had lost a brother, sister, mother or father to the mutineers. Even six days later they were still slaughtering whoever came to hand, and proud of it.

The king had escaped but gave himself up when his advisors convinced him that the English would not find him guilty of trying to harm them. Two of his sons and another prince were also found, and although aided by 3,000 Indians, they surrendered to a force of 150 Brits, under the command of a lieutenant, William Hodson. Hodson had the princes loaded in a cart and a bit later, perhaps fearful that the crowd would turn against them, he ordered the mob to lay down their arms. Amazingly, although scorning the British, they complied. The arms were loaded in a cart and the march continued to within a mile of Delhi. Here Hodson turned to his second, Lt. Macdowel, and pretended that he was certain they would never make it back, and that it was essential to resolve the problem then and there. He ordered the princes stripped of their clothes and he personally shot all three. The Sikhs shouted in glee and the mob simply silently dispersed. A captured eunuch, said to have been the king's favorite, was likewise dispatched. In camp Hodson, enriched by the princes' rings and swords, was welcomed as a hero. The murderers of children and women had been murdered, and rightly so.

Lawrence, back in the Punjab, was kept up-to-date concerning the executions and looting. He who had brought order to the Punjab by killing hundreds now wrote to whomever he could, to plead for justice and an end to the murder in Delhi. He was not listened to. Gallows were dressed everywhere and they served for weeks. Many of the soldiers had seen the blood-splattered walls in Cawnpore, many had seen the wells filled with women, children and babies, all had witnessed the killing and amputations of their comrades in arms. Only a handful felt the slightest pity. But in the end Lawrence gained cause. Delhi was transferred to Punjab jurisdiction, his jurisdiction.

Now was the time for looting, the result of which would alas remain with the looters, not the troops that had bled and died. Fat inhabitants were tortured until they revealed where they had stashed their treasures. Houses were measured to find secret rooms. Servants were bribed or threatened until they divulged where the money and jewels of their masters were hidden. One house alone was said to have concealed thirteen wagonloads of treasure. In another, jewels were found behind a load of onions. In still another, jewels worth thousands of pounds were unearthed.

The murders were so widespread and all-inclusive that faithful sepoys had to be given special armbands to wear so as not to be shot. Weapons were routinely protected from the damp by being fired into prisoners. Other prisoners were led to rivers to be shot so the bodies would not have to be carried, just tipped into the water. Mop-up operations continued throughout the whole continent by men fired by the memory of Cawnpore, and the last words most of the mutineers heard was *Remember Cawnpore, you bloody nigger!* One deeply religious man recited the Bible while bayoneting an estimated twenty prisoners. Elsewhere sepoys were tied and branded, stabbed in the face and roasted over fires. The memory of Cawnpore and Delhi seemed to grow, not decrease in time. And details of the martyrdom of children and babies in newspapers fired new recruits who landed in Calcutta, straight from London, each vowing to avenge English women. No matter how many would eventually perish, in a country of 150,000,000 the surface was barely scratched. During this time Havelock, sick with dysentery, called for his son Harry and died in his arms.

The King of Delhi, Bahadur Shah II, was given a two-month long trial, found guilty, and exiled to Rangoon in the company of one of his sons. His ancestors live there to this day.

Nana Sahib staged his own suicide, by drowning in the Ganges, after the fall of Cawnpore. He was later reported to have fled to Nepal where he died of fever in 1859. Another story had him dying in 1906 at the age of 81, having become a religious wiseman who lived in a cave.

John Nicholson, in one of Fate's twisted asides, was mourned by the Indians he had allowed into his presence, to whom he had paid no attention, whom he had whipped when they spread out before him as if he were a god. Now they fell to their knees sobbing.

Nicholson's full life can be found in my book *John (Jack) Nicholson.*

RICHARD BURTON AND JOHN SPEKE
The Discovery of the Source of the Nile
1858

Richard Francis Burton (1821–1890) was an eminent Freemason explorer. The catalyst for the expeditions of Richard Burton and John Speke was the Greek geographer known as Ptolemy who in 150 A.D. produced a map which showed, thanks to information gleaned by the Greek explorer Diogenes, the existence of a mountain range with twin peaks, from which two rivers flowed to form the Nile. Burton took on Speke in his attempt to find the mountains and the exact sources of the Nile. The Nile had posed problem since the pharaohs. It not only crosses the most desolate, hottest deserts in the world, it not only never dried up in summer, but, against all logic, it flooded Egypt during the hottest months, making Egypt the breadbasket of the ancient world, the reason for its being a prime Roman conquest, as well as giving Cleopatra sway over Caesar and Marc Antony.

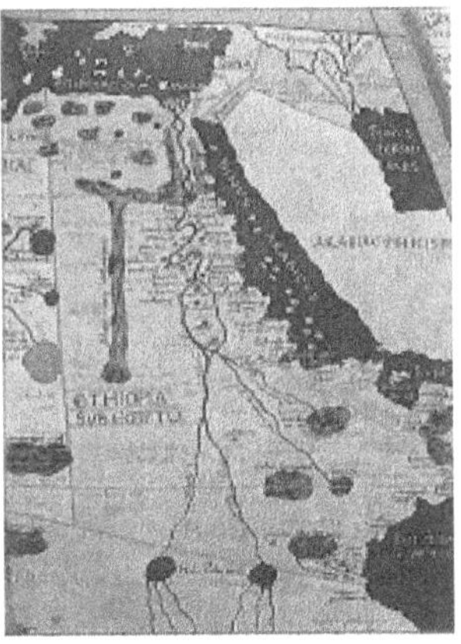

Ptolemy's map

Burton, tall and swarthy, had become known when he successfully made a hajj to Mecca, disguised as an Arab merchant. Aged 37, he went so far as to have himself circumcised, an extraordinarily painful process during adulthood. Mecca was, and is today, a city closed to infidels. Had he been caught, he would have been torn to pieces. He certainly had one of the richest sex lives known to western man: Already, as an adolescent, he and his older brother accompanied their father, a hypochondriac, throughout Europe in search of spas, the two boys entertaining themselves in a steady succession of whorehouses while daddy took the waters. It was Burton who translated and brought to us the *Kama Sutra*, the content of which he had turned into practical knowledge since his balls dropped, and to go on from girl-love to boy-love was, for him, a step towards Nirvana.

The first question that comes to mind concerning the discovery of the origin of the Nile is simply why not sail up the river to its source? This had been tried in 1850 by Andrew Melly, a millionaire who died of fever. In 1851 Andrea De Bono made his way up the cataracts, selling captured lions and human beings, until stopped by malaria. Giovanni Miani tried in 1860, paying his passage by selling ivory but turned back too due to malaria and hostile tribes. Now it was Burton's turn.

Burton could apparently speak Arabic and Persian so well he could pass for someone from both peoples. He is said to have spoken 29 other languages, including Hindustani, Gujarati, Punjabi, Sinhi, Saraiki, Marathi, Sanskrit, Portuguese, Spanish, German, Icelandic, Swahili, Hebrew, Aramaic, Latin, Greek, French and Italian. He believed in British superiority, a normal sentiment in that the British were everywhere on the planet and everywhere successful. In addition, he loved the desert and Arab dress.

Speke, as tall as Burton at 6 feet, had blue eyes and light hair. Even later, when they were implacable enemies, Burton described him as being courageous, perseverant and energetic. Their first experience together was harrowing:

Somalia then, as today, had a notorious reputation for violence, founded, it seems, on their seizing a man's genitals and unmanning him with a single thrust of a knife. Burton, Speke and two aids had camped along the shore of the Somalian town of Berbera. Perhaps because it was feared that they were a British vanguard whose purpose was to deprive the Somalians of their wealth--their slave trade--or perhaps simply to steal their possessions, the explorers' two tents were attacked in the early morning. There were four men in two tents, Burton, William Stroyan, Speke and G.E. Herne. Hearing someone outside his and Burton's tent, Stroyan went out and was immediately hit on the head with a sword while a spear was thrust through his heart. Burton exited and received a spear that pierced him from one cheek through the other, destroying teeth and cutting across the roof of his mouth. Speke had come out of his tent firing, his gun killing several Arabs until he was wrestled to the ground and tied. He later wrote that when someone groped at his privates he was certain that they would be cut off. Instead, to Speke's inexpressible relief, the man was only searching the area preferred by Arabs when hiding knives. A man nevertheless ran up and planted his spear into Speke's chest, several times, the last thrust aimed at Speke's heart that he was able to deflect with his tied hands, badly injuring them. The man, furious, jabbed the spear into his thigh, to the bone. Although certain this was the end, Speke righted himself and ran down the beach through a hail of spears. He found Burton and

Herne pushing off in a boat. He joined them and they rowed across to Aden, under British rule. Miraculously, Speke was back on his feet in a few weeks. Burton's wounds would take months to heal.

Facially scarred for life, Burton and Speke set out for Zanzibar. Both men were alike in one instance, they both had dominating mothers, and fathers in retreat. Fathers, absent due to work, alcoholism or who die early, coupled with the aforementioned mothers, are classic in the creation of homosexuals, although this is far from being a full-proof formula. Otherwise both men were totally different. Only in one instance did Speke lose his head and strike a porter, while Burton regularly beat his. Burton hated Africans, Speke, like Livingston, genuinely liked them. It would turn out that Speke was often right in his premonitions. He wanted, for example, to explore Lake Victoria, the veritable source of the Nile, before Lake Tanganyika, while Burton agreed with their sponsor, the Royal Geographical Society, that an inland ''sea'' the Society had just become aware of, Lake Tanganyika, should come first. Speke did make the mistake, however, of cutting back on sums spent on beads and cloth, absolutely essential in buying food and paying passage through hostile lands, which caused huge problems later. He refused, too, to buy a portable boat, a miscalculation that would land them in trouble multiple times.

In Zanzibar they recruited around 140 men. When they shoved off for the mainland the British consul, a thoroughly good man, whispered to Speke, ''Good luck. I would not travel with that man (Burton) under any condition.'' How Speke felt about Burton at the time is unknown because Burton was his superior, and it was Burton who had chosen him over hundreds of other candidates. That said, Speke had nevertheless made it known to intimates that Burton had sexually propositioned him, a possibility that, knowing what we known about Speke's honesty, we have no reason to doubt.

Richard Francis Burton

''Of the gladdest moments in human life is the departure upon a distant journey into unknown lands. Shaking off with one mighty effort the fetters of habit, the leaden weight of routine. The blood flows with the fast circulation of youth, excitement gives a new vigor to the muscles.''

The Royal Geographical Society wanted both men to bring back specimens of animals and plants. Burton didn't hesitate to broaden the mandate to include anthropological discoveries, including the measurement of native penises (although he hated the natives to see him naked because what they saw, in comparison to them, inevitably brought on mirth). For his part, Speke examined vaginas, and commented on those sewn shut until the girls' suitors saw fit to force them.

They made their way over and through incredible physical obstacles, forests, deserts, torrents and marshes only veritable heroes could surmount, Henry Stanley among them. The same was true of diseases, especially smallpox that slaughtered thousands, malaria and ulcers (chiefly of the feet and ankles), although they would both come back alive, which was far from the case of those who lost their lives in Africa, about whom we know little because they hadn't succeeded. In Burton's case he came down with a sickness that deprived him of the use of his arms and legs, for four months, leaving him unable to walk without aid for a further eleven. Speke nearly went blind, and for months had to be led by hand. Strangely, his eyes got better when, trying to extract an insect from his ear, he did himself such harm that his face, down to his shoulder, "became contorted," in Speke's words. But the infected area seemed to have drawn away the infection from his eyes.

They made it to Tanganyika, the first whites ever. (When an Arab was told of the "discovery" of the lake he said, "What are you talking about? We've known it was there for generations!") They stayed in a town on the lake, Ujiji, where Stanley would soon meet Livingston, a center of Arab slave and ivory trade. They were offered girls by their parents, the price nothing more than a loincloth.

John Speke.
Peter Sagal wrote, in a 1990 article for the *L.A. Times*, that Burton was blithely open about his sexual experiences, while Speke "had no interest in

women'' and ''there is no more reason to assume that there couldn't have been a sexual element between them than there is to assume there was one.'' As their friends and Burton's wife destroyed all letters and journals of a compromising nature, we'll simple never know.

They had heard from several travelers that at the northern end of Tanganyika there was a river that flowed out of it, supposedly the source of the Nile. Boats were hired and Burton, extremely sick, went there with Speke. Alas, either the reports had been false or Burton and Speke had made a mistake in understanding--Burton claimed that Speke spoke no African languages, and as for Burton, his Arabic had been tested by an Arabist who found it rudimentary, but he was tested again by a friend who found it excellent. Burton's fluency in African language is not known. There was indeed a river, but it flowed *into* Lake Tanganyika. Disappointed, they returned to Ujiji where it was decided that Speke alone, with porters, would investigate the huge lake to the northeast, Lake Victoria. Hiring a boat, he navigated to the north of the lake where he found a river that flowed *out* of it, to the north, the beginning of the Nile. When Speke returned to tell Burton, Burton fell into days of depression. They returned to Zanzibar, both so sick they were carried into the town. From there Speke made his way to what should have been glory. Burton, ill, followed later.

No one will ever take from Speke the fact that it was he--due to Burton's illness--who first made the vitally important discovery of the source of the Nile. Yet today there is one biography of Speke, half a dozen of Burton. The reason seems to be due to a simple promise: Speke had given his word not to go to the Royal Geographical Society without Burton. But he did so. Burton accused him of being a lying cad, following up his accusation by belittling him to RGS members, by giving interviews poisoning Speke's well, and later by writing books in which he smeared Speke. Speke, less audible, was soon vilified. Added to this was Speke's early death, just six years after his discovery. Once underground, Burton let out all stops in his vilification. Had Burton not been crippled they would have found the source of the Nile together. As it is today, the name of Burton is known by all, that of Speke known to a few.

Burton and Speke were among those in a line, a very long line, of courageous, thoroughly fearless, totally indomitable, curious, tenacious and wonderfully intelligent British who made Britain the world's greatest power for generations.

Burton had at first admitted Speke's discovery of the source of the Nile, before lambasting Speke, putting in doubt his triumph and labeling him a disloyal liar. Speke in turn divulged that Burton had hit on him and

Burton, for his part, insinuated that Speke was an in-the-closet homosexual.

While stationed in India General Napier had asked Burton to visit three local whorehouses supposedly frequented by British soldiers, whose prostitutes were exclusively boys. Whether Napier had made the request to Burton because he was aware of Burton's sexual proclivities, or whether it was due to his excellence in languages, is unknown. There was a Napier Report, but whether it was on paper or delivered orally is also unknown, as the report is lost to us. The precision of the report is such that Burton is believed to have been a participant in the sexual happenings. The contrary would be surprising as Burton was by then known by one and all for his no-holds-barred sexuality. In an often-cited passage of the report, Burton reveals that uncastrated boys were preferred (many of the prostitutes were eunuchs) because one could grab their balls and use them as reins in guiding the movement of the lads' buttocks. Although such recondite knowledge is beyond my personal understanding, it does indicate that Burton followed what was going on from close up.

Burton later went on to give us a version of the *Kama Sutra* and the *Arabian Nights* in 16 volumes (!), and he was working on what he called his *magnum opus, The Scented Garden*, already 1,282 pages long, *said to have been* a defense of homosexual activity. Some suggest that he never touched his wife *in that way*, but she was devoted to him to the end. She had him given last rights, maintaining that he was still alive, despite his heart attack at age 69. The possibility of his still being alive is refuted by most. At any rate, Burton was an atheist, and her ignoring his wishes to be buried with no religious rites is in itself an act of ignorant barbarity, one enforced by her destroying his *magnum opus* and his other ''filth'' as she called it.

After his discovery of Lake Victoria Speke returned there to glean additional proof of its being the source of the Nile, in the company of James Grant. Part of the journey was through the land of a king whose family had reigned supreme over the enormous region for 400 years. His capital was known for its huge structures, its clean streets and a superb agricultural system that had banished famine since living memory. He had never seen a white man and when he heard that Speke was coming with presents, he sacrificed 400 of his subjects in thanks. When presented with guns he had Speke try one out on four cows that Speke, a renowned marksman and avid hunter, immediately shot dead. The king then gave a rifle to a child and told him to kill the first man he came across outside the king's huge complex of huts. The child came back, laughing, mission accomplished. Speke assisted, helpless, as one to three of the king's wives were led away, daily, to have their heads bashed in, for errors in kingly etiquette, such as the wife who served a certain kind of fruit that another, specific wife, was supposed to give him. The king used Speke for sexual advice, unsatisfied with both the length and endurance of his member. For endurance, Speke told him the less often he honored his wives the stronger would be his lust. As for size, the king had Speke draw him nude which, if the drawing is exact, left the king with decidedly non-African dimensions. Anyway, Speke told the king that a stick of any length did the job, but the king didn't believe a word.

James Grant

The king's mother, enormously fat, also desired Speke's medical knowledge and didn't hesitate to strip naked for his examination. He gave her quinine and counsel, thanks for which she offered him two girls. There seems no doubt that Speke had them both, and he fell in love with one, but was repulsed when she admitted that her interest went only as far as his wealth.

Speke eventually got back to Lake Victoria and returned with proof that he had been right. But it was Burton who received a knighthood. As a final humiliation Burton organized a debate between them both, moderated by Livingston, Livingston who also believed that Speke was mistaken about the source of the Nile, this because Speke and Grant hadn't descended the river far enough from Lake Victoria to convince him (the reason Livingston would soon leave the find the veritable source himself, leading to his disappearance and ''discovery'' by Stanley, and Livingston's ultimate death).

The day before the debate, Speke went hunting, his favorite pastime. He laid his shotgun against a wall that he climbed up on. He then reached down to retrieve it by the barrow. Somehow it went off, shooting him through the upper chest. The day before he had been with Burton and Livingston to plan the debate, but certain that both men would do what they could to demean him, he had stormed out shouting ''I've had enough!'' Now, dead, the rumor was that he had taken his own life, although most people doubt that Speke, who had suffered so greatly during his expeditions, would have done such a thing. Others felt that he was at the end of his rope and did, indeed, kill himself.

Burton's wife had a tent monument raised above both their graves.

Speke was honored with an obelisk.

Spike's Obelisk/Burton's Tomb.
''The more I study religions the more I am certain that man never
worshipped anything but himself.''
Richard Francis Burton

HENRY STANLEY
Stanley Meets Livingston
1871

Nothing can ever fill the abysmal, heartrending emptiness of loss felt by a child abandoned. Such was the case for Stanley, an invisible *A* for Abandoned etched into his forehead throughout every moment of his life. We know that Stanley had friendships, but how deep, how lasting, will remain a mystery. His search for Livingston, an old man he genuinely loved, and the search for himself ran parallel. Only the first was a success. Were there consolations along the way, other than truly extraordinary adventures, we can only hope.

His mother, a cold unloving heart, farmed him out to his grandfather Moses Parry who cared for him well, but he died when the lad was 7. The boy perhaps felt responsible because he had broken a jug and Moses had said he would see to his punishment when he returned from the fields, something the boy prayed to God wouldn't happen--it didn't because it was in the fields that Moses Parry dropped dead. An uncle took him in until the day when, promising to take him on a visit to his Aunt Mary's, he took him instead to a huge building of stone behind an iron gate. He left the boy behind that gate, vowing that Mary would soon be there to fetch him. Only 9 years later did the gates reopen, and the lad of 15 was freed.

Stanley

In the interim he was educated. To what extent is not known, but when he came out he found employment as a teacher in the school of a relative, Moses Owen. He taught English, history and geography during the day, after which Moses taught him math and Latin. During the boy's free time he read from Moses's large library, and Stanley later wrote that his learning environment took up 18 hours of each day. So we know that he had been educated to a certain degree in the Workhouse. We also know that the children slept two to a bed, that every sexual perversion known to man took place, that the boys were rough and their language filthy, and we know they were beaten with birches. Stanley was favored by the headmaster who eventually placed him over the boys whom Stanley too mercilessly birched. In his autobiography Stanley tells us that during one flogging by the headmaster he was able to overcome him, to break the master's glasses and then flog him in turn until he no longer moved. Most biographers believe the story is apocryphal but on at least one occasion he met ruffians far bigger and tougher than he, who threatened him. He told them they'd regret it if they didn't let him pass. Something in Stanley's eyes made them back down.

Throughout all of his young years there was not the slightest indication of real love--although he had had some luck with his grandfather, with the headmaster who seems to have recognized his intellectual superiority and encouraged his thirst for learning, and with Moses Owen. From women there was nothing. When he came upon his mother years later he wrote, ''I directed a shy glance at her and perceived she was regarding me with a look of cool, critical scrutiny. Her expression was so chilling that the valves of my heart closed as with a snap.''

During one of his peregrinations he came upon a sea captain who offered him $5 a month as a cabin boy. He was 17 and a window to life had miraculously opened. He sailed from Liverpool to New Orleans, and the life of adventure that lay beyond, a destiny unknown to most men. He was a mere boy, but a boy who decided that he had but one life, a life he would fill to overflowing.

Stanley was born John Rowlands on the 28th of January 1841 in Wales. His mother, perhaps part domestic, part whore, had four bastards, John the first. Two fathers seem to have been possible, both drunks. We won't dwell on his name or family because he would soon abandon them both and rebuild himself in a new land, with a new name. Of his former life he would only carry his quest for learning and a love of books, a way of losing himself in the persona of others.

Yet his Dickensian past accompanied him on the boat headed for New Orleans. The captain's plan was to work a boy to the bone, to show him utter contempt, with the aim of having him jump ship at the first port, thusly forfeiting his salary. This he did. Now 18, he went along the docks, requesting employment with the plea, ''Do you want a boy, sir?'' Someone eventually did. He was taken in at $25 a month, leaving him, after room and board, $15, a fortune, not only for the boy, but also for the times. What strikes one is that his heart had not as yet been cauterized. The power of hope and promise in youth seems immeasurable. Only sexually does he seem to have been damaged, although unless one leaves candid written traces of one's adventures, as did Cellini and Roger Casement, one can never know what went on under blankets and in back alleys. He had jumped ship with another cabin boy who had immediately taken him to a bar-cum-whorehouse. He bolted. Caravaggio had taken to the sexually obscure and infinitely exciting shadows of desires and sighs when far younger than Stanley, but Caravaggio had lived in a sexually omnisexual society (19), not a dark Workhouse of loathsome sexual filth.

The man who took him in then was a wealthy cotton broker, Henry Hope Stanley, called Hope, whose name Stanley took for his own. Hope gave him work as a clerk and encouraged the boy in his reading, introducing him to Shakespeare, Byron and Irving. Reading would always be a refuge for Stanley, a way of escape, of separating himself from others. Certain psychiatrists maintain that reading is a boy's attempt to find himself back into the comfort of the womb, a theory that is highly plausible to some. Be that as it may, Stanley's catastrophic boyhood and lack of love in general--a mother's love in particular--made him mistrustful of affection from wherever it came, and never would he be able to get along with anyone but himself--with the exception of Livingston, and that for a short time and under harrowing conditions. Hope Stanley took him into his home, installed him at his dinner table, until something went so wrong that Hope forbad the mention of Stanley's name in his presence.

Years of wandering followed, very briefly summarized here because we know so little. He was sent to work on a plantation owned by a friend of Hope Stanley. He left to work on boats plying the Mississippi, recounting, in his autobiography, stories of knife fights, showboat gambling, shootings and robberies (where the incident concerning the ruffians took place). He stated that it was because he had been called a coward that he joined the Civil War on the Confederate side. He then went over to the Union before again deserting. There followed work on merchant ships, trips to Barcelona and France, and even passage back to Liverpool where he decided to see his mother. But she was horrified when he arrived, dirty and dirt-poor. She accused him of humiliating her in front of her friends and new husband, and ordered him away, with the gift of a single shilling. Stanley wrote that he was enraged by the rejection. He returned to N.Y. where he again enrolled in the Union army. He saw horrifying carnage, was taken prisoner, and witnessed, firsthand, death by typhus and dysentery. He himself became ill numerous times, during one of which he had fallen unconscious in a field and had been found by an incredible rarity, a family that put him to bed and nursed him back to health. He worked on the family farm when better, and then found a place as a lawyer's clerk for a judge, Hughes, until one night the drunk judge attempted to kill his wife with a hatchet. Stanley intervened and lost his job. He became a cook on the *North Carolina* where he met 15-year-old Lewis Noe, the ship's messenger. Noe was of special importance because he is the only person who is known to have written honestly about Stanley. Noe described him as cold, aloof, excellent in penmanship and always reading. The encounter, for Noe, would turn out to be the most unfortunate in his life.

Stanley had a two-pronged plan: one was to become a journalist, the other was to go to the Middle East in search of fortune, promising Noe riches in gold and jewels. To get there both boys needed money. Stanley hit upon the scheme of having Noe enlist in Civil War armies, collect the bounty offered for enlistments, desert, and then begin again elsewhere. Noe agreed until his family found out and brought an end to a practice that would have seen the boy, sooner or later, in front of a firing squad. Stanley then made the rounds of newspapers, trying to get taken on thanks to articles he wrote about the war. He was offered a trial as a printer, a toehold. While preparing a meal for fellow employees he burned himself. From then on the resultant scar became a wound from an Indian arrow, his first attested lie. He met a freelance journalist, William Cook, with whom he traveled down the Platte River to Omaha, the purpose being to put them both into physical form for their next adventure, a voyage to the Middle East. In N.Y. Stanley looked up Noe. Promising Noe's family, as he had Noe, diamonds and rubies, he received their consent to take their son, now 17, with him. Noe met Cook who immediately took a disliking to the boy because he felt Stanley's preference for the lad over himself. Even so, it was Noe that Stanley put to work during their passage on the *Yarington* to Smyrna, Turkey, while Stanley spent the days on a lounge chair reading.

Stanley, said to have had a wonderful ear for languages, studied a Turkish grammar and learned enough to be understood. He hired two horses for a trek into the interior of Turkey, mounts for himself and Cook, while Noe walked alongside. Convinced of his inferior status, Noe finished by creeping away in the dead of night. Caught by Stanley, now 25, and Cook, the same age, he was tied to a tree, his shirt ripped off, and his back lashed by Stanley until he drew blood, a remnant of what he had both undergone and meted out in the Workhouse. Even Cook, who watched, instantly recognized the homosexual nature of the sadomasochistic attack. Later Noe would write that he had put up with it all because he was in a strange land, unable to speak the language, and still only 17. He was certainly, too, small, perhaps the reason he was chosen for the infamy to follow. Stanley made him promise to obey him from then on, ''even if I tell you to cut a man's throat,'' wrote Noe later.

Because their horses fell while climbing a steep summit and were too hurt to continue, Stanley decided to steal others. A passing Muslim on a horse, with a second horse following, was stopped by Stanley who told him something in Turkish. They went to an enclosed area where, Noe recounted in the *New York Sun*, the man immediately went for Noe's genitals. Stanley then struck the man with a sword, the aim being to split his head open, but as the man had stuffed his turban with material to keep his head warm, the blow only felled him to his knees. He was able to grab hold of Stanley who lost his drawn gun. It fell near Noe whom Stanley told to pick up and shoot, which he did. But the gun was empty. Hearing the click, the Muslim ran off, his face covered in blood. Knowing what awaited them, the three took the horses and decided to put as much distance as possible between themselves and the people who would soon be coming.

They were nonetheless caught, beaten, tied and blindfolded. They were taken to an encampment where they were again beaten and used for target practice. The man whom they had tried to kill, unarmed, screamed his indignation and spurred the tormentors on. As the bullets neared, and Stanley certain they were as good as dead, an old man rode up and gave orders for the shooting to stop. Noe piteously asked Stanley if they would be killed, to which Stanley could only shrug. They were lain out at the foot of three stakes. Ropes were tied around their necks and to the stakes, so that if they moved they would strangle themselves.

Later that night the inhumanity continued. Three boys came up, stripped Noe naked, and each raped him. Stanley, who undoubtedly had witnessed such scenes during his stay at the Workhouse, looked on. The morning after the ignominy, the three boys turned to Mecca and prayed.

By all rights all three Europeans should have then been put to death as the easiest way out of the situation for the Muslims. Instead they were taken to a town a five-hour ride from there and put in prison. Here an episode nearly as sickening as the rapes took place. A Turk guard hit Noe in the stomach, doubling him up. ''Henry, I've been hit,'' said the boy to Stanley ... who *laughed,* something that Stanley admitted doing in his autobiography.

The boys were saved by the local governor who sent them to Constantinople where they sued the Turks for a huge sum of money, maintaining that they themselves had been robbed of an important amount of gold. The Turks, wanting good relations with America, said they would do their best to compensate for the injuries. The Turk Stanley had nearly killed was locked up and, as far as we know, the key was thrown away. Stanley and Noe left Cook to collect what loot the Turks would eventually turn over. Stanley borrowed money he never intended to repay and the two went to Paris and then to N.Y. via Liverpool where Stanley again visited his mother, telling her he was now an officer in the U.S. Navy. The money he had ''borrowed'' allowed him to offer teas and dinners. In N.Y. he split up definitively with Noe, Noe the archetype of the kind of relationships Stanley would have, throughout the rest of his life, with boys he could easily dominate. Surprisingly, it was proved in Turkish courts that Noe had been raped. Stanley was awarded $14,000, $1,200 of which the Turks eventually turned over, minus the money the American consul had himself lent Stanley, that he recouped through his own efforts. Years later Noe would accuse Stanley of the aforementioned acts of brutality, but by then Stanley was the man who had found Livingston, and no one was listening to Noe. As for Noe, he went on to marry and became a newspaper man for the *Brooklyn Times* as well as for the *Associated Press.* He was interviewed until the end of his life, at age 82, by Stanley biographers.

Stanley was finally taken on by the *Missouri Democrat* as a reporter. He covered the Indian wars, meeting Custer, Wild Bill Hickok and General Sherman. His articles were noticed by the *N.Y. Herald* that engaged him to cover the war in Abyssinia were Brits had been taken hostage. Stanley was always described as being lucky, and in a way he was, being in the right place at the right time, but in the essentials he is one of the most heartbreaking human beings in human history.

He now sailed to Suez and then joined British troops in Abyssinia. He marched alongside them, taking incredible risks, two months over mountains and through forests to Magdala where the hostages were freed and the emperor of Abyssinia committed suicide. He returned during the rainy season, again taking great risks, back to Suez where he sent off his story. He was the first of the reporters back from Abyssinia and thanks to a cut in transmission that lasted a week, his was the first story of the war and its outcome to reach N.Y. Such were the events he described that no one believed what the *Herald* published until confirmation from other reporters came through a week later. He was treated as a hero, but his luck was only beginning. Dr. Livingston had gone missing in Africa, and as more and more people were becoming concerned about his mission there, Stanley was the *Herald's* natural choice to go to Africa to find him.

While waiting for the *Herald* to decide on the steps to take in the disappearance of Livingston, he traveled to Paris where he invited his mother and his half-sister Emma to spend a few days, both found to be ''simple'' by those who met them. Why he would care to impress either is a mystery, since for both women he was nothing but a meal ticket, and he would remain so to the end. A case in point is that he got Emma a job as a servant in the household of Katie Gough-Roberts, the woman he planned to marry. Now, Katie was one of many of Stanley's female romantic interests, all of whom he treated with *virgo-intacta* innocence. He admired ''ladies'' of a certain class but although some historians describe his interest as bisexual, others believe he was caving in to societal pressures so as not to be classed as a queer. Indeed, at that very moment he was trying to get Edwin Balch's parents to allow their boy to accompany him in covering the opening of the Suez Canal. The parents naturally hesitated, perhaps due to the fact that the boy was 14. When this fell through Stanley turned to Edward King, a rooky journalist whom Stanley convinced to see him off at the Gare de Lyon on his way to Marseille and then Suez. Stanley continued to write to Katie letters that were intercepted by his sister Emma and destroyed because she felt certain that, once married, Stanley would cease backing her and Mom financially. Emma even went so far as to tell Katie that Stanley was already married.

The owner of the *Herald*, James Gordon Bennett, decided to launch an expedition to find Livingston, but wanted to put it off for a year so that interest in Livingston would grow to a red-hot level. Bennett was a journalistic genius, who invented celebrity interviews, the profuse use of illustrations, society gossip--sensational, libidinous news and huge incredible headlines, like the headline reserved for the New York visit of the nattily dressed Haitian ambassador: ''A GORGEOUS NIGGER IN N.Y.'' Bennett provoked fights when he got drunk, he discarded his clothes on the way home so he could arrive naked, and when seen pissing in the fireplace in front of his fiancée, he was horsewhipped by her brother. Later Bennett funded an expedition to find the exact site of the North Pole and when the explorers went missing, he sent off a Stanley-like reporter to find them. The men had frozen to death and Bennett brought them home to an immense (and well publicized) funeral. Later, accused of having been the cause of the deaths through lack of sufficient funding, Bennett got on his yacht and sailed to Europe until things cooled down. Bennett finally married, for the first time, at age 73.

It was Livingstone's love of exploration which would provide the catalyst for the discovery of the White and Blue Niles. Born in Scotland and put to work in a cotton mill as age 10, Livingstone attended school despite his 14 hours at the factory every day. He studied medicine and attended divinity school. He wanted to work as a missionary in China but was prevented by the Opium Wars. He went to South Africa instead, and was so badly wounded by a lion when trying to protect his converts' sheep that his left arm was disabled for life. He was one of the very first to cross the whole of Africa, from the Atlantic to the Indian Ocean, despite malaria, dysentery, sleeping sickness and physical obstacles that made the trek murderous (300 men would die accompanying Stanley on his search for Livingston--one of whom could just as easily have been Stanley himself). Livingston thought that the best way to end slavery was to open up Africa to international trade. He thusly decided to explore the Zambezi River as a major trade route, but the river proved to be impassable. As an explorer, the consensus seems to be that he was an incompetent leader, self-righteous, secretive, moody and totally beyond criticism. A colleague who would follow in his steps, John Kirk, claimed he was out of his mind. Although John Speke and James Grant had found the origin of the Nile, Livingstone believed them wrong and set out to prove that the origin was farther south. He suffered from all the above ills, plus pneumonia, cholera and ulcers. In fact, he was eventually saved by the Arab slavers he had come to fight. Livingston lost contact with the outside world for 6 years; only 1 of his 44 letters made it through to Zanzibar, a letter put up for sale in 2010 where it sold for £28,800. Livingston's suffering from his African expeditions weakened his health until his death, and it was thought that Stanley's depressions dated too from his sick spells in Africa. Livingston made a convert of a chieftain who learned enough English to translate the Bible into his native tongue, although what the chieftain learned about Christianity changed nothing concerning his daily life, multiple wives included. It was in Zambia that Livingston would eventually die of malaria and dysentery, his followers paying for his body to be repatriated to England, except for his heart, interred where he died. In 2002 he was named one of one hundred Great Britons. *And* he had found the time to produce six children before his wife died, at his side, during one of his expeditions.

As this chapter is an overview of Stanley's life, there is no question of going into a day-by-day description of his trek into the interior of Africa in search of Livingston. The whole idea was mad, anyway. Finding a single man somewhere in the center of an entire continent, an area the size of Australia, was too crazy for words. Only two insane unrealistic souls like

Bennett and Stanley would have considered such folly longer than it took to drink a cup of tea.

Stanley set out from Zanzibar, an island 46-miles-long and 9-miles-wide in some places, with two whites, one Scotsman and one American, and around 250 stark-naked porters. It soon became apparent that Stanley was a man unto himself, one who needed absolutely no one else. When historians later asked themselves why he set out with even two whites, the only possible reason found was that by tradition all expeditions centered around an intimate circle of white leaders. Of the whites who accompanied Stanley, then or later, *none* would come back alive. Stanley was a small man, 5' 7'', physically nothing in comparison to the men he commanded, yet a fist of iron was needed and not only did he have it, he now had the occasions he so relished to beat and flog to his heart's content. The terrain the swampy, the rainfall torrential, the forests had to be axed to make passage, and how he crossed the swaying bridges with donkeys and two horses remains a mystery. Mist, fog, red ants, wasps, along with fever, cholera, malaria, sleeping sickness and his own personal ignorance so abominable that he did nothing to stop tsetse flies from biting him. He lost 40 pounds his first week. When he came down with fever the expedition stopped. When the other two whites did, there wasn't the slightest pause. When a porter fell to the wayside he was abandoned, synonym to death for which Stanley would later be scorned.

On one occasion the American, in cahoots with the Scotsman, shot at him through his tent, such was their hatred for the tyrant. Where other men would have cringed, Stanley smirked. He took the arm away and warned the two that if they stepped out of line again he would have them hanged, and if anything happened to him in the future there would be 200 porters to testify to the authorities. When the Scotsman fell ill he was left at a village, grateful that he could finally rest and so sick he didn't care if he did die. Both Stanley and the American knew that without medicine he didn't have long, which was the case.

There is no doubt that Stanley was both tenacious and fearless. How he could control so many men, twice his size, is an enigma, and brings to mind mahouts, Indian boys who have absolute control over their elephants. During the trek he came upon the Wagogo, a tribe of ferocious savages who demanded payment from those who passed through their land. Stanley forked over $160. Then, traveling through Wagogo territory, he became incensed by their arrogance and in one village he flogged those who approached too closely. The American tried to cool him down, but in the end only a relapse of fever ended Stanley's vindictive frenzy. Why these warriors didn't kill him is a second enigma. A third is why, throughout his whole travels, tribes demanded payment of passage when they could have had the totality of the 8 tons of equipment, goods and gold he was transporting--all simply by slitting his throat? During the exploration of the Sahara, Arabs regularly murdered explorers for their possessions, infinitely less valuable than Stanley's, and they were so used to death that they rode over the bones of the 8,000 blacks who died yearly when crossing from Central Africa to Libya, where they were sold into slavery, at times even playing ball with their skulls during periods of rest.

The American became ill. Stanley ordered him to mount a donkey and had porters walk beside him and prop him up so he wouldn't fall off. After nonetheless falling to the ground several times, each time begging Stanley to let him return home, in piteous terms Stanley himself revealed in his book, the American was freed to return, perhaps because Stanley knew the boy's end was near. Death came a few days later. (I won't go into the details of the boy's begging, found, as I said, in Stanley's own autobiography, because Stanley's reaction to it was too dehumanizing, too disgusting.)

Always accompanied by boys, on this trip Stanley had a faithful Arab lad, Selim, and a small black child, Kalulu. In pictures taken of both it seems clear that they would have taken care of Stanley's sexual needs without Stanley ever having to fear public exposure. But this is pure speculation on my part as most biographers never doubted his being sexually repressed to a point that he was inoperative. Victorian sexuality was the strangest to have existed in our society. On the one hand most men seemed to have put women on pedestals and succeeded in controlling their urges, while on the other hand there were never so many male brothels. The sending of telegrams exploded when it was found out that men could hire the boys who delivered them for a few kopeks, a boon for the men, and badly needed additional income for the boys. After all, what a healthy lad did by himself in the privacy of his own room could just as easily be turned into profit, especially as the assignations lasted literally just minutes. Men were perhaps pushed by societal demands to marry, but how can one explain the extraordinary number of those like Oscar Wilde, Wilde who craved boys, craved having sex with them and watching, voyeuristically, them having sex together, yet he married, and there seems to be no doubt that he had a problem in ''honoring'' his wife?, his life and the period covered in my book *The History of British Homosexuality*.

How far Stanley went with his boys is and will remain unknown--unless lost correspondence comes to light. Selim, very young but still much older than Kalulu, was deposed by the latter--who looked no more than 8--due to Kalulu's superior intelligence and because, as Stanley writes, Kalulu not only did everything imaginable for Stanley's comfort, he was able to foresee what would bring Stanley pleasure and fulfill his every desire: ''I have but to express a wish and it is gratified,'' Stanley wrote.

With Kalulu.

The suffering of the porters was horrendous, especially the outbreaks of smallpox. When they died, others were bought. When they ran away Stanley paid to have them hunted down and then chained together by way of iron neck collars--becoming, instantly, slaves. The natives were armed because they were under constant attack from tribes and thieves, yet not one ever turned an arm against Stanley.

Weeks and months went by as he traveled through the dense forests and across plains so arid that porters dropped to the wayside through thirst. From Arab caravans he would occasionally have news of the old bearded missionary, Livingston, usually reported in the area of the town of Ujiji. Selim became dangerously ill with smallpox and to sustain himself he drank a mixture of milk and sugar. As sugar was precious, Stanley had given orders that it was not to be touched. He mercilessly flogged the boy who survived thanks to the resiliency of his youth. Once he was back on his feet Stanley beat him again when he stole a single fruit ''to discourage the others,'' wrote Stanley.

Finally, after nearly 1,000 miles and 236 days, they caught the sight of beautiful Lake Tanganyika, the site of the town of Ujiji. At the entrance Stanley ordered rifles shot off and the Stars and Stripes unfurled. An old bearded white man dressed in a red jacket and sporting a navy cap came towards him.

''Doctor Livingston I presume?''

''Yes.''

''Doctor, I thank God I have been permitted to shake hands with you.''

''I feel thankful that I am here to welcome you.'' In an area the size of Australia, he had indeed found the needle in the haystack.

What followed was a true love affair. Stanley had finally found a man worthy of him. Their first meeting had been solemn and would later be ridiculed (the ''I presume'' even became part of the repertoires in musicales), but Livingston's reputation of being a misanthrope who would turn his back on Stanley, and Stanley's fear of being rejected, had led to the formality. Later Stanley would admit that he would have preferred to turn ''a somersault,'' before Livingston. Also, he wrote that he hadn't wanted to show weakness by being too ebullient in front of the porters, now down to around 50, half chained by the neck. Stanley was determined to stay a single day, to deposit the goods he had brought Livingston, get a signed letter, proof of his having found the great man, and then leave. Instead he found a father, and for the very first time became a son. They enchanted each other with anecdotes and Livingston confessed that as he had recently been robbed of all his possessions, he was literally facing starvation before Stanley's arrival. Stanley told Livingston that he had been sent by the *Herald* on a humanitarian mission to enable Livingston to continue his good works; there was no mention of the scoop and the additional wealth in advertising it would bring to Bennett's newspaper.

Livingston had become known in Victorian times thanks to his writings and his ability to bring Africa to life to the reader. As an explorer he had discovered but one small lake, and as a missionary he had had but one convert, who recanted when Livingston went away.

Six days later Stanley wrote in his diary, ''...he is benevolently paternal ... almost tender, though I don't know much about tenderness...'' and crucially, ''the consequence is that I have come to think myself somebody, though I never suspected it before.'' Besides the goods Stanley had brought, he had what remained to him divided into two piles and asked Livingston to choose the one he wanted. He then accompanied him on a tour of Lake Tanganyika. They were both hard, determined men, Stanley a pessimist who believed in a wrathful, vengeful God, Livingston an optimist who truly loved Africa and Africans, a believer in redeeming love. In one location their boat was met by stone throwers. Stanley wanted to shoot at them. Livingston refused, replying that they were beyond the reach of the stones, ''let us thank God for that.''

They spent four months together, and although Stanley discovered that Livingston was no living angel, they parted father and son, perhaps the closest relationship either had had till then, certainly the closest Stanley would ever come to the purity of love.

On the way back Stanley came across the Wagogo again who were setting out to fight a neighboring tribe. Stanley admired their headdresses of ostrich and eagle feathers, their ankle bells, spears and shields. There were over a thousand to Stanley's 50 men, and Stanley had a large supply of weapons and ammunition, guns that could have helped the Wagogo, yet they let Stanley through unharmed.

Stanley and his men made their way over flooded lands, through forests and torrential rains, and hostile tribes that demanded payment. Continuous fevers and deaths among the porters, torrents that needed fording, harassed by insects, the ever-constant terror of dying, all of which would have felled most mortal men. Yet he held strong, his aim now the telling of his story in the *N.Y. Herald*.

When he reached Zanzibar he came face to face with Livingston's twenty-year-old son who had set out with three others sponsored by the Royal Geographical Society to bring aid to Livingston. Stanley filled them all in, but due to disputes between the three, two offered resignations and Livingston's boy returned home. Stanley paid Selim 33 pounds for his work and sailed on to Marseille with Kalulu.

In Paris he was feted by the American ambassador and had lunch with Sherman who told him his accomplishment was greater than his own march to the sea. When Stanley asked him if they had met before, Sherman said Never. Stanley then repeated part of the speech Sherman had given in Stanley's presence during the Indian Wars that Stanley had covered. Sherman was naturally bowled over. The British were unhappy that an American had found Livingston, and the Royal Geographical Society was furious that Livingston's own son had given up trying to find his father. Americans immediately believed Stanley's *Herald* stories, the British maintained that Livingston's letters were not only fakes, but they were not Livingston's style at all. Stanley's family sent letters begging for money, and then insulted him when the sums were deemed insufficient. That said, he was given a £2,000 advance for his future book, a huge sum (£255,000 in 2022). The book came out under the title *How I Found Livingston*. At a formal gathering in England of rich aristocrats, when one of whom made the mistake of sneering at him, he informed them that they were all arrogant nobodies; he bowed and walked out. Newspaper articles followed about his illegitimacy, his refusal to admit a Welsh birth; his small size was even a reproach, all of which fully justified Stanley's cynicism of a dog-eat-dog world.

He was admitted into the presence of Queen Victoria, "This lady to whom in my heart of hearts next to God I worshipped." He was given the Royal Geographical Society's highest award. The Society apologized for having doubted him, and Mark Twain, present, saluted the RGS "as the very pinnacle of human nobility."

In his superb book *Stanley*, Frank McLynn writes, "Stanley was the sort of person who ignores a hundred plaudits to worry away at a single insult," and it was true. His three-month stay in England, despite the success of his trek, despite his book and his awards, was a disaster.

Bennett learned that Stanley would earn a minimum of $50,000 for his book and promised lecture tour. Bennett was a truly bigger-than-life person, who won the very first trans-oceanic yacht race, who organized the first polo match in the United States and who founded the first cup given for ballooning, among other accomplishments. But he had his human foibles, as related, and inexplicably decided he would bring Stanley down from his pedestal, a deserving descent because, in Bennett's mind, it was unfair that Stanley now had enough money for the rest of his life while Livingston had spent thirty years in Africa and had hardly a penny to his name. The comparison was of course ridiculous, and only Bennett's jealousy of Stanley's fame can explain his actions. So when Stanley started on his lecture tour the *Herald* was there to curb what Bennett found to be Stanley's arrogance by maintaining that Stanley was dull and spoke ''too fast in his eagerness to bore his hearers.'' All of which seems to have had a grain of truth. Stanley worsened things by putting out a statement that he had been born in America and that he had said, Doctor Livingston *I believe*, not *I presume*. To 19ᵗʰ century ears the *I presume* brought howls of laughter, becoming a Broadway must for comics.

Back in Africa Livingston was found dead kneeling in front of his bed. His heart was put in a tin box and buried where he'd died. The body was dried in the sun, sewn into sailcloth, placed in a bark sarcophagus, and carried by pole to a waiting ship. In Southampton it was given a twenty-gun salute and taken by train to London where Livingston lay in state. At the funeral the coffin was preceded by two of Livingston's sons, and followed directly by Kalulu who had known him well. Livingston had wanted to prove that the Lualaba River was the source of the Nile, and it was now suggested that Stanley take up the gauntlet. *The Telegraph* offered £6,000 if the *N.Y. Herald* would offer the same. Bennett, afraid of being deprived of a great story, sent a one-word telegram: ''Yes.'' Stanley had well over a thousand offers from volunteers, and wound up selecting three from the working class who would give him no trouble, two brothers, the Pococks, and a lad named Barker. A boat, detachable in five sections, was built.

In ways, the trek this time out was easier because he had more men, 347, although by the end 181 would be dead. He was now also fluent in Swahili. His three white volunteers, who would show themselves helpful and valiant, all died too, of fever. He made for Lake Victoria that he decided to circumnavigate. Leaving the main of his men on the shore, he went off in his boat with twelve others.

What Stanley described as the most desperate day in his life took place as he landed on an island called Bumbire. Natives suddenly appeared and forcefully shored his boat, along with its occupants. Stanley's initial reaction was to open fire, but an Arab aid told him he could have what he wanted--food to continue the circumnavigation--through negotiation. This went on for several hours when suddenly some of the natives--there were over a thousand--grabbed the oars. Stanley still permitted the talks to go on but when their chief told them to seize the guns, Stanley gave orders for the boat to be pushed into the lake. Stanley doesn't explain how this was done without their being massacred, but they were able to row beyond the reach of the native's arrows, using the torn-up seats as paddles. They were chased by canoes but Stanley, apparently the only one armed, turned his elephant gun on them, killing men and sinking their canoes. If this were not harrowing enough, Stanley returned to his base camp and methodically drilled his men on how they would teach the Bumbire a lesson. He returned with 230 porters, 50 trained in firing. As the Bumbire came to the beaches screaming and shooting arrows, Stanley and his men mowed them down. They paddled back to the base camp to celebrate, after which Stanley led them to Uganda. Along the way the natives, hearing of the massacre of the Bumbire warriors, were spectacularly welcoming.

Set up for life financially, having experienced fevers so severe his life had repeatedly been in danger, armed but nonetheless aware that there was nothing he could do should the thousands of warriors in a tribe decide to kill him, he had nevertheless set out to discover if the Lualaba was the veritable source of the Nile. To get to the Lualaba they would have to go through an area never explored by either white men or Arabs, Arabs who were everywhere else on the continent. At one place they went through the territory of a man known as the Black Napoleon. Mirambo was 5' 11'' and so meek in appearance that Stanley thought a joke was being played on him. Yet the man whom Stanley described as being handsome and soft-spoken was accompanied by 15,000 men armed with rifles, all young, all unmarried. Mirambo told Stanley they would not separate until they had become blood-brothers, which was the case, and when they did split up they tried to outdo each other in gifts. When Stanley got to Ujiji he was deeply saddened by the absence of Livingston. There was an outbreak of smallpox which was killing 50 inhabitants of Ujiji per day, many of them Stanley's men. Another sad event, never explained, was the desertion of Kalulu who was accompanying him. The boy was caught and eventually pardoned.

At a place called Kaesong Stanley met an Arab slave and ivory merchant known at Tippo Tip, an extraordinary person who controlled a huge region. Tippo Tip recruited hundreds of young Africans that he had circumcised as a sign of allegiance to him. As Stanley's mission was to chart the Lualuba, he was glad to learn from Tippo Tip that another explorer sent by the Royal Geographical Society, Verney Lovett Cameron--to see if the Lualaba emptied into the Congo or was the source of the Nile--had given up for lack of canoes. Since Tippo Tip had accompanied Cameron part of the way, Stanley now hired him for $7,000 to do the same for him. They set out with 146 of Stanley's men and 500 of Tippo Tip's. Stanley and 36 crack shots left in his boat, while others followed by canoe, and still others trekked along the banks.

Hampered by attacks of smallpox, pneumonia and dysentery, three bodies per day were thrown into the river. From the river banks natives shot volleys of poisoned arrows and sent out canoes to destroy them, but Stanley's barrage of gunfire killed so many that each attack petered out. When Stanley and his men stopped, they constructed stockades and posted snipers in surrounding trees to ward off attacks. Stanley even organized night attacks in order to weaken the enemy and capture their huge canoes so that more and more men would be able to float down the river. Finally Tippo Tip decided that he and his men had had enough, and told Stanley they were leaving. Stanley's own men wanted to return with Tippo Tip and both Stanley and the Arab had to threaten to shoot any deserters. Stanley nonetheless gave the remaining porters a bonus of cloth.

Stanley's leadership was stupendous. Mirambo had been dubbed Napoleon, but the true Napoleon was Stanley who matched the former one down to his size. As cited, he trained his men to become marksmen. He had a real grasp of strategy, and more than fearless, he had heart. Not the bleeding humanistic kind to be sure, but one that was undaunted. For Stanley nothing counted outside the goal he had fixed for himself. He had had success and knew it for the chimera it was; worse, success had led to intolerable humiliation--and for a man, any man, nothing is more painful than humiliation.

Mirambu and Tippo (Tippu) Tip

As he descended what he now believed to be the Congo, the attacks from the banks and from launched canoes never ceased. Greeted everywhere with the cry of ''meat, meat'' he could only wonder at the kind of death that would be reserved for him before being carved up and served steaming. The attacking natives had never seen a white man. Their drums-- that destroyed the silence and unnerved Stanley--warned downstream tribes of the arrival of a man with a face the color of the moon, and his mysterious fire sticks. The natives had never known of an armada like Stanley's, which was there for purposes other than war, and generations of infighting had established borders between the tribes that were hermetically sealed--anyone who failed to respect these was asking for annihilation.

Stanley came to what would be called Stanley Falls, seven cataracts. To get past them he had to make trails, 15 feet wide, by chopping through jungle. This he repeatedly did, an act of immense difficulty. Half his men did the cutting while the other half held off attacks that were incessant.

The very worst came at the foot of the last cascade where he confronted four monstrous canoes, each with 80 rowers and 500 men, a total of over 2,000 warriors. Quasi certain that this would be the end, he nonetheless had his men hold off their fire until the last second, the poisoned arrows raining down on the shields he had raised on both sides of his own canoes, before he gave the order to fire. Even while showing such incredible courage, he was certain that they would be overrun by the sheer numbers screaming as they approached. Yet not only were they not destroyed, once the warriors began to back off Stanley ordered his men to attack, he in front. They docked the boats and went to the cannibal village where, Stanley wrote, they loaded up on fantastic amounts of food. Ivory was found, of a value of $18,000, that Stanley offered to his own warriors in its entirety. Later Stanley calculated that this had been his 28th combat.

There would be a total of 32 combats before the last cascade, in the middle of which Frank Pocock drowned. Stanley had said of him, ''The coolest man and the happiest I ever saw.'' Bennett had added: "He is a brave, honest, manly, patient young Englishman.'' Frank had spent three years with Stanley, friends to the end. His death caused Stanley to have a nervous breakdown.

They eventually reached the Atlantic, exactly 999 days after setting out.

Stanley's next adventure concerned another of life's seemingly endless incredible people, Emin Pasha. Born Eduard Schnitzer in Germany, he passed his medical exams to become doctor but for unknown reasons was not licensed to practice. Furious, he went to Albania, under Turkish rule, and did so well he became physician to the Albanian governor. A brilliant man, Schnitzer spoke seven languages, was a superb pianist and chess player, and seduced the governor's wife with whom he fled back to Germany--along with her four children and six slaves. Discovering that he couldn't support them all, he fled again, this time to Khartoum where he became the physician of General Gordon who appointed him governor of lower Sudan, an area known as Equatoria. So as not to be found by those looking for him in Germany and Albania, he claimed he was a Turk (he had converted to Islam) named Emin Pasha. Shortly afterward Gordon was assassinated and Emin wrote an S.O.S. to a newspaper saying that although he was stranded, he was holding down the fort for Britain. The British government decided that a Livingston-style expedition should be organized to save and supply Emin in arms and munitions, and who better to send than Stanley?

Stanley had been giving a world lecture tour at an immense $10,000 that he halted the moment he was contacted. He set out yet again for Zanzibar with lads of his choosing. Not the humble lads he usually preferred but those having a military background and upper-class education, and who were, certainly by accident, handsome. He also took along his 17-year-old valet. One of his choices was James Jameson, 33, the rich son of a whisky magnate who volunteered £1,000 (128,000 in 2022 dollars) for a place with Stanley, assuring him that he was an habitué of Africa, having big-game hunted there. Later Stanley divided up his expedition. Jameson was left behind with a group of men, and while awaiting Stanley's return Jameson paid for a girl of 11 whom he offered to cannibals to kill, cut up and cook, so he could record it all in his notes. When told later, Stanley refused to believe the story until he rifled through Jameson's affairs and found drawings and a detailed description of the incident. Happily, Jameson soon died of fever. Major Edmund Barttelot was also chosen. A psychopath who had a 25-year-old white mission boy beaten to death (we don't know why) and numerous blacks killed or beaten--he soon went insane.

The expedition consisted of 805 men plus Tippo Tip whom Stanley had hugely bribed. There were tons of stores, guns and munitions. The travel conditions were as horrible as already described, with jungle, torrents, rain, diseases, fevers, dysentery and atrocious ulcers, hostel tribes firing poisoned arrows and porters who ran off with supplies and guns, one of whom was shot when found in order to impress the others. The blacks were also beaten within an inch of their lives when Stanley's gentlemen felt like it, and badly accepted Stanley's advice to have them flogged on the back and not the legs as the legs could become infected and slow them down.

They were the first whites to see Mbuti pygmies, just over 30 inches in height. Stanley had already used up his nine lives and what kept him going and still alive was a true mystery of human determination and abnegation and madness, especially since he could have remained at home in his manor, as rich as Croesus.

Yet he did come upon Emin Pasha, at Lake Albert, and as with all the great men he had encountered, they too hit it off from the beginning. By then, alas, Stanley's stocks had been so reduced that the visit had been hardly worth it. On the other hand, where Stanley had found Livingston in dire straits, Emin Pasha had an army, thanks to Gordon, and millions of dollars in ivory, that Stanley had been ordered to bring back. These few paragraphs summarize still more months of sufferance in Stanley's life, and although Emin Pasha had most certainly suffered less than Stanley, Emin had nonetheless led a life most men wouldn't have even dreamed of. A huge banquet was organized, with pre-W.W.I cheer between British and German officers, in honor of Stanley and Emin Pasha.

The next day found Emin Pasha in the hospital. Drunk, he had apparently fallen over the railing of his hotel, although Stanley and most others believed he had tried to kill himself. Before leaving Germany he had stolen his mistress's jewels and she had filed complaints. When she read in the papers of his showing up in Zanzibar she wrote to him promising to destroy him. Happily, thanks to the ivory and his back pay, he had enough to pay her off and enough to mount an expedition of his own into the Congo. There his sixty servants were killed and he was beheaded. Those who had known him in Europe mourned the death of a charming pianist doctor. Those who had known him in Africa rejoiced at the end of a man so tyrannical and murderous that even the Arabs refused to sell him slaves.

King Leopold of Belgium had never stopped giving Stanley a retainer of £1,000 a year. Now he wanted him to return to Africa and, at the head of troops, unite south Sudan with the Congo. While thinking this over Stanley went to Cairo to write his best seller, *In Darkest Africa*, a book that would seal his fame and his fortune. In the meantime Leopold was losing a fortune with his investments in Africa until the day when a Brit invented an air-filled tire so his boy could ride his bicycle more comfortably. The tire caught on and its inventor, Dunlop, would bring wealth, thanks to rubber, to those investing in Africa, the first of whom was Leopold. Ivory was bringing in millions too, just from the manufacture of piano keys and billiard balls. Stanley went to Brussels to talk things over with Leopold and then crossed over to London. His book and a speaking tour in America brought him 1 million dollars more and, during all this, he wedded. How much was due to Victorian obligation, how much was sexual pleasure, is of course not known. He seemed to genuinely want a baby and, at the same time, he genuinely wanted to return to Africa. How a place of slavery, of every form of atrocious death, of cannibalism and every kind of inhumanity could keep pulling him back like a monumental magnet is a true conundrum. Those who had accompanied him on former explorations and had returned to Africa, succumbed to fevers. Most were very young in comparison to Stanley, and soon he was the last one left standing. His life with his wife was in disarray, for many reasons among which were her efforts to make him a member of Parliament, thusly removing any possibility of his returning to Africa, or so she believed. He fled her and went to Pau near the Pyrenees. His half-sister Emma, as illegitimate as he, had an illegitimate son that she allowed Stanley to adopt (buy). The boy, Denzil, was baptized with water from Lake Albert. Stanley devoted himself to the child, decided on giving him the love he hadn't himself known.

In Africa Leopold had mounted a war against slavers, under Captain Francis Dhanis, that Stanley applauded. Dhanis had been victorious thanks to the help of the Batetela tribe, 10,000 cannibals who ate those captured on the battlefield.

Denzil became the focal point of his life. Stanley refused to allow the boy gifts of toy guns, and because of the wars in South Africa Denzil, at age 6, was already stating his hatred of the Boers. Stanley traveled extensively with the lad, Switzerland, France and Italy, spending much time in the fresh air of the mountains. The day he died Denzil had asked him if he were happy. ''Always when I see you,'' Stanley had replied.

The boy would always be protected by the man who had been an orphan and who had lived a checkered life.

But what a life!

DENIS BROWNE
Gallipoli
1915
Rupert Brooke

As a youngster Denis Browne was a boy of multiple talents who, at age 15, played the organ and ran the choir of his family church. He won a Classics scholarship at Rugby, turned down one in mathematics at Harlow and accepted a third at Cambridge. He became close friends with Edward Marsh, Marsh who was a member of the Apostles (11) and Churchill's private secretary for 21 years, Marsh greatly appreciated for the organization of his all-male orgies, which at times concluded the meetings of the Apostles when a chosen few withdrew to the privacy of Marsh's digs (32). Marsh obtained a commission for Browne and for Rupert Brooke, both lovers from early school days.

It was on the island of Skyros that Brooke died in Denis's arms, from a mosquito bite that infected. ''At 4 o'clock he became weaker, and at 4:46 he died, with the sun shining all round his cabin, and the cool sea-breeze blowing through the door and the shaded windows. No one could have wished for a quieter or a calmer end than in that lovely boy, shielded by the mountains and fragrant with sage and thyme.''

Denis went on to the Dardanelles where he was wounded and later killed during the Gallipoli Campaign. The last letter he'd written was found in his wallet: ''I'm luckier than Rupert because I've fought. But there's no one to bury me as I buried him, so perhaps he's best off in the long run.''

Dennis Browne

Of the two men, Brooke was by far the best known, Brooke startlingly good-looking, for whom boarding-school boys lusted. He was president of the Cambridge Fabian Society and a founder of the Marlowe Society, a drama club in which he acted in its plays. How many students were members thanks to the club's literary appeal and how many were there--boys and girls--drawn by Brooke's looks can't be known. Born in Rugby, in 1887, he is reputed for his First World War poetry, appeals for young men to engage in the services and commit mass suicide, his most celebrated poem being this:

If I should die, think only this of me:
That there's some corner of a foreign field
That is forever England. There shall be
In that rich earth a richer dust concealed;
A dust whom England bore, shaped, made aware,
Gave, once, her flowers to love, her ways to roam,
A body of England's, breathing English air,
Washed by the rivers, blest by suns of home.

Rupert Brooke.
Bisexual, having perhaps fathered a daughter on a visit to Tahiti (25), Brooke was an Apostle and part of the Bloomsbury Set, along with homosexual friends E.M. Forster (32) and John Maynard Keynes (28), Keynes who represented the British Treasury at Versailles in 1918 and when he couldn't protect the German people from financial catastrophe, he resigned. Keynes was open about his homosexuality, and won disfavor among his numerous lovers when he married a ballerina in Diaghilev's Ballets Russes in 1925, a marriage that lasted 20 years. He died of a heart attack in 1946.

T.E. LAWRENCE
Damascus
1918

I loved you, so I drew these tides of men into my hands
and wrote my will across the sky in stars
To earn you Freedom, the seven-pillared worthy house,
that your eyes might be shining for me
when we came.
Lawrence's gift to Selim Ahmed--Dahoum

Lawrence is our Everest, and I have no desire whatsoever to scale its heights. Yet the fact remains that he was a hero, and for those who share my preference, he was, in part, *our* hero. We know for certain he loved a boy, Dahoum (Selim Ahmed), perhaps the unique joy of his life. If the relationship went beyond friendship cannot be known. How Dahoum felt about Lawrence cannot be known either, as what Dahoum felt was an inextricable tangle of many sentiments: the pride of being in the service of an Englishman, his gratitude for the education that Lawrence offered him, wide travel at the side of his mentor, and freedom from even the shadow of

want, as Lawrence cared for his every need. For both it was adventure and shared harmony, a moment more exhilarating than any temporary sharing of desire, even if there is no greater happiness than that found in the arms of one's belovèd.

Lawrence by Augustus John.

Lawrence began his career in Cairo as a cartographer, and it was Ronald Storrs, a Foreign Office official, who got him permission to visit Faisel, one of the sons of Hussein, the powerful Sharif of Mecca, so powerful in fact that Hussein demanded, for his aid in ridding the region of Turks, that he be made king over not only today's Saudi Arabia, but also Palestine, Syria, Lebanon and Iraq. The British agreed, but specified that the details would be decided during a conference to take place after the war. In reality, the British and the French had already divided the Arab world between themselves in a treaty negotiated by the British Parliamentarian Mark Sykes and the French diplomat François George-Picot, giving, in grossly general terms, today's Saudi Arabia and Iraq to England, and today's Syria and Lebanon to the French where they had roots dating back to the Crusades. (Even then the English and the French had been entwined, through the love affair between Richard Coeur de Lion and Philippe II (32 and 33).)

Lawrence had a great deal in common with Storrs, literature, interests in art and archeology, even music, and both would remain friends until Lawrence's death. But whereas Storrs appreciated the finer things in life, Lawrence neither smoked nor drank, he dressed carelessly, didn't like meat (although, apparently, he wasn't a vegetarian), and he never fit in, which is the case for many if not most homosexuals, especially those who love their recruits but would rather die than show it, like Jack Nicholson in India (17). Storrs on the other hand was cut out for high society. Lawrence ate only to fuel his body, he was ascetic, decided, certain of his destiny, and as usual when one's destiny is accomplished, he detested every minute that followed his success. In fact, his success would destroy him.

He met Hussein's son Feisal at Wadi Safra. If it were not love at first sight for Lawrence, it certainly resembled it. As Lawrence wrote in his book, Feisal was tall, slim, with a perfectly trimmed black beard, drooping eyes, and hands that continually fidgeted with a dagger at his waist. In age Lawrence was 28, Feisal 33. Lawrence immediately knew that this was the man, and decided that from then on he would do anything in his power to see Feisal to Damascus where he would declare himself ruler, thusly shattering the Sykes-Picot Treaty. Feisal asked Lawrence how he found the encampment, and Lawrence answered, ''too far from Damascus,'' which earned him Feisal's loyalty from then on, because Feisal correctly read the love for the Arabs in Lawrence's face.

Feisal

And there had to be love in order to overcome Arab failing. They stole whatever wasn't nailed down, from friends as well as foe. They fought exclusively for gold, the idea of a nation being foreign to them. Their nation was their family, clan and tribe, even if they continually wreaked vengeance through incessant blood feuds within the very same family, clan and tribe. They were supreme slave owners--black slaves that cared for their fields of dates, prepared their bread, freeing Arab wives to look after the goat herds while the men made war.

The Turks were disciplined, something the Arabs never ever were. The Turks, too, were barbaric to a point that shocked the Arabs who would never harm a woman or a child, while a Turk pasha would sit back in comfort while an Arab encampment was slaughtered to the last man, woman and baby, after raping, or even while raping the women. The encampment would be set on fire and the bodies cast into the flames.

It was then, too, that Lawrence met the enormously powerful and enormously dangerous chieftain Auda Abu Tayi, a warrior who fought against his own Arabs, cutting out the still-beating hearts of his enemies and biting into the throbbing flesh. He had wives and sons without number and was in the pay of the Turks because they hadn't been able to kill him.

Hawk-nosed, his beard as pointed as Feisal's own, his eyes flashing, he was like Lawrence, fearless and a charismatic leader of men.

Auda Abu Tayi

Lawrence and Auda decided to blow up Turkish trains and rails. In one incident they came across a Circassians goatherd. Circassians were a Caucasian people who had sought exile from the Russians--who had conquered Caucasia in 1864--by seeking refuge in Turkey. Blue-eyed and fair skinned, their women were known for their beauty and got top price for Ottoman harems, and their boys were no less handsome. As the Arabs systematically slit the throat and robbed the clothes of whomever they came across, Lawrence wanted to save the boy but he couldn't tie him up because he would have died of thirst, yet had he freed the lad, he would have warned the Turks. So Lawrence had the soles of his feet cut with a dagger, obliging him to crawl home, where his feet would eventually heal.

It was Feisal who suggested that Lawrence dress as an Arab.

The Bedouins gorged themselves on the boy's herds, and once again Lawrence recognized how different they were from him. They didn't put meat aside for later, and indeed had trained their camels to eat it when available. The same was true with water that they would drink until bloated, with no thought of rationing it for future use. They wasted ammunition by announcing their arrival by firing in the air. They would be friendly to Lawrence but he would never be accepted as one of them, and could never, either, totally accept their ways, their heartless slitting of captives' throats, the filth of their jokes and personal habits. On the other hand, he appreciated their ''voluntary and affectionate'' sexual relations among themselves, which Lawrence found preferable to their visiting prostitutes and bestiality with animals, he later wrote. At the same time, the treachery of his own people towards the Arabs, as in the Sykes-Picot Treaty, distanced him forever from his native land.

He was exiled in his mind from his own country, and that since his youth. The tragedy is that he found no replacement. The tragedy is that he had nonetheless returned ''home''. The tragedy is that one can't go back. He should have exiled himself elsewhere, free from the humiliations he had known at home and in Arabia both.

Lawrence's father was Sir Thomas Chapman, an Englishman living in Ireland, the father of four girls whose governess was Sarah Lawrence, the woman he loved and who would give him five illegitimate sons, concrete proof of an erotic attachment. It was her name that T. E. Lawrence, her second son, adopted. Of strict morals, she was one of life's paradoxes, a deeply religious woman, herself illegitimate, who produced five bastards, a term of little import during the Renaissance in Italy (8) but shameful in Victorian Britain. In fact, had his father had the means of sending his boys to his own school, Eton, they would have been prevented from entering by their illegitimacy, one of life's countless injustices. Sarah seems to have consoled herself by repeating that God hated the sin but loved the sinner. Called Ned by the family, born in Wales, he would only learn of his illegitimacy later in his youth.

It is an incontestable fact that homosexuals disdain collective sports, favoring the individuality of swimming, athletics and bicycling--and as a boy Lawrence lived for his bicycle. His brothers Frank and Will, tall and of extreme beauty, preferred team sports, rugby and cricket, which made them popular, unlike Ned, the eternal loner. He seems to have been a practical joker and, as determined and inflexible as his mother, was often in opposition to her, earning him whippings, as it was she the family disciplinarian, perhaps why he himself, later in life, allowed himself to be beaten by boys he rigorously chose to mete out the punishments. His brother Arnold said, later, that she had tried to break Ned's will. As his father had some money, the boys were looked after by nannies, and despite the discipline, the boys were said to have loved both parents, and were deeply loved in return. Lawrence was sent to a local Oxford school, close enough so that he and his brothers could sleep at home, thusly avoiding the bullying, arrogance and sexual slavery of boarding schools, something his father was obviously familiar with (6). Ned was said to have spoken French fluently at age 6 and had started Latin at age 5, both of which claims could possibly have been true. His father seems to have been an ideal companion, fulfilling his sons' needs, giving Ned, for example, his first bike and then accompanying him on long rides. Ned joined the army on a sudden impulse at age 16, disliked it, and was bought his freedom--apparently possible at the time--by his father. At age 18 his father had a cottage built for him so that he could be on his own, an immeasurable gift of love and understanding. At also 18 he cycled through the north of France, and studied French medieval fortifications, making drawings and taking pictures. He then returned to go to Oxford University.

An Oxford education is extraordinary to American eyes. After exams and an interview, one is accepted or not. A student has rooms, usually a sitting room and a separate bedroom; he can be served breakfast, lunch and dinner; and there is someone, a kind of valet, to see to his needs, the luxury of which, or lack of luxury, depending on the students' parents' wealth. A student is assigned a tutor for a weekly hour who directs his studies, a man with whom he may remain in close contact throughout his entire life. The best minds taught at Oxford, men of immense experience, authors of renown. But as in all institutions, everywhere, some intellectually weak ones got through, stodgy old pussies it was a student's bad luck to draw. He had a best friend, Vyvyan Richards who himself claimed he loved Lawrence at first sight, something Lawrence didn't see or pretended not to see, even when Richards made his dedication to Lawrence obvious. Richards wrote that Lawrence was either sexless or unaware of sex. Michael Korda, in his wonderful book *Hero--The Life and Legend of Lawrence of Arabia*, writes that Lawrence was not so much sexless ''as armored against sexual temptation,'' and Korda feels, as did Lawrence's brother Arnold, that ''Lawrence died a virgin''. There was an Officer Training Corps at Oxford that Lawrence joined, spending a great deal of time practicing with his pistol. Richards claims that he went swimming in winter, breaking the ice, which suggests to some that he was attempting to control his sexual urges.

In 1909 Lawrence set out to explore the Middle East, a harrowing journey fraught with dangers, as he could have been murdered anywhere along the route he traveled, his clothes, stripped from his dead body and sold, as was the custom then, or at the very least he could have had his money and pistol (he carried one) stolen. He studied Arabic in preparation for the trip, did the necessary reading, talked with those who knew the region (and at Oxford scholars in the know were numerous and available).

His father gave him a huge $10,000 in today's money. He sailed to Port Said and then to Beirut, from which he took the train or walked--a total of 1,000 miles--staying with inhabitants, Arabs honor-bound to welcome him, but once he left their tents he became game for robbers. He also stayed in missions. In Palestine he noted the wonderful farms of the Jews and hoped that more would come to perpetuate agriculture there. His letters home, especially to his mother, were warm-hearted, optimistic, wonderfully young in their enthusiasm, showing no fear because he was an absolutely fearless boy. His letters were so fresh and clean that one wishes to end the story of his life here, as far as possible from the deceptions, intrigues, murders, massacres and masochistic self-imposed suffering on the horizon.

He was often ill and could have died from cholera and malaria that he had already contracted. The heat was in the 120s and body lice ubiquitous. He was shot at, and a newspaper even claimed he had been murdered; he had his camera stolen and was beaten over the head by a man who robbed him of his remaining possessions and would have shot Lawrence had his pistol not refused to fire. As Korda so perfectly puts it: to a hero ''a life-threatening encounter is merely a challenge to be overcome, a step forward in his apprenticeship--the more frightening and the more physically punishing the better, provided he survives.''

He handed in his thesis on Middle Eastern archeology and won a First Class. One easily understands why Richards loved such a boy, a boy of undaunted determination.

He went off on another bicycle trip around France, this time with his brother Frank. They did 50 miles a day, and Lawrence read, read and read, writing his mother that it was his way to ''go beyond one's miserable self.'' Truer words never spoken.

After winning his brilliant First in archeology at Oxford, Lawrence went on a three-year-long dig to the Hittite site at Carchemish. There were two water-boys present, one being the love of his life, Dahoum, a boy aged 14 to Lawrence's 21. The boy was both handsome and well built, good natured and intelligent, and could read a little Arabic. His real name may have been Salim Ahmed. He certainly genuinely appreciated Lawrence who took him back to London for a short visit to meet the family. They traveled to Aqaba where together they bathed in the sea. One wonders if Lawrence had a premonition that in a few years he would become master of the entire region, that he would take Aqaba at the head of Auda's bandits. Lawrence was at the dig for three years, an enormous length of time with the boy he loved. How intimate was their friendship cannot, of course, be known. The poem at the beginning of this chapter was for Dahoum, the promise and deliverance of independence, but from the beginning of his relationship with Dahoum Lawrence had also tried to help Dahoum's people. At the

Carchemish site Lawrence had received advice from his doctor-brother Bob in how to vaccinate the Arabs against smallpox, a horrible plague then, one of the world's greatest mass murderers, and he cared for those with cholera, which killed 90% of its victims, another plague that could have killed Lawrence too, one he tried to treat while he himself suffered from bouts of malaria.

Dahoum by Francis Dodd.
Lawrence met Dahoum when he was 14, young and inexperienced enough for Lawrence to feel comfortable in expressing his intimacy, especially as Lawrence knew that Arabs, in the absence of women, shared an uncomplicated sexuality. He taught the boy to read and write, and in 1913 he brought Dahoum to Oxford to meet his family, both staying in a small house in the back of the garden.

As stated at the beginning of the chapter, Lawrence's plan was to get Feisal to Damascus, all the while raiding the Turk railway, 800 miles of line, which would oblige the Turks to dedicate huge forces in its protection. His success was complete. The Arabs got their loot and fulfilled their blood lust by slaughtering nearly every living thing on the trains, women and children excluded--those that hadn't perished in the train's fall. As winter set in, he decided to visit the garrison town of Deraa, a known rail center he planned to destroy in better weather, a decision that would mark him for the rest of his life. The rape of women is horrifying, and I in no way mean to lessen it by saying that for a man it is a life-ending experience, a destruction so complete that only suicide can put an end to his suffering, physical suffering first and then, to the last day of his time on earth, mental anguish. In Deraa Lawrence would be raped multiple times by multiple rapists.

He had set off for Deraa with a single companion who had killed a score of Turks and who had such a price on his head that he was forced to leave Lawrence on the outskirts. Dressed in dirty Arab robes, Lawrence entered alone. Seeking information that would help with an attack on the town, he made his way to what looked like an airfield. There he was stopped by soldiers who were indifferent to his story of his being a Circassian. He was taken to a room and ordered to clean himself, and await the orders of the Bey. Later he was taken to a room where a sweaty fat man had him stripped naked and began to caress him. Lawrence kneed him in the groin and the Bey, the moment the pain had sufficiently subsided, took one of the soldier's bayonets and plunged it into Lawrence's side. Lawrence was then dragged to a room and stretched over a bench where he was whipped, the torturers claiming that after 10 blows he would cry for mercy, after 20 he would plead for the Bey's caresses. The pain was indescribable, and at times they would pull his hair and head back so he could see the damage, his back covered with blood. He did cry out for mercy, and when finally they righted him, they whipped him too over his groin, buckling him again in pain. They then spread his legs and, as he himself wrote, ''rode me like a horse''. Lawrence admitted to feeling ''a delicious warmth, probably sexual, was swelling through me''. He erected and the men, seeing it, hit him again across the groin with the whip. They splashed him with water and pulled him back to the Bey's bedroom where the Bey called them fools for thinking he would want to touch the bloody mess. He was taken from the bedroom, where one of the youngest, handsomest of the guards was ordered to remain. He was pulled through the streets to an Armenian's house where the Armenian was ordered to clean and bandage him. The soldiers left, one inexplicably whispering in his ear that the door to the house was not locked. From somewhere he found clothes and made his escape, to the indifference of those he passed. There was no explanation as to why he hadn't been killed when the Bey bayoneted him. In fact, the whole episode is one huge enigma.

This was his first sadomasochistic experience and he had enjoyed it, certainly a revelation to himself, yet why he would write about it is another mystery. Why he chose to talk about the incident, later, to Bernard Shaw's wife Charlotte Shaw, is strange too, compounded by the fact that she had entered into a *mariage blanc* with her husband, refusing penetration.

During this time Allenby took Jerusalem and gave orders for Lawrence to join him. It was in Jerusalem that Lawrence was reunited with Storrs and where Storrs presented him to the man who would make him world famous, Lowell Thomas.

Thomas was a story in himself. A former gold miner, now a newspaper man with a master's degree from Princeton whose former president, Woodrow Wilson, asked him to make a film that would make the war popular to the American public. Later Thomas's lectures showing dashing Bedouins and camels became the talk of America. He took over the Madison Square Gardens for weeks and, combined with his book *With Lawrence in Arabia* he made millions. When someone asked him about

Lawrence's purported modesty, Thomas answered, ''Lawrence had a genius for backing *into* the limelight.''

Heartbreakingly, Lawrence lost two of his servants, two boys intensely in love with each other, inseparable, their hands always intertwined, ''for the happiness of feeling one another,'' Lawrence wrote. One was Daud who froze to death one night during a campaign, the other was Farraj who received a bullet in the spine, and because he was unmovable Lawrence drew his pistol to his head, ''Daud will be angry with you,'' said Farraj, his last words before Lawrence pulled the trigger. ''Salute him for me.'' Heartbreaking, intolerable pain impossible to imagine. It was said that only with these two boys and Dahoum could Lawrence be himself, Dahoum who seems he have remained at the dig at Carchemish where he died of typhus in 1916.

From here on Lawrence was alone and bereft of love, and would remain so to his death.

The stories in all of my books evoke the wondrous sharing of knowledge, adventure and physical meshing of males among themselves, yet from here on I will go faster because there was no more love for Lawrence, just corporal pain and, later in civilian life, sadomasochistic ejaculation.

At the head of Arab troops Lawrence came upon the massacre of Tafa, a village slaughtered by 2,000 Turks. What struck the Arabs was the number of bayoneted babies strewn seemingly everywhere, the women, their thighs spread, and one, heavily pregnant, who had been pinned to a wall upside down, by bayonets. From one of the dwellings a child came stumbling towards them, blood gushing from her throat. One of Lawrence's men jumped from his camel and ran towards the girl who screamed, ''Don't hit me, Baba!'' A child from the man's own family, he took her in his arms where she expired. The man mounted his camel and charged at the retreating 2,000 Turks. Lawrence made to stop him but Auda prevented him with his hand. He rode towards the troops who watched him coming, in total silence, as did the Arabs too. Only when he was nearly on them did they open up with a machine gun, killing him and his horse. Lawrence gave the *No prisoners* order and the slaughter began. Lawrence wrote that the Turks fought magnificently and that the Arabs were repulsed several times, but in the end ''we killed and killed'' bashing ''in the heads of the fallen and of the animals, as though their death and running blood could slake the agony in our brains''. Some of Lawrence's men had not heard the *No prisoners* order and 200 Turks were found roped together. We cannot know what Lawrence would have done had an Arab not been found next to them, taken prisoner during the fighting and pinned ''out like a collected insect''. ''Who did it?'' Lawrence asked. The man looked towards the prisoners. As the Arabs opened fire, slaughtering the 200, the man died.

Lawrence and the Arabs were brothers as never before, and as such they moved towards Damascus. On the way they went through Deraa where Lawrence had been sodomized. Most of the Turks had fled but those left had their throats slit, down to the patients in the Turk infirmary.

His entry into Damascus was met with cheers and crying. The assembly of Arabs that followed was perfect chaos, throwing of chairs, Lawrence separating Auda from a Druse who attempted to kill him, Auda stopping a man who tried to put a dagger into Lawrence. Lawrence had decided to keep Feisal outside of Damascus for his safety, and Allenby had decided to keep his troops clear of Damascus too, but Lieutenant-General Chauvel, at the head of an Australian army, had entered the day before, so it was technically he the first to liberate Damascus. Lawrence wrote that he did what he could to help those in hospitals, but some patients had been dead so long that their bodies had to be scraped from the floors with shovels. When the commanding doctor screamed his indignation at Lawrence, Lawrence broke into laughter, a tick he had in times of extreme crises, he wrote, and received a slap on the face. It was true that since leaving Deraa he had had three hours of sleep.

This and the slaughter that preceded it, and his eventual failure to give the Arabs the freedom he had promised, made him, Korda so justly relates, an unclean being in his own eyes, something so soiled that no amount of scrubbing would ever cleanse him again.

Allenby arrived the next day, Feisal too, who learned that the Sykes-Picot agreement would be enacted.

Faisal asked Lawrence to take part in the 1919 Paris Peace Conference which produced the Treaty of Versailles, its retribution against Germany so severe that it paved the way for W.W. II.

In 1919 Lowell Thomas's film and photographs involving Lawrence premiered in New York, Thomas invited to show the presentation in England by the king himself. The show only skirted Lawrence's role in the Arab uprising until Thomas saw to what extent Lawrence, dressed as a Bedouin, ''captured the public's imagination'' (34). In 1920 Thomas changed the name of his spectacle from *With Allenby in Palestine* to *Lawrence in Arabia,* Lawrence present to offer Thomas his full support.

Afterwards Lawrence worked directly with Winston Churchill and in the Colonial Office, but wrote his friend Robert Graves, of *I, Claudius* fame, to tell him of his boredom. He grew increasingly outspoken in his support of Arab independence, making him a pariah in France and suspect to Churchill.

He changed his name to T.E. Shaw, taking that of Charlotte Shaw, her husband George Bernard Shaw having helped Lawrence edit his masterpiece *Seven Pillars of Wisdom*, and under than designation he joined the Royal Tank Corps., followed by the RAF.

In 1935, in an attempt to avoid two cyclists, both 14, Lawrence, helmetless, crashed his motorcycle, killed at age 46, Churchill present at his burial.

The love of Lawrence's life seems clearly to have been Dahoum. Lawrence wrote to Charlote Shaw, ''I've seen lots of man-and-man loves: very lovely and fortunate some of them were'' and spoke of ''the openness and honesty of perfect love'' that he'd witnessed during the war between soldiers. About his rape in Dera he wrote feeling ''a delicious warmth, probably sexual, was swelling through me'', which most probably led to later beatings at the hands of boys paid to do so, Lawrence biographer Lawrence James noting his '''strong homosexual masochism''. In 1992 the London *Daily Telegraph* stated that it had uncovered evidence that Lawrence was not only homosexual, but actively so (39), while many biographers believe he was asexual--the outward hostility against homosexual-love displayed by the people who practice it the most, in their schools and the privacy of their bedrooms, the British themselves. It was during his time in the Tank Corps that Lawrence was given floggings by several recruits, the most notable of which was a Scottish boy, John Bruce, floggings that ended in Lawrence ejaculating, Bruce who wrote that Lawrence paid him £3 per thrashing.

John Bruce

GEORGE MALLORY
Everest
1920s

George Mallory, 1886-1924, was the son of a well-off clergyman and his younger brother was a W.W. II Air Force Commander named Trafford.

At age 13 Mallory won a scholarship in mathematics to Winchester College where one of his teachers, R.L.G. Irving took him and a select group mountain climbing in the Alps each year. He went to Cambridge in 1905 and became intimate with the Bloomsbury Set (28), including the Strachey brothers, Rupert Brooke, Maynard Keynes and Duncan Grant. Of Mallory Lytton Strachey wrote, ''*Mon dieu*--George Mallory! He's six foot high, with the body of an athlete by Praxiteles, and a face--Oh incredible--the mystery of Botticelli, the refinement and the delicacy of a Chinese print, the youth and piquancy of an unimaginable English boy.'' All of these men were homosexual, as was Mallory, many married for Victorian societal reasons.

At age 9 Mallory entered the Winchester preparatory boarding school, followed by Oxford. Founded by Henry VIII, Oxford and Cambridge are referred to together as Oxbridge, schools for the rich and aristocratic where the dons, following a Middle-Ages custom, were not married, but where an inexhaustible supply of highborn boys were at their disposal. Lads were trained academically and homosexually on courses of Greek and Latin classics, the first step of which were the prep schools of Repton, Harrow, Winchester and others. Oxbridge were ruled by dons, professors who lived in the upper-class world they created in their image, exclusive, privileged to an unbelievable extend because they could do as they pleased with university monies, live in lavish surroundings, kowtowed to like emperors by teachers and staff. Margaret Thatcher ended their paradise in the 1980s by asking the question What-the-hell-are-they-doing-with-Britain's-money?, and, when she found out, she put a stop to it.

Schools were homosexual settings in the 1800s where the highborn went to do boys, where learning was far less important than playing both musical beds and sports, the athletic heroes of which were chosen to be Fag Masters and had their pick of the prettiest lads, employing them to bring them off manually or lying on their stomachs, and whose influence was reinforced by handing the lads, post-orgasm, to their friends for their personal gratification. In tandem with the mediocrity of an education in both Oxford and Cambridge, was the poor physical condition of the writers, poets and other aesthetes, of the 1800s and early 1900s, that frequented both schools. Yet they were convinced of their excellence, even if many were nothing but arrogant wimps, often moneyed, who paid for rent-boys in pre-W.W. II Germany and Italy, an easy task in those years where a lad would sell himself for the proverbial Hersey Bar (while after the war most boys sold themselves for even less because they were *starving*) (14). Many Oxbridge boys didn't see war because physically unfit to be induced, poor eyesight, bird-breasted chests, precocious varicose-veins, girlish biceps. The exceptions were spectacular: Rupert Brooke, Byron and several others, yet even Byron was only attractive when illness brought his weight down to human levels (35). Few of the men from Oxford and Cambridge resembled the boys seen in gymnasiums or on the wrestling mats, although the boys they paid for were often physically splendid. Proud of the clothes they donned for extravagant meals and the robes they wore in the inner chambers of their rooms, coquettish and swishy, most Oxbridge boys wouldn't have turned on even a girl, let alone far more demanding males-- effeminate twits that make England, today, the last place virile males seek out their own, although there are, and have always been, remarkable exceptions, one of which was tall, strong and vigorous Mallory.

Tutors and students took sherry together and shared meals, after which what naturally happened when young men wished to please their masters did happen, consisting most probably of little more than mutual masturbation, but when it took place one time it was hard to see how the inexperienced student could (or would dare to) ward off a second and then a third occasion, and so on, which meant, in the end, that it was a disgraceful debasement of what should have been a striving towards academic excellence. It was putrid exploitation, exploitation that Mallory may have had to agree to under his tutor Arthur Benson, as will be seen. In the Greek way the lover served as a tutor, whose quest was to instruct the boy as well as sexually share acts of love, but the difference was that the boy always chose the man, and that the man was but a few years older, handsome thanks to boys being physically trained, from childhood, to care for their bodies, whereas in Cambridge and Oxford the tutors were flabby, pale-skinned, often androgynous wrecks. We know nothing of Byron's sexual encounters with his tutors, although they most certainly took place, but we do know he had the consolation of lads younger than he, for whom his experience, eloquence, fine clothes, wealth, title and tastes made him a god, a god who willingly released them from their virginity if they had managed to keep it till then, which, knowing boarding schools that catered to lads 12 and over, was highly improbable.

About his own schooling, John Addington Symonds wrote: ''The talk in the dormitories and studies was of the grossest character, with repulsive scenes of onanism, mutual masturbation and obscene orgies of naked boys in bed together. There was no refinement, just animal lust.'' The first order that Makepeace Thackeray received on his first day at school from a schoolmate was ''Come & frig me,'' he wrote later.

How much the men who left both universities, to become truly great warriors and administrators, owed to Oxford and Cambridge training cannot of course be known, but there were many who thought that bonding through the exchange of sexual favors was destined to ready the graduates for their role as builders and leaders of the British Empire, an inane belief but one supported, in a way, by Plato who had Aristophanes put this in one of his plays: ''While they are boys they love men and like to lie with them and embrace them, and these are the best of the boys and youths. The evidence is that it's these boys, when they grow up, who become the best men in politics.''

Many of these aristocratic pansies were in no way comparable to the admirable *men* who died at Thermopylae and in the ranks of the Sacred Band of Thebes, nor those who fought in the Crimea and Gallipoli, like Denis Browne, who ruled the seas for generations and made the second most populous country in the world, India, a democracy, who were decimated in the First World War and saved England from disaster in the Second, and most assuredly had nothing to do with the homosexual trio of fops, Blunt, Burgess and Maclean, who betrayed their country to the murderous Soviets. (32)

Winchester, Mallory's school.

In boarding schools and universities today, boys can do what they want as long as they are discreet and there is no sexual exploitation, a form of don't ask/don't tell, which is the way it should be. Boys should be left alone, in the sense that adults must be excluded because they can force boys by their positions (priests and headmasters), their sweet talk (as men are infinitely more experienced and knowledgeable than boys), money and other forms of pressure and coercion. The rule of older boys poses a conundrum because young lads can be drawn to their prowess, especially when they're successful athletes, the key to Mallory's success. Older boys can show responsibility in the Greek way, become a teacher and protector, which Mallory certainly was, encouraging the boy to greater heights. In such extremely rarified cases, who can rightfully cast the first stone?

About Winchester Mallory wrote to his parents: ''It's simply lovely here; life is like a dream.'' At Winchester he became an athlete, excelling in group sports like soccer and cricket, and was the school's best gymnast, thanks to which he developed the Praxiteles body so admired by Lytton Strachey. Another boy described him as ''smooth-chinned, pre-Raphaelite-looking young man''. At Winchester he was introduced to a school master who took him climbing in the Alps during the summer, Andrew Irving, 27, Mallory 17. Of Mallory Irving later wrote: ''He had a strikingly beautiful face. Its shape, its delicately cut features, especially the heavily lashed thoughtful eyes, were extraordinarily suggestive of a Botticelli Madonna." They spent weeks in the mountains together, just the two of them. This, Irving repeated with other boys, over a period of five years. Then, in 1930, two of his young climbers fell to their deaths, and his days of mountain climbing with boys came to an end.

Andrew Irving

Mallory went to Oxford in 1905, majoring in History. His tutor was Arthur Benson, there to guide his studies during three of his four years at the college. Benson found Mallory "a fine looking boy" and was struck by the "extraordinary and delicate beauty of his face," quotes brought to us by Peter and Leni Gillman in their excellent *The Wildest Dream*, 2000. "A singular, more ingenuous, more unaffected, more genuinely interesting boy I never saw. He is to be under me, and I rejoice in the thought," commented Benson. It was apparently Benson who introduced the boy to the Bloomsbury Set, and all it encompassed (28).

Mallory by Duncan Grant.

Benson was homosexual, a man who strongly believed ''in friendships 'across the generations' which brought together 'youth and age' '', the Gillmans tell us. ''He went further, referring to 'romantic attachments' which were to be conducted with 'seemliness and decorum'.'' Men who have power over the young, whom the young need to advance, scholastically, was the disgusting legacy of those times in Oxford, Cambridge and elsewhere (6). How hard Benson pushed himself on Mallory, and how far Mallory allowed him to go, can of course never be known.

A photo of Mallory taken by Duncan Grant. Mallory asked Grant for copies of the photos he took, stating, ''I am profoundly interested in the nude me'', an interest in himself that was lifelong.

Benson introduced Mallory to Charles Sayle, a homosexual and intimate friend of Rupert Brooke and Maynard Keynes, who in turn introduced Mallory to the Apostles, the Apostles a Cambridge University discussion group founded in 1820, originally 12 in number, from which came the name. Meetings are held Saturday evenings, refreshments consisting of coffee and Whales, sardines on toast. Undergraduate members, the most numerous, are called embryos, former members angels. The group's papers are kept in a cedar chest they've dubbed the Ark. Eleven of the original 12 were buried in the same cemetery, proof of the group's cohesion until death. Some of the subjects of debate were ''Is self abuse bad as an end?'' (most voting *No!*) and one debate was entitled, ''Achilles or Patroclus,'' supposedly meaning lust against friendship. (11)

Homosexual traitors Kim Philby, Guy Burgess, Donald Maclean and Anthony Blunt were Apostle members, among other Apostle traitors, most of whom were homosexual. Maynard Keynes was a man whose obsession with numbers led to his noting his blowjobs, his wanking and his passive pursuit of sodomy. He loved Mediterranean islands where lads were cheap and boy whorehouses common (36). The license to fuck children was part of an Englishman's aristocratic rights, the basis being English Boarding Schools where they themselves had been plugged even before reaching puberty (6).

Charles Sayle later claimed that Mallory had become one of his swans, code for his having given himself to Sayle. Sayle was the founder of the Climbers' Club in which Mallory organized a trip to the mountains in North Wales, in the company of three of Sayler's other swans, one of whom was Rupert Brooke, the others George Keynes and Hugh Wilson. A high point of the climb was when they all bathed naked together after a day's efforts, as photographs he took testify. George Keynes wrote that ''They were the best days of my life.'' Mallory's younger brother Trafford had begged to come along, but Mallory refused--one wonders why? Mallory then joined a rowing club with Rupert Brooke.

Mallory was very homosexually active and didn't lack in easily accessible bodies, as everyone was not only doing it, ''it'' was ''in'', and to not participate left one out of liberal university and academic society. One could claim that he participated because he was obliged to do so, wishing not to be a social pariah. The truth seems that Mallory was an enthusiastic, perhaps a leading, character in what went on in the Bloomsbury Set, and we know that his sexual presence was sought by Duncan Grant, the Strachey brothers, the Keynes brothers, and numerous boys on the skirts of the set. The pleasure was amplified because there was always an element of conquest, of the gradually-building-up arousal that followed from one's first meeting, to the final conclusion in the warmth of a shared bed. The conquest of a boy was not unlike the conquest of Everest, the exciting part being the preparation and the scaling. There were no saunas and bathhouses used for sexual encounters back then (37), no possibility of instantly meeting and mating as today, on the streets, in gyms, swimming pools and porno cinemas; and picking up someone in a park could get a man hanged until 1885, imprisoned afterwards. The ease of sex today can also be compared to Everest today, where those with money can literally get themselves all but carried to the summit of the peak.

Mallory posed in the nude, and not only for Grant Duncan, and one can be certain that what went on before and afterwards involved a shared orgasm. The true mystery is why biographers should try to hide or explain away (''adolescent curiosity'', ''a passing bisexuality'') what has been perfectly natural since before, far before, the Ancient Greeks. Mallory was merely part and parcel of the intellectually advanced among us, a man who accepted himself and life for what it was. That he married is a normal outcome of the omnisexuality that has existed up to our own age (25). The Greeks preferred boys but copulated easily with women (8), and the Spartans were obliged to seed women in order to produce the soldiers who would one day stand for them as they now stood for their officers (21). The Romans were completely omnisexual, taking what happened to be at hand, be it a male or female slave (9). Afterward, religion put the mark of Satan on anything to do with homosexuality, even when priests often became priests due to the easy access to choirboys. Mallory's form of omnisexuality is the path of the future, when boys can decide with whom they'll share their bed for the night, thanks to that infallible compass, the direction that points their erect phallus (38).

James Strachey was extremely candid about his relations with Mallory. He wrote that Mallory ''insisted, before we parted, on copulating. He seemed so very anxious, I submitted.'' The experience hadn't been a good one for James, and later Mallory tried to remain his friend by writing him, ''You had better forget that I was ever your lover.''

He met Geoffrey Winthrop Young, a mountaineer and Eton and Cambridge graduate, a man who preferred rough-trade, especially boxers, and Mallory. In 1909 they went off to the Alps together, for a few months of climbing, including a stay at Chamonix.

Geoffrey Winthrop Young.

When Mallory graduated from Oxford his dream was to become a teacher at Winchester, but the headmaster appears to have told him that he was not teacher material. He was offered a position at the prep school Charterhouse, teaching History, Math, Latin and French. James's older brother Lytton Strachey tried to bed Mallory at Charterhouse itself, but James wrote that Mallory got out of it by saying there would be no place private enough at Charterhouse. Everyone who knew Mallory knew that when he wanted someone he *always* found both the time and place. Lytton himself wrote Duncan Grant: ''The copulation never come. I would have given worlds for an embrace.'' In another letter to Grant, Lytton wrote: ''I reached here yesterday in a state bordering on collapse,'' due to his inability to seduce Mallory.

Mallory went on his sixth trip to the Alps in 1912, during which there were three deaths, the bodies found by his lover Geoffrey Young, about one of which Young wrote, ''He looked like a young god, lying at rest on a rock after bathing.'' One had simply to slip, or to lose a grip on a rock, in order to fall to one's death. With the equipment they had, mountaineering was insanely dangerous, and took place only because of the recklessness of youth. Boys wore tweeds (some wore ties!) and thick boots, ropes were made of easily ruptured hemp and attached to any outcropping, while pitons weren't even invented until 1920 (and were then shunned as being unmanly, an artificial means of cheating). The use of duck down was just being experimented with.

As Irving had done when Mallory was a student, Mallory now too began to take students on climbs, all of whom were the personification of beauty, magnificent specimens of British manhood.

Mallory, on the left, and Siegfried Herford, an example of British beauty, 1914.

Boots worn at the time, these found on Mallory's dead body.

Sex between boys is easy because boys are carbon copies of each other. They know exactly what to do sexually. This rarely goes beyond sexual discovery and experimentation in countries that do not have boarding schools because societal pressures literally push boys into the arms of girls. But in British dormitories, what followed sexual discovery was years of sexual intimacy, with only minor exploration with girls that a lad could pay for, and only those with a serious heterosexual bent chose to pay for what they could get for free each night thanks to their roommates. What was easy among themselves became far more complicated on that unknown continent which was women. Everything, there, had to be learned anew, and psychologists maintain that boys who have not known girls from the very start of their sexuality will never experience the fullness of love, the intensity of orgasm, that they knew nightly with boys. Public college boys who married were rarely fully sexually content, and either they had boys on the side or they depended heavily on masturbatory skills.

Mallory met Ruth Turner and they married in 1915. The love was most certainly sincere on both sides, even if, the night before the wedding, Mallory bathed nude with Duncan Grant and Geoffrey Young, Young who was also his best man.

The war came, and the deaths of Denis Browne and Rupert Brooke, as reported earlier. Mallory came through the massacres during his military service, 1916-1918, after which he returned to teaching at Charterhouse.

Everest was designated the highest mountain in the world in 1856, and was named after the surveyor, George Everest. The first man interested in climbing Everest was Francis Younghusband in 1893. In 1921 the Royal Geographic Society decided the time ripe to conquer the mountain, and Mallory was invited, in part thanks to the intervention of Geoffrey Young. Younghusband chaired the Mount Everest Committee, responsible for the planning. The exclusive coverage of the event, sponsored by *The Times* and royalities on books and photos brought hope of wealth to the planners. Travel was an immense hassle back then, but far worse were the hazards as yet unknown to the first climbers. The incredibly convoluted glaciers, the terrible heat ''radiating from the glacier like a furnace'', write the Gillmans, and sun reflected from the ice, all in contrast to freezing temperatures at night. The ridges, the cols, precipices seen and unseen, training the porters--although already some Sherpa were treasured like brothers among the climbers; human relations between the men themselves, each an individual often out to advance his own career; quarrels, disputes, but the beauty was such that Mallory wrote, ''I have been half the time in ecstasy.''

The first attempt fell far short of the goal due to sheer fatigue, the ''wind like a hurricane'', and one man who had already lost feeling in his feet.

Everest in 1922 was put into immediate planning, beginning with a request for Mallory to give a series of lectures on the first attempt, keeping for himself 25% of the proceeds. This time the climbers had better equipment, woolen coats, windbreakers and ski-boots. Compressed oxygen made its appearance. At 29,000 feet there was 1/3rd of the oxygen found at ground level. Mallory viewed oxygen as artificial and a way of cheating. He would change his mind, but not during this trip. (Others argued that ''goggles, thermos flasks and warm boots'' were just as artificial, note the Gillmans.)

This time the problem was frostbite, from which every man suffered. The leader, George Finch, was also downed by dysentery. Two of the men used oxygen, thanks to which they traveled higher than all the others, and during one bitter-cold night in their tents the men discovered they could revive themselves by using it.

One last attempt was decided on, this one led by Mallory, two Brits and fourteen porters. It had snowed heavily and on the way up an avalanche broke loose that buried them all, Mallory having the time to think ''the matter was settled.'' It wasn't for him but seven men were killed. Back in London Mallory was blamed for taking 17 men up the mountain, which ''was fifteen too many'' stated a mountaineer. Geoffrey Young offered his compassion, and Younghusband told him he would have led the group in the same way.

Following his return Mallory went back to the lecture circuit, talking to packed houses and receiving 35% of the proceeds, which amply covered what he lost when he left Charterhouse. Still more income came through articles he penned. The circuit went on to N.Y., where pictures of Mallory show him as handsome as ever. He toured eastern America and Canada. He returned to lecture at Cambridge and to prepare the climbing season of 1924.

Despite the avalanche deaths and the opinion of several climbers that Mallory was unqualified to climb Everest, some noting his chronic absentmindedness, his notoriety closed the door on any attempt to exclude him, especially as the expedition had to be a financial success--all of their salaries depended on it--and only Mallory could assure that there would be maximum media coverage.

Ruth and Mallory took a far bigger home, but he could hardly cover the cost of it and that of his growing family. He had a daughter, about whom he wrote to a friend, ''I can't claim any great interest (in her).'' A second daughter came later, followed by his deeply desired son John. All three children became accomplished mountain climbers.

The Everest expedition was in a financial hole too, until a film executive, John Noel, offered £8,000 (£381,000 in 2022) for photographs and film rights.

The major event at the time was the selection of a new team member, and the choice went to a second-year Oxford student, a member of the rowing team, a superb athlete, supremely beautiful, the boy who would perhaps be Mallory's last love, Sandy Irvine, about whom Mallory said he had ''a magnificent body for the job,'' we learn from Julie Summers's book *Fearless on Everest*, 2009.

Mallory and Sandy Irving

Ruth and Mallory's marriage was in an increasingly unhappy state, the finances still bad and Mallory was often away on the lecture circuit, or alone writing, or absent teaching, yet the root cause was that a man could not satisfy himself with a woman or women after having known adolescent first-love in the arms of another boy, the memory and happiness of which would never leave him for long. Mallory's letters to Ruth were extremely loving, but in reality he had little left to offer her, other than facile words and ersatz tenderness. Few men had a sexual side as blatant as Mallory, as testified in his posing for artists and friends nude, and the moment it became warm on an expedition he would strip totally naked, naked among the other fully-dressed trekkers. On trips with friends it was always he who initiated the skinny-dipping, one fully frontal view of him showing a splendid all-boy physique (the image, alas, too poor in quality for publication). Dressed or naked, with Ruth or no-holds-barred sex with boys, Mallory was not overawed by Victorian modesty. And the letters and diaries left by former lovers prove his lust for those of his sex.

A not so elegant Mallory at right.

Peter and Leni Gillman state that Sandy was ''spectacularly heterosexual'', and, of course, that may have been the case. Biographers seem to sigh with relief when they can prove that the subject of their books put his dick in the right emplacement, a way of according him a clean bill of health. Sandy does come out, concerning Mallory, as a fine young heterosexual man, and as nothing has filtered through concerning his prep-school dormitory years nor his friendships among the famous Oxford Blue Boat rowers, we will accord him the benefit of the doubt, and be pleased that Mallory had the beauty of Everest and the beauty of Sandy before his eyes at the end.

So Mallory's choice of Sandy may have been a one-sided wish to be with the handsomest and by-far youngest member of the climbing team. As the reader knows, nothing in human relationships is more mysterious than men's sexuality, meaning we'll never know if they shared intimate moments together. We do know that on the 6th of June 1924 Mallory and Sandy set off to reach the summit of Mount Everest.

Mallory was found 75 years later. Sandy never.

WILLEM ARONDEUS
Who shouted out before a Nazi firing squad, ''Let it be known that homosexuals are not cowards.''

Willem Arondeus was the homosexual icon and ideal for each of us who wishes to incarnate the good inherent in our way of love. Born in the Netherlands in 1894, he participated in the bombing of the Amsterdam public records office wherein were stored public documents, the identity of Dutch Jews among them, the source of information for the Gestapo. Painter and author, he was betrayed by an unknown informant, arrested and shot in 1943. In 1984 he received the Resistance Memorial Cross and was named a Righteous Among the Nations in 1986, his name placed in Yad Vashem, Israel's official memorial to the victims of the Holocaust.

ALAN MATHISON TURING
Enigma – W.W. II

The hallowed Olympus of homosexual icons includes not only the world's greatest sculptors, Phidias, Praxiteles, Michelangelo and Cellini among others, the foremost artists, including Caravaggio, da Vinci and Botticelli, writers from Homer to Tennessee Williams to Truman Capote, philosophers like Nietzsche, as well as mathematicians and logicians, one of whom is Alan Matheson Turing, a founder of computer science.

Born in London in 1912, Turing graduated from Cambridge and won a PhD in mathematics at Princeton, helped to break the code of the Nazi

Enigma machine, thusly saving the lives of thousands, who was himself arrested, under British law, for his homosexuality in 1952, underwent chemical castration, and committed suicide at age 41 by taking cyanide.

Alan lost his boyhood friend when he was 17, which may have played a role in his atheism, or perhaps, like Nietzsche, he simply wanted to be honest with himself. His contribution to humanity was recognized in 1999 by *Time* magazine that named him one of the 100 Most Important People of the 20th century. At Cambridge, Alan studied under another outstanding homosexual, Ludwig Wittgenstein, an Apostle, his life covered in my book *Homosexual Secret Societies*.

The mindboggling hypocrisy concerning the acceptance of homosexuals is especially atrocious in Britain, its public schools (private in American English) and its universities--Eton, Harlow, Winchester, *et al.*, Oxford and Cambridge--are hotbeds of no-holds-barred debauch, covered in detail in my book *Boarding School Homosexuality*, while outside those sanctuaries men in Britain were hung and beheaded for homosexuality from the time of Henry VIII to the last two executed in 1835.

In our times we have gay marriage and Internet that has utterly destroyed the religious nonsense that plagued my youth, forbidding me to even touch my body, yet the mindless Tartufferie continues on, with those responsible for Turing's death attempting to anesthetize responsibility by publicly *pardoning him*, in 2013, not accusing themselves, and then issuing an opiate in the form of a £50 Bank of England note with Turing's portrait in 2021, while continuing *to send their sons to be sodomized* in the hundreds of thousands at the hands of those in which the lads should have the greatest confidence, priests, 6,000 priests recently accused of sexual crimes in the U.S. alone, the church paying out *$3 billion* to abuse survivors, while outside the States over $4 billion in settlements to 5,000 cases in 2020 were shelled out, according to Catholic Church BishopAccountability--all of which is but the tip of the despicable iceberg of the still-functioning scumbags who continue to whisper into their victims' ears, ''Christ had his John, just like I have you.''

The sanctuaries of schools like Eton and universities like Oxbridge
have allowed students to discover their sexuality without the
interference of self-serving adults, something Alan Turing took full
advantage of.

DE LATTRE
The only Frenchman to command American forces in W.W. II

It's humbling to relate the life of the war hero Jean Joseph Marie Gabriel de Lattre de Tassigny, 1889-1952, because he was of vital importance in freeing France, de Lattre equal to Marshal Montgomery with whom he shared the command of the Ground Forces in Western Europe from 1948 to 1950, the only French general of W.W. II to command United States forces, as well as being named commander-in-chief of all French Forces in Germany from 1945 to 1947. Like Montgomery he had his quirks, perhaps even more so, perhaps equal to General Patton as a loose cannon.

A graduate of the French Naval School and Saint-Cyr, he was wounded a first time at the beginning of W.W. I by shrapnel from a munitions explosion, followed a month later by a lance. The following year, 1915, he was wounded 5 times during the 16 months he was at Verdun.

In 1939 he was promoted to Brigadier General, the youngest general in France, and following the Armistice of 22 June 1940 he fully backed Maréshal Philippe Pétain at Vichy, inaugurating field schools and military instruction centers for the training, military and physical, of what would be his main interest, youth centers he would establish the remainder of his career, that he would often visit, hold snap inspections, fond of organizing basketball games, some participants observing, later in memoirs, that the more the youths were naked, the keener his interest. He set up a similar center in Tunisia from 1941 to 1942.

When the Allies landed in North Africa he was imprisoned by the Germans but escaped to join de Gaulle's Free French in London in 1943. He was put in charge of 365,000 men that he united with the French Forces of the Interior (F.F.I.) already in France, and they, plus volunteers, formed an army of 400,000 that liberated Lyon and Strasbourg, after which four U.S. divisions were placed under his orders. From 1945 to 1947 he was commander-in-chief of French Forces in Germany, as said.

Montgomery, Eisenhower, Zhukov and de Lattre in Berlin in 1945.

From 1950 to 1951 he commanded French troops during the First Indochina War where he was described as the Gallic MacArthur, handsome, stylish, flamboyant and egocentric to the point of megalomania, vain but brilliant. He came up against the Vietminh General Giap, and the first of the hundreds of thousands that would eventually die in Vietnam began, one of whom was de Lattre's son, killed when his father ordered him to defend an inconsequential town ''at all costs''. 92,500 French lives were lost, a total of 400,000 for all participants.

In 1951 de Lattre went to the Pentagon to request American aid, without which he knew that France had no chance against the Vietminh, and offered the reasoning that would eventually see 58,220 American boys killed: if Vietnam falls all of Southeast Asia will fall to communism. ''Three-hundred thousand wounded. The amputations, the blindness, the terrible scars of body and mind. Men looking down at the space where their legs used to be,'' wrote Robert Caro in his magnificent *Lyndon Johnson*, vol. 4. But at the time of De Lattre's request for aid Americans were busy in

North Korea and the French folded their tents after Điện Biên Phủ. Giap remained a power in Vietnam only second to Ho Chi Minh, and died recently, in 2013.

De Lattre died of cancer in 1951 and his state funeral lasted five days, with halts at Les Invalides (Napoleon's Tomb), the Arc de Triomphe and Notre Dame, Dwight D. Eisenhower and Marshal Montgomery among the pallbearers. Bells ran out and flags were at half-most, while at his birthplace his 97-year-old father, blind, ran his hands over his son's coffin, over the posthumous marshal's baton and over his boy's kepi. The coffin was laid to rest beside that of de Lattre's son Bernard, killed eight months previously, at age 23.

A French icon, perhaps one day a complete biography of de Lattre's life will be written, when people finally accept that homosexuality and soldierly valor have gone hand-in-hand since Achilles and Patroclus, Alexander the Great and Hephaestion, Frederick the Great (14) and the great Charles XII of Sweden (40).

WILFRED THESIGER
Arabian Sands
1959

Wilfred Patrick Thesiger, 1910-2003, was called the latter-day Lawrence of Arabia, and in truth they could have been twins. Both were inveterate travels and explorers, both war heroes, and both loved an Arab boy, Dahoum in Lawrence's case, bin Kabina in Thesiger's. Bin Kabina and his companion, Salim bin Ghabaisha, had at first forced their presence on Thesiger, the three then becoming inseparable. Both Lawrence and Thesiger were secret about their loves, Thesiger only saying, later, ''He was like my son,'' states James Maw who interviewed Thesiger. James Maw believed that Thesiger's love for the boy had been platonic because Thesiger was a solitary soul and sought purity and the cleanness of the desert, points that held true for Lawrence as well.

Bin Kabina and bin Ghabaisha. Of Ghabaisha Thesiger wrote: ''He was loyal, generous and afraid of nothing. He was a wonderful man to travel with.''

An extract from Thesiger's 1959 book *Arabian Sands* suggests that Thesiger's attraction to both boys went well beyond the platonic: ''Bin Kabina was accompanied by the boy I had noticed the night before. They were about the same age. This boy was dressed only in a length of blue cloth, which he wore wrapped around his waist with one tasseled end thrown over his right shoulder, and his dark hair fell like a mane about his shoulders. He had a face of classic beauty, pensive and rather sad in repose, but which lit up when he smiled, like a pool touched by the sun. Antinous must have looked like this, I thought, when Hadrian first saw him in the Phrygian woods (13). ''He told me his name was Salim bin Ghabaisha and he asked me to take him on. Bin Kabina urged me to let him join us, saying that he was the best shot in the tribe and that he was as good a hunter as Musallim, so that if he was with us we should feed every day on meat, for there were many ibex and gazelle in the country ahead of us. 'He is my friend. Let him come with us for my sake. The two of us will go with you wherever you want. We will always be your men.' ''

Thesiger

Thesiger lived to be 93 and for his 90th birthday both bin Kabina and bin Ghabaisha were flown to his retirement home in Surrey.

Thesiger's father had been a British consul-general in Addis Ababa and it was there that Thesiger was born. He studied History at Oxford and was the captain of the Oxford boxing team--no easy task--and Treasurer of the Oxford University Exploration Club. A group of nomads, the Danakil, cut off the testicles of the men they killed, as trophies. Thesiger said that it reminded him of his days at Eton, with its fagging and flogging, and how he had been used sexually. When an Arab held up the trophies of four men he had thusly mutilated Thesiger said, ''It was equivalent of an Etonian who had just won his school colors in cricket'', what took place in dormitories full covered in my book *Boarding School Homosexuality*.

Thesiger joined the resistance against the Italians in Ethiopia and captured a garrison of 2,500 Italian soldiers, for which he was decorated. After the war he traveled extensively throughout Africa and Arabia, and his first book, *Arabian Sands*, concerned his exploration through the unknown regions of the desert interior of Arabia, a land ruled by tribes whose vendettas never ended, and who massacred infidels, for their goods, for their disbelief in Allah, and for the sheer pleasure of the killing. Both the Romans and the Ottomans had been defeated by these tribes, along with diseases, chiefly dysentery from filthy water. Thesiger copied the Arabs in everything they did, down to their toilet rituals (down to squatting to piss), sleeping with a dagger and rifle, dressing and walking as they did, his Arabic perfect (although it's unclear if he'd had himself circumcised as Richard Burton had had done), but even with all these precautions he was most probably never taken for an Arab, so one surmises that he survived by being simply tolerated by the Arabs, and by avoiding the most hostile among them. It is said that he was called Mobarak bin London, the Blessed One, son of London. About his love of the desert he said, ''I was exhilarated by the sense of space, the silence and the crisp cleanness of the sand. I felt in harmony with the past, traveling as men had traveled for untold generations across the deserts, dependent for their survival on the endurance of their camels and their own inherited skills.''

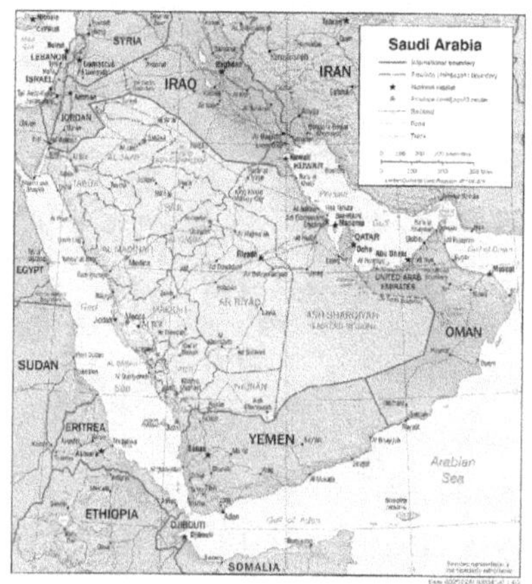

The lands Thesiger explored, areas in the center of the map that are slightly less grey.

EDWIN GALLAGHER
Alive to Thrive.

Ed Gallagher, born in 1957, was an American football player for the University of Pittsburgh from 1977 to 1979. Unable to reconcile his image of himself as an athlete with gay urges, he attempted suicide, which left him paraplegic. ''I was more emotionally paralyzed then, than I am physically now,'' he stated on CBC Radio's *The Inside Track*. He founded Alive to Thrive, an organization designed to help parents and leaders understand how suicide can be prevented. Ed died of a heart attack in 2005, aged 48.

Edwin Gallagher

MARK BINGHAM
September 2001

Before enrolling in the best all-around university in America, the University of California at Berkeley, where he played on its champion-winning rugby team while assuming the presidency of his Chi Psi fraternity, Mark had been the captain of his Los Gatos High School rugby team, no easy task because unbridled, testosterone-driven high-school athletes are the most difficult to manage. Mark outed himself at age 21, formed his own company, the Bingham Group, with plans to operate on both coasts, Mark playing rugby in San Francisco while founding a rugby team in N.Y., the Gotham Knights.

On the 11th of September 2001 Mark's United Airlines Flight 93 took off, minutes before two airplanes crashed into New York's twin Trade Center towers, followed by the announcement from the plane's cockpit that the plane had been hijacked, its destination the White House or the Capitol Building. Mark and fellow passengers Todd Beamer, Tom Burnett and Jeremy Glick decided to take the plane back from the terrorists, all four men over six feet, Mark himself 6'4''. The men managed to break into the cockpit, but not before the plane was forced downward, the crash site a National Memorial today.

Mark, Todd Beamer, Tom Burnett and Jeremy Glick had not been alone in the participants' attempt to take back the plane, their combined heroism in stark contrast to the miserable and dangerous spectacle offered by the place their heroism saved, Washington D.C., from 2016 onward.

BRETT JONES
A Navy SEALS hero married in 2011
and BILLY SIPPLE
A United States Marine Corps hero

The Navy SEALS (Sea, Air and Land Teams) became world famous when they killed Bin Laden, and may be the world's number one intervention force, all heroes.

The story of Brett Jones is heartrending because he was a SEAL who accidently outed himself by leaving an I-love-you phone message to his sailor lover. He left the Navy in 2003, after having been thrown out of his home by his Air Force pilot father and mother when he was an adolescent, due to his homosexuality. ''My mom told me homosexuals go straight to hell'' and ''My dad said he wasn't going to have me infecting our family with that disease.''

He married a former detective, Jason White, and inherited the detective's 13-year-old son, Ethan, all three forming a seamless bond. They decided to settle down in Alabama where they were treated like lepers, their son's classmates even passing him messages in school with Bible verses concerning his two dads' sins.

Brett's close SEAL buddies supported him but not the corps, and a Navy investigation into his sexuality ended only thanks to the intervention of equal-rights lawyers and several congressmen.

Jones and White married in Indiana in 2011, White's dad embracing his boy. White's son, straight, became a pilot. He calls White, Dad, and Jones, Brett. As Brett worked in security in Afghanistan and Iraq, and White was a cop, they opened a security company. The company, and their new lives, are a success.

Brett, Brett and Brett on the far right.
Stated Brett playfully: ''I didn't fuck half my squad. Maybe, like, a quarter at most.''
During duty in Afghanistan a teammate not so playfully changed his radio call-sign from ''Bad Monkey'' to ''Gay Gay''. Afraid his team couldn't be counted on in a life-or-death situation, Brett requested an early return home.

That a man with Brett's qualifications couldn't be accepted for himself, other than among those who knew him, does not bide well for the acceptance of homosexuals. The armed forces have tried every possible way of gaining the tolerance of straights for gays, using strategies like ''mutual gaze aversion'' (avoiding eye contact) and averting their eyes to a neutral direction in locker rooms when confronted with nudity (a demand outrageous to the point of being sick). It remains probable that heterosexuals will never be comfortable in situations in which they feel others are ogling them, showers and saunas the last male fortresses where they can be themselves. ''We're all crammed together in the showers and I don't want to worry that some gay guy is staring at me,'' said one airman. ''Servicemen who were trained to be cool under fire were unsettled by the thought of a homosexual glancing their way in a shower, afraid some guy might want to see him as a woman'', the above quotes from Bruce Bawer's *Place at the Table: The Gay Individual in American Society* and from David Zucchino's article in the *Los Angeles Times*.

Freedom is showering outside where no one's going to judge the size of your dick or check out your ass, the reason most straights resist the presence of homosexuals.
Homosexuality in the military is covered in my books *The History of Homosexuality in the Armed Forces* and *Sailors and Homosexuality*.

''BILLY'' SIPPLE

Oliver Wellington ''Billy'' Sipple, born in 1941, was a U.S. Marine Corpsman who served and was wounded in Vietnam before joining Harvey Milk's campaign team. On September 22, 1975, he wrestled a gun from the hands of a woman who had been able to get off a shot at President Gerald Ford, Billy perhaps saving Ford's life, the bullet ending up in a taxis driver who survived. Billy was deep in the closet at the time, but Milk felt that Billy's heroic act was a perfect occasion to turn the spotlight on gays, stating, ''It's too good an opportunity. For once we can show that gays do heroic things, not just all that caca about molesting children and hanging out in bathrooms'' (an example William Haines, the most successful actor of his times, tried for picking up a six-year-old on a beach, taking him home and putting his tiny genitals into his mouth, the story covered in my book *Hollywood's Homosexual History*, and George Michaels, picked up at a public urinal as recently as 1998).

Milk's selfish outing of Billy ended Billy's desire to lead the life of a heroic Marine, not a heroic gay who saved a president, an outing that terminated Billy's relationship with his mother, and even Ford himself only sent Billy a thankyou note when the publicity fallout over his refusal to do so forced his hand, although it's true that Ford was basically known for his ability to walk and chew gum at the same time.

Billy didn't sue Milk for outing him, but he did sue *The Washington Post* for $15,000,000, a suit he lost, and his family did end by taking him back, at the end of the long spoon generally reserved for the Devil, his brother writing, ''Our parents accepted it. That was all. They didn't like it, but they still accepted. He was welcomed. Only thing was: Don't bring a lot of your friends.'' In truth, when he tried to contact his mother she hung up on him and his father, besides telling his ''good'' son to ''Forget you have a brother'', refused to let Billy attend his mother's funeral.

Losing all will to live, Billy Sipple was found dead in his San Francisco apartment in 1989, the cause unspecified.

Had Milk not outed him, Billy may have been around on the 27th of November 1978 to stop Milk from being shot to death.

MATTHEW PACIFICI and HUDSON TAYLOR

Matthew Pacifici, born in 1993, was an American soccer player known for his work with AthleteAlly, an LGBT grouping of athletes that promotes inclusion, refuses discrimination and gives aid to athletes. AthleteAlly was founded by Hudson Taylor, a former wrestler and wrestling coach, who took it on himself to come to the defense of gays harassed by bullies, Hudson, straight, wanted an organization of other straights that straight athletes and coaches could adhere to, the aim to help gays confront homophobic badgering. AthleteAlly visits elementary schools, junior highs, high schools and college campuses to encourage allyship--harmony between differing sexual orientations. AthleteAlly promotes pride nights, workshops, all devoted to non-discriminatory policies. Taylor and his organization has received numerous awards, Taylor himself named ''Greatest Person of the Day'' by Huffington Post. In 2012 he was named Alumnus of the Year from his Maryland University alma mater. He's married. He is, proudly, this book's unique straight hero.

The picture of Hudson Taylor between two pics of Matthew Pacifici, two worthy and honorable men.

Matt won his reputation as a goalkeeper when he played for Davidson College. Taken on by South Carolina's Columbus Crew in March 2016, he was kicked in the forehead by a teammate the following July, ending his soccer career. He didn't come out during his playing time because as a third-string player it would have made no difference to the outside world, but it might have cost him his place on his team, or any future teams, and it would certainly have cost him sponsors, not to speak of the potential displeasure among his teammates, the exact combat of Athlete Ally.

He's in a relationship with his lover Dirk Blanchat, stating that ''it makes me the most happy ever in my life.'' About coming out, he said, ''I think that every time you have a story like Robbie Rogers (his life found in my book *Homosexual Athletes*), or mine or whoever it may be, it makes it easier for the next generation. Everyone has that deep-down fear they won't be accepted, so the more athletes that can come out, the easier for future people to follow.''

Blanchat and Matt/Dirk.
Is there a word, other than bliss?
''There's no perfect time to come out. I waited until I was 24,'' said Matt. ''Now I'm absolutely at the spot where I'm very willingly and happy to help raise awareness in any way for the LGBTQ community.''

JACK MACKENROTH
Outgames

Born in 1969 in Seattle, Washington, Jack Mackenroth was an American swimmer, model and gay pornstar, a premed student at the University of California, Berkeley, who dropped his studies in medicine in favor of two degrees, in Fine Arts and in Sociology, after which he went on to study Fashion Design at Parsons School of Design, to work with Tommy Hilfiger, Levis and Weatherproof Active Wear, opening his own menswear store in New York, ''Jack''.

Jack's perfect face and beard, Jack swimming medal winner and Jack with a buddy.

Throughout the 90s he posed on the cover and inside *Men's Fitness, Men's Journal, Men's Health, Genre, blue, L'Uomo Vogue, refresh, POZ, Gloss* and others, his designs in *Elle*. He was a competitive swimmer in elementary, high school and university, earning three All-American titles as well as putting in a record time for the breaststroke in the 4x50-meter relay at the Masters World Championships in 2006. In 2009 he competed in the Outgames (41) in Copenhagen and in 2010 the Gay Games in Cologne, where he won seven medals. He was diagnosed with the gay plague in 1990 and spent the rest of his life in campaigns like Living Positive By Design. He fought discriminatory behavior against gays and for projects, like Housing Works, that provided homes for gay-plague sufferers, his homage in this book just a token recognition of his heroism.

Jack Wet Platinum Man of the Year, he was diagnosed seropositive in 1990 at age 19 and came out in 2008 in *Project Runway*.
His modeling beauty led to his taking selfies of himself for the most ardent of his fans, that he later monetized, something Walt Whitman said every boy should do in order to gain life experience and a little pocket change.

In 2018 Jack began doing pornography though his OnlyFans webpage (42), one of the most exciting in the industry, and was elected Wet Platinum Man of the Year for 2015, Wet Platinum a sex lubricant. He participated, as said, in *Project Runway*, a popular talent show where competitors complete to create the best clothes, limited by time, material, budget and themes.

Jack as sex icon.
To better care for gay-plague victims, Jack returned to school for a degree in nursing, making him a homosexual hero.

POSTSCRIPT

Homosexuals have their own culture, living standards and ways of life, freed from the commitment and financial burdens of wedlock and the responsibilities of raising children (which are gigantic in this day and age), unless they go through the hurdles of tying the knot, mostly societal hurdles in civilized countries but nonetheless daunting enough to make men think more than twice before doing so. In non-civilized countries homosexuals are still condemned to death (a form of genocide, the countries practicing it listed in *Wikipedia* under ''Capital Punishment for Homosexuality''), legalized murder practiced in Britain by hanging until 1861, arrests for which continued in Tasmania until *1984* (43), while *Brokeback Mountain* filming site, Wyoming, saw the torture-killing of a gay University of Wyoming student in 1998, and in Texas in 2018 a jury recommended the sentence of 10 years' *probation* for the murderer of Daniel Spencer, 32, whose own parents denied that Daniel had even been gay. Canadian filmmaker Xavier Dolan (44) and Canadian pornstar Gabriel Clark (45) were warmly received when they came out in high school, but a high-school student today in the States would have to possess undaunted courage and Popeye biceps to admit to locker-room buddies that he preferred them to the girls his pals where talking about plugging that night, locker-room showers and saunas a retreat where straight boys don't want their asses and inner thighs sized up. The disastrous 2016 election results in the U.S. are not merely a call for vigilance in the protection of the gay rights that the men in this book have fought tooth and nail to gain, but are a serious warning that Nazi-style pink triangles are not beyond possibility, Berlin the most openly gay culture in the world until the rise of Hitler (14).

The problem is *people*, 70% of the Republicans, who voted-in the 2016 miscreant, still willing to support him, while the British democracy that founded other democracies throughout the world, notably in South Africa and the greatest democracy on Earth, India, continues to kowtow to Royals put in place exclusively through *the accident of birth*, one of whom wished to take the place of the kotex of his mistress, while his youngest son played pool naked with Vegas whores, yet 70% of Brits continue to support their shenanigans and this blatant denial of democracy itself.

The conundrum is as great in Australia which has the most exclusive form of bromance outside of Ancient Greece, mateship, a beer advertisement during a rugby match proclaiming: ''Mates, mates, they're what the country's made of / they're what your wife's afraid of'', yet few countries are more homophobic. Canada is a clear example of an open, intelligent, homo-tolerant society, legalizing gay marriages in 2005 (against 2015 in the States), with hopes open for Tasmania which allowed gay marriage in 2017 and is on the road to some of the most progressive pro-LGBT rights of any nation (43).

Despite serious anti-gay bias which impairs the economic growth of gays, a 2017 Christopher Carpenter and Samuel Eppink study for *Southern Economic Journal* stated that gays earn 10% more than straights, this despite the fact that many employers do not find gays manly enough, while Lesbians have always made more than heterosexual women thanks to what employers call their inherent manliness and their devotion to work and not the kids they won't be producing. Homosexuals are often better educated because they meet far more different kinds of men, men from various horizons as nothing is a better social leveler than sex, and they travel far more, and farther afield, than straights, the search for sexual adventure often the reason, and, lastly, most know that in order to compensate for discrimination they need to be university educated.

Other homosexual giants could also have figured in this book, da Vinci one of them, his works covered in my book *Homoerotic Art*, as were Cellini and Caravaggio (my books *Cellini* and *Caravaggio*), Michelangelo (*Renaissance Homosexuality*), Magnus Hirschfeld (*German Homosexuality*), and *scores* of others, in homage of whom Apple president Tom Cook stated, ''I'm proud to be gay and I consider being gay among the greatest gifts God has given me'', seconded by CNN's Anderson Cooper who proclaimed, ''I think being gay is a blessing, and it's something I am thankful for every single day.''

SOURCES

(1) See my book *Michael Hone His World, His Loves.*

(2) See my book *Cesare Borgia, His Violent Life, His Violent Times.*

(3) See my book *Louis XIII.*

(4) See my book *Renaissance Homosexuality.*

(5) See my book *Homosexual Warriors.*

(6) See my book *Boarding School Homosexuality.*

(7) See my book *Henry III.*

(8) See my book *Greek Homosexuality.*

(9) See my book *Roman Homosexuality.*

(10) See my book *TROY.*

(11) See my book *Homosexual Secret Societies.*

(12) See my book *Alcibiades.*

(13) See my book *Hadrian and Antinous* for more on both men.

(14) See my book *German Homosexuality.*

(15) See my book *American Homosexual Giants.*

(16) See my book *Gay Genius.*

(17) See my book *John (Jack) Nicholson.*

(18) See my book *Capri: Homosexual Paradise.*

(19) See my book *Caravaggio.*

(20) See my book *The Garden of Allah.*

(21) See my book *SPARTA.*

(22) See my book *The Sacred Band.*

(23) See my book *The HomoErotic Couples who have Enriched the World.*

(24) See my book *TROY* or the fully-illustrated *The Trojan War*, for the entire story, which I consider my best works.

(25) See my book *Omnisexuality, the Death of Straight and Gay Sex.*

(26) See my book *The Essence of Being Gay.*

(27) See my book *CELLINI.*

(28) See my book *The Bloomsbury Set.*

(29) See my book *ARGO.*

(30) See my book *Alexander & Hephaestion.*

(31) See my book *Five Renaissance Wonders.*

(32) See my book *The History of British Homosexuality.*

(33) See my book *French Homosexuality.*

(34) *Wikipedia.*

(35) Byron's life covered in my book *Venice*, where Byron spent a good number of lustful years.

(36) See my book *Mediterranean Homosexual Pleasure.*

(37) See my X-rated book *Hustlers.*

(38) See my book *Phallus.*

(39) No one would have believed that milquetoast Maynard Keynes had been sexually active until his detailed diary came to light. As for Lawrence, he was, on the one hand, so sexually discrete that his closest friends thought he was asexual, while those responsible for his beatings intimate that they had been often and not always private.

(40) See my book *Charles XII of Sweden*.

(41) The World Outgames originated in 2006 when the Gay Games left Montreal for Chicago and the Outgames was established to replace them. The Outgames are more than just games in which anyone can participate, they also include cultural events such as conference, concerts and film screenings, all dealing with human rights and homophobia. Any sexual orientation is allowed. The first games took place in Montreal in 2006, the second Copenhagen in 2009, followed by Antwerp, but the 2017 Miami games were canceled in 2013, at the last minute, athletes in transit, most certainly unable to recover travel costs, certainly the end of the Outgames.

(42) See my book The *All-Male Porn Industry*.

(43) See my book *Tasmania*.

(44) See my book *Venice*, where Dolan received his awards.

(45) See my book *All-Male Pornography*.

SOURCES FOR THE GREEK AND ROMAN SECTIONS OF THIS BOOK

The major Greek and Roman sources consulted or used in the writing of this book:

<u>Aelianus</u> was a Roman author and teacher of rhetoric who spoke and wrote in Greek.

<u>Aeschylus</u>, of whom 7 out of perhaps 90 plays have survived. His gravestone celebrated his heroism during the victory against the Persians at Marathon and *not his plays*, proof of the extraordinary importance of Greek survival against the barbarians (sadly, he lost his brother at Marathon). He is said to have been a deeply religious person, dedicated to Zeus. As a boy he worked in a vineyard until Dionysus visited him in a dream and directed him to write plays. One of his plays supposedly divulged too much about the Eleusinian Mysteries and he was nearly stoned to death by the audience. He had to stand trial but pleaded ignorance. He got off when the judges learned of the death of his brother at Marathon and when Aeschylus showed the wounds he and a second brother had received at Marathon too, the second brother left with but a stump in place of his hand. In one of his later plays Pericles was part of the chorus. The subjects of his plays often concerned Troy and the Persian Wars, Marathon, Salamis and Xerxes (Xerxes is accused of losing the war due to hubris; his building of the bridge over the Hellespont was a show of arrogance the gods found

unacceptable). In *Seven against Thebes* he relates the destinies of Oedipus' two sons who agree to become kings of Thebes on alternate years. Naturally, when the time comes for them to change places the king in place refuses, which leads to both boys killing each other. *Agamemnon* is an excellent retelling of the Trojan War, as Agamemnon sails home to be murdered by his wife Clytemnestra. In *The Libation Bearers* Agamemnon's boy Orestes returns home to destroy his father's assassins, Clytemnestra and her lover Aegisthus. In *The Eumenides* (the Kindly Spirits) Orestes is chased by the Furies for having killed his mother. He takes shelter with Apollo who decides, with Athena, to try the boy before a court. The vote is a tie, but Athena, preaching the importance of reason and understanding, acquits him. She then changes the terrible Furies into sweet Eumenides.

__Anacreon__ was born in 582 B.C. and was known for his drinking songs.

__Andocides__ was implicated in the Hermes scandal and saved his skin by turning against Alcibiades in a speech that has come down to us called, what else?, *Against Alcibiades.*

__Aristobulus__, c. 375-301 B.C., a Greek historian who accompanied Alexander the Great on his campaigns. He was also an architect and military engineer, and a friend of Alexander. He rebuilt the tomb of Cyrus the Great. His writings only survive through Arrian and Plutarch.

__Appian__, who lived during the reigns of Trajan and Hadrian, was a Roman historian of Greek origin. He was a friend of Fronto, Marcus Aurelius' tutor and, perhaps, lover. He left his book, *Roman History*, which describes, among other events, the Roman civil wars.

__Aristophanes__, my preferred playwright, is, naturally, the father of comedy. He wrote perhaps 40 plays of which 11 remain. He was feared by all: Plato states that it was his play *The Clouds* the root of the trial that cost Socrates his life. Nearly nothing is known about him other than what he himself revealed in his works. Playwrights were obliged to be conservative because part of each play was funded by a wealthy citizen, an honor for the citizen and a caveat for the author. He was an exponent of make-love-not-war who saw his country go from its wonderful defeat of the Persians to its end at the hands of the Spartans. Along with Alcibiades and Socrates, Aristophanes is featured in Plato's *The Symposium* in which he is gently mocked, proof that he was considered, even by those he poked fun at, as affable. *The Acharnians* highlights the troubles the Athenians went through after the death of Pericles and their defeat at the hands of Sparta. *The Peace* focuses on the Peace of Nicias. *Lysistrata* tells about the plight of women trying to bring about peace in order to prevent the sacrifice of their sons during war, occasioning the world's first sex strike. When Athens lost its freedom to Sparta, Aristophanes stopped writing plays.

__Arrian__, c. 86-c.160 A.D. A Greek historian and philosopher, his *The Anabasis of Alexander* is today's best source on Alexander the Great's campaigns. Born in Bithynia, home of Antinous, he became a Roman citizen. He was a friend of Emperor Hadrian who appointed him to the senate. He is known as the young Xenophon thanks to the clarity of his writing, or because it was a name he chose due to his love for the great writer. Eight of his *oeuvre* exist.

<u>Athenaeus</u> lived in the times of Marcus Aurelius. His *Deipnosopistae* is a banquet conversation *à la Platon* during which conversations on every possible subject takes place, filling fifteen books that have come down to us.

<u>Ausonius</u> was a Latin poet and teacher of rhetoric, around 350 B.C.

<u>Bion</u> was a Greek philosopher known for his diatribes, satires and attacks on religion. He lived around 300 B.C.

<u>Callisthenes</u>, c. 360-328 B.C., was a historian who accompanied Alexander during his Asiatic expedition. His great uncle was Aristotle who obtained the position of court historian for him. His praises of Alexander turned to critisizme when Alexander took on Persian clothes, manners and demanded that his men bow to him. Accused of treason, he was tortured, and later died in prison.

<u>Cassius Dio</u>, 155 A.D. to 235 A.D., was a noted historian who wrote in Greek and published a history of Rome in 80 volumes, many of which have survived, giving modern historians a detailed look into his times.

<u>Chares</u> of Mytilen was part of Alexander the Great's court. He wrote a history of Alexander in ten books, dealing mainly with his private life. Fragments come to us thanks to Athenaeus.

<u>Cicero</u> was born in 106 B.C. and murdered by Mark Antony in 43 B.C. Michael Grant said it all when he wrote, ''the influence of Cicero upon the history of European literature and ideas greatly exceeds that of any other prose writer in any language.''

<u>Cleitarchus</u> was active in 4th century B.C. His work was completely lost but much quoted by Diodorus, Quintus Curtius, Justin and Plutarch.

<u>Cornelius Nepos</u> was a Roman friend of Cicero. Most of what he wrote was lost, so what we know comes through passages of his works in the books of other historians.

<u>Ctesias</u> was a Greek historian from Anatolian Caria, and the physican of Artaxerxes, whom he accompanied in his war against his brother Cyrus the Younger. He wrote a book on India, *Indica* and Persia, *Persica*. The fragments we have of his writing come to us through Diodorus Siculus and Plutarch.

<u>Curtius</u> [Quintus Curtius Rufus], 1st century, has but one surviving work, *Histories of Alexander the Great*. Nothing else is known about him. His book is uniquely isolated, in that no other ancient work refers to it.

<u>Diodorus Siculus</u>, 1st century B.C., also known as Diodorus of Sicily, a Greek historian who wrote *Bibliotheca historica*, the first half of which

170

covers history up to the Trojan War, the second half up to Alexander the Great's death.

Diogenes of Sinope (aka Diogenes the Cynic) comes to use through extracts of his writing passed on by others, as nothing he wrote has survived. He had a truly remarkable life, at first imprisoned for debasing the coins his father, a banker, minted. Afterwards he pled poverty, sleeping in a huge ceramic jar, walking the streets of Athens during the day with a lighted lamp, saying he was in search of an honest man, and teasing Plato by noisily eating through his lectures (later Plato claimed he was ''a Socrates gone mad''.) On a voyage he was captured and sold as a slave in Crete to a Corinthian who was so entranced by his intelligence that he made him his sons' teacher. It was in his master's household that he grew old and died. Plutarch tells us he met Alexander the Great while Diogenes was staring at a pile of bones. In answer to Alexander's question he said he was searching for the bones of Alexander's father, but could not distinguish them from those of a slave. Alexander supposedly said that if he couldn't be Alexander he would choose to be Diogenes. He was the first man ever to claim to be ''a citizen of the world.'' He urinated on people, defecated where he would and masturbated in public, about which he said, ''If only I could banish hunger by rubbing my belly.'' The word cynic meant dog-like, and when someone questioned him about it he said he too was dog-like because he licked those who helped him, barked at those who didn't, and bit his enemies. Rogers and Hart wrote these lyrics about him: There was an old zany/who lived in a tub; he had so many flea-bites/he didn't know where to rub.

Eratosthenes, c.276-c.194 B.C., was a Greek mathematician, poet and astronomer, a geographer who invented the discipline of geography. The first person to calculate the circumference of the Earth and the distance between the Earth and the Sun. He dated the Trojan War at 1183 B.C., centuries before the current evaluation of between 1280-1180.

Eupolis lived around 430 B.C. An Athenian poet who wrote during the Peloponnesian Wars.

Euripides may have written 90 plays of which 18 survive. His approach was a study of the inner lives of his personages, the predecessor of Shakespeare. Due to his stance on certain subjects, he thought it best to leave Athens voluntarily rather than suffer an end similar to that of Socrates. An example: ''I would prefer to stand three times to confront my enemies in battle rather than bear a single child!'' He was born on the island of Salamis, of Persian-War fame; in fact he was born on the very day of the battle. His youth was spent in athletics and dance. Due to bad marriages with unfaithful wives, he withdrew to Salamis where he wrote while contemplating sea and sky. When Sparta defeated Athens in war, it did not burn the city to the ground: Plutarch states that this was thanks to one of Euripides' plays, *Electra*, put on for the Spartans in Athens, a play they found so wonderful that they proclaimed that it would be barbarous to destroy a city capable of engendering men of the quality of Euripides. (The real reason was to preserve the city that had twice saved Greece from Persian victory.) Euripides was known for his love of Agathon, a youth praised for his beauty as well as for his culture, and would later become a playwright. Aristophanes mocked Euripides for loving Agathon long after he had left his boyhood behind him. (Remember, not everyone followed boy-love to the letter. The idea of men loving boys until they grew whiskers did not always hold true. Boys grown ''old'' could shave their chins and butts; some men just preferred other men, hairy or not, while most men impregnated boys but other men adored being penetrated.) Plato says that Agathon had polished manners, wealth, wisdom and dispensed hospitality with ease and refinement.

<u>Herodian</u> wrote a history of Greece entitled *History of the Empire from the Death of Marcus*, in eight books. Thanks to him we learn a great deal about Elagabalus.

<u>Herodotus</u> was contemporary to some of the events that interest us here. Cicero called him the Father of History, while Plutarch wrote that he was the Father of Lies. His masterpiece is *The Histories*, considered a chef-d'oeuvre, a work that the gods have preserved intact right up to our own day, a divine intervention that would not have surprised a believer like Herodotus (it's also a book I reread every year). Part of his work may have been derived from other sources (what historian's work isn't?) and the facts rearranged in an effort to give them dramatic force and please an audience. Much of what he did was based on oral histories, many of which themselves were based on early folk tales, highly suspect, naturally, in all their details. Aristophanes made fun of segments of his work and Thucydides called Herodotus a storyteller. Surprisingly little is known about his own life. For example, he writes lovingly about Samos, leading some to believe that he may have spent his youth there. Born near Ionia, he wrote in that dialect, learning it perhaps on Samos. He was his own best publicist, taking his works to festivals and games, such as the Olympic Games, and reading them to the spectators. As I've said, many people doubt that he actually went where he said he went and saw what he said he saw. But the same was true of Marco Polo who causes disbelief to this day simply because he never mentioned eating noodles in China or seeing the Great Wall or even drinking Chinese tea. No historian, then as now, can write a book on ancient occurrences without referring to Herodotus' observations. An amusing example of recent discoveries that give credence to Herodotus is this: Herodotus wrote about a kind of giant ant, the size of a fox, living in India, in the desert, that dug up gold. This was ridiculed until the French ethnologist Peissel came upon a marmot living in today's

Pakistan that burrows in the sand and has for generations brought wealth to the region by bringing up gold from its burrows. Peissel suggests that the original confusion came from the fact that the Persian word for marmot was similar to the word for mountain ant.

__Isocrate__ was a student of Socrates who wrote a speech in the defense of Alcibiades during a trial that took place after his death.

__Josephus__, 37 A.D. to around 100 A.D., was a historian born in Jerusalem. He fought against the Romans and was captured by Vespasian who kept him as his interpreter and, later, Josephus even assumed the emperor's family name, becoming a citizen (Titus Flavius Josephus). A Jew, he turned against his people and helped Vespasian's son Titus to loot the Second Temple. His works include *The Jewish War* and *Antiquities of the Jews.*

__Justin's__ personal history is largely unknown. His Latin places him in the second century, under the Roman Empire. He wrote histories concerning Philip II and other Macedonian kings. Much of what we know comes from other historians who related his works.

__Juvenal__ was a satirical poet who wrote *Satires.*

__Lucan__ (Marcus Annaeus Lucanus) lived from 39 A.D. to 65 A.D., a short life due to his being ordered by Nero to commit suicide because of his role in the treasonous Piso conspiracy. In hopes of a pardon, he implicated his mother among others, all of whom followed him in death. He was a poet, a close friend of Nero until the emperor grew tired of him and his poetry, after which Lucan's writing became insulting, insults Nero was said to have ignored.

__Lysias__ was extremely wealthy and contemporary with Alcibiades. He founded a new profession, logographer, which consisted of writing speeches delivered in law courts. One of his speeches was *Against Andocides*, another was *Against Alcibiades.*

__Memmius__ was an orator and poet, and friend of Pompey but eventually went over to Caesar.

__Mimnermus__ was born in Ionian Smyrna around 630 B.C. He wrote short love poems suitable for performance at drinking parties.

__Myron of Priene__ is the author of a historical account of the First Messenian War.

__Onesicritus__, 360-290 B.C., was a Greek historian who accompanied Alexander the Great on his campaigns throughout Asia. He was helmsman on one of Alexander's boats and did such a good job that he was awarded with a crown of gold, along with Alexander's admiral Nearchus.

__Pausanias__, a Greek historian and geographer, famous for his *Description of Greece*. He was contemporary with Hadrian and Marcus Aurelius. He's noted as being someone interested in everything, careful in his writing and scrupulously honest.

Phanocles lived during the time of Alexander the Great. He was the author of a poem on boy-love that described the love of Orpheus for Calais, and his death at the hands of Thracian women.

Quintus Curtius Rufus: see Curtius

Theopompus, 380-315 B.C. Born in Chios, he lived in Athens and was a student of Isocrates. He knew Alexander and went to Ptolemy Egypt after his death. What we know of his works comes from quotes from later writers. He wrote a *History of Philip.*

Philemon lived to be a hundred but alas only fragments of his works remain. He must have been very popular as he won numerous victories as a poet and playwright.

Pindar's great love was Theoxenus of Tenodos about whom he wrote: ''Whosoever, once he has seen the rays flashing from the eyes of Theoxenus, and is not shattered by the waves of desire, has a black heart forged of a cold flame. Like wax of the sacred bees, I melt when I look at the young limbs of boys.'' He lived around 500 B.C. and celebrated the Greek victories against the Persians at Salamis and Plataea. His home in Thebes became a must for his devotees.

Plato was a major source for this book, along with Xenophon, Thucydides and Plutarch. Plato's most famous work is the Allegory of the Cave. Humans in the cave have no other reality than the shadows they see on the walls. If they looked around, they could see what was casting the shadows and by doing so gain additional knowledge. If they left the cave they would discover the sun, analogous to truth. If those who saw the sun reentered the cave and told the others, they would not be believed. There are thusly different levels of reality that only the wisest are able to see; the others remain ignorant. It's basically thanks to Plato and Xenophon that we know what we do about Socrates. Plato's perfect republic is ruled by the best (an aristocracy), headed by a philosopher king who guides his people thanks to his wisdom and reason. An inferior form of government, one that comes after an aristocracy, is a timocracy, ruled by the honorable. A timocracy is in the hands of a warrior class. Plato has Sparta in mind, but it's unclear how he could have found this form of government better than, for example, a democracy. The problem may be that we know, in reality, so little about Sparta. Next comes an oligarchy based on wealth, followed by a democracy, rule by just anyone and everyone. This degenerates into a tyranny, meaning a government of oppression, because of the conflict between the rich and the poor in a democracy.

Pliny the Younger was the Elder's nephew. He witnessed the explosion of Vesuvius. He was a lawyer and a letter writer, many of which remain, vital historical sources of the times. His letters concerning Trajan are of special importance. Under Trajan he worked side by side with Suetonius.

Plutarch was born near Delphi around 46 A.D. to a wealthy family. He was married, and a letter to his wife even exists to this day. He had sons, the exact number unknown. He studied mathematics and philosophy in Athens and was known to have visited most of the major Greek sites mentioned in this book, as well as Rome. He personally knew the Emperors Trajan and Hadrian, and became a Roman citizen. He was a high priest at Delphi and his duty consisted of interpreting the auguries of the Pythoness (no mean task). He wrote the *Lives of the Emperors* but alas only two of the lesser emperors survive. Another verily monumental work was *Parallel Lives of Greeks and Romans* of which twenty-three exist. His interest was the destinies of his subjects, how they made their way through the meanders of life, the Jekyll/Hyde struggle of virtue versus vice. A small jest, he went on, often reveals more than battles during which thousands die. His writings on Sparta, alongside those of Xenophon, are nearly all we possess concerning that extraordinary city-state. His major biographies are the *Life of Alexander* and the *Life of Julius Caesar*. Amusingly, Plutarch wrote a scathing review of Herodotus' work in which he stated that the great historian was fanatically biased in favor of the Greeks who could do, according to Herodotus, no wrong.

No gratitude can ever be enough for what this man has given us, although in the case of the Greeks we must never forget that he was writing *500 years after the events*.

Polybius, around 200 B.C. to 118 B.C., was a Greek historian whose *The Histories* covered the period from 264 to 146 B.C. He was a friend of Scipio Africanus. He details the ascent to empire of Rome, and was present at the destruction of Carthage.

Polyenus was a Macedonian known as a rhetorician and for his books on war strategies, called *Stratagems*, the stratagems of the most celebrated Greek generals. He lived in the 2nd century.

Sallust was a Roman historian and politician, 86 B.C. to about 35 B.C. One of his works concerned Catiline and he wrote *Histories* of which only fragments remain.

Satyrus was a philosopher and historian whose Lives come down to us thanks to Athenaeus and Diogenes.

Seneca (Lucius Annaeus Seneca) lived around 4 B.C. to 65 A.D. He was the advisor of Caligula, Claudius and Nero who forced him to commit suicide for supposedly planning his overthrow. He is known for his philosophical essays, letters and tragedies.

Simonides of Ceos was a Greek poet born about 550 B.C. Besides his poems, he added four letters to the Greek alphabet.

Suetonius (Gaius Suetonius Tranquillus) lived around 69 A.D. to 123 A.D. He was a truly great Roman historian known for his *Twelve Caesars*, his only extant work. Pliny the Younger says that he was studious and totally dedicated to writing. He was highly favored by both Trajan, under whom he served as his secretary, and Hadrian who fired him for having an affair with the Empress Vibia Sabina.

<u>Sophocles</u> was the author of 123 plays of which 7 remain, notably *Oedipus* and *Antigone*. An Athenian born to a rich family just before the Battle of Marathon, he was a firm supporter of Pericles. He fought alongside Pericles against Samos when the island attempted to become autonomous from Athens. He was elected as a magistrate during the Sicilian Expedition led by Alcibiades, and given for function the goal of finding out why the expedition had ended disastrously. Sophocles was always ready and willing to succumb to the charms of boys. Plutarch tells us that even at age 65 ''Sophocles led a handsome boy outside the city walls to have his way with him. He spread the boy's poor himation--a rectangular piece of cloth thrown over the left shoulder that drapes the body--upon the ground. To cover them both he spread his rich cloak. After Sophocles took his pleasure the boy took the cloak and left the himation for Sophocles. This misadventure was eventually known to all.'' He died at 90, some say while reciting a very long tirade from *Antigone* because he hadn't paused to take a breath. Another version has him choking on grapes, and a final one has him dying of happiness after winning the equivalent of our Oscar at a festival. The first of his trilogy--called the Theban plays--is *Oedipus the King*. Here the baby Oedipus--in a plot that goes back to Priam and Paris at the founding of Troy--is handed over to a servant to be killed in order to prevent the accomplishment of an oracle, an oracle stating that he will kill his father and marry his mother. He does both after solving the riddle of the sphinx (which creature becomes four-footed, then two-footed and finally three-footed?). His mother, when she finds out she's been bedding her own son, commits suicide and Oedipus blinds himself. In *Oedipus at Colonus* Oedipus dies and we learn more about his children Antigone, Polyneices and Eteocles. In *Antigone* Polyneices is accused of treason and killed. His body is thrown outside the city walls and the king forbids its burial, under pain of death. Antigone does so anyway and, faced with death, she commits suicide, followed by the king's son who was going to wed her, followed by the king's wife who couldn't face losing her precious son. (Whew!)

<u>Tacitus</u>, around 56 A.D. to 117 A.D., was a historian who wrote *Annals* and *Histories*, concerning Tiberius, Claudius, Nero and the Year of the Four Emperors. He is known for his insights into the psychology of his subjects.

<u>Theocritus</u> was a Sicilian and lived around 270 B.C. In his 7th Idyll Aratus is passionately in love with a lad. His 12th Idyll refers to Diocles who died saving the life of Philolaus, the boy he loved, and in whose honor kissing contests were held every spring at his tomb. In his 23rd Idyll a lover

176

commits suicide because of unrequited love, warning his belovèd that one day he too will burn and weep for a cruel boy. Before hanging himself the lover kissed the doorpost from which he would attach the noose. The boy treated the corpse with disdain and went off to the gymnasium for a swim where a statue of Eros fell on him, coloring the water with his blood. In his 29th Idyll a lover warns his belovèd that he too will age and his beauty will lose its freshness. He is therefore advised to show more kindness as ''you will one day be desperate for a beautiful young man's attentions.'' Although lads are often disappointing, it is impossible not to fall madly in love with them. In the 30th Idyll the poet states that when a man grows old he should keep a distance from boys, but in his heart he knows that the only alternative to loving a boy is simply to cease to exist.

<u>Theognis</u> was born around 550 B.C. His poems consist of maxims and advice as to how to live life. Fortunately, a great deal of his work has come down to us, most of which is dedicated to his belovèd, the handsome Cyrnus.

<u>Thucydides</u> was an Athenian general and historian, contemporary with the events he described. What he wrote was based on what actually happened; there was no extrapolating; no divine intervention on the part of the gods as was the case with Plutarch. An example of this was his observation that birds and animals that ate plague victims died as a result, leading him to conclude that the disease had a natural rather than supernatural cause. His description of the plague has never been equaled, the plague that he himself caught while participating in the Peloponnesian War. He is thought to have died in 411 B.C., the date at which his writing suddenly stops. He admired Pericles and democracy but not the radical form found in Athens.

<u>Tyrtaeus</u>, a rare Spartan writer, left us an account of the Second Messenian War. The purpose of his poetry was to inspire Spartan support of the Spartan state. Athenians claimed he was of Athenian birth. Pausanias maintained that the Athenians had sent him to Sparta as an insult, because he was both crazy, lame and had one eye. Herodotus wrote that he was only one of two foreigners to be given Spartan citizenship.

<u>Xenophon</u>, born near Athens in 430 B.C., was a historian and general. His masterpieces are *The Peloponnesian Wars* and *Anabasis*. He loved Sparta and served under Spartan generals during the Persian Wars. Like the Spartans, he believed in oligarchic rule, rule by the few, be they the most intelligent or wealthy or militarily acute. He spent a great deal of time in Persia alongside Cyrus the Younger who raised an army, among whom were Xenophon's 10,000 and other mercenaries (all of which is the subject of *Anabasis*). After Cyrus' death Xenophon and his ten thousand made their way back home, the breathtaking account of which ends his *Anabasis*. The Athenians exiled him when he fought with the Spartans against Athens

but the Spartans offered him an estate where he wrote his works. His banishment may have been revoked thanks to his son Gryllus who brilliantly fought and died for Athens.

OTHER SOURCES

Abbott Jacob, *History of Pyrrhus*, 2009
Ady, Cecilia, *A History of Milan under the Sforza,* 1907.
Aldrich and Wotherspoon, *Who's Who in Gay and Lesbian History,* 2001.
Aristophanes, Bantam Drama, 1962.
Aronson, Marc, *Sir Walter Ralegh*, 2000.
Baglione, *Caravaggio*, circa 1600.
Baker Simon, *Ancient Rome*, 2006
Barber, Richard, *The Devil's Crown--Henry II and Sons*, 1978.
Barber, Stanley, *Alexandros*, 2010.
Beachy, Robert, *Gay Berlin*, 2014. Marvelous.
Bellori, *Caravaggio*, circa 1600.
Bergreen, Laurence, *Over the Edge of the World. Magellan.* 2003
Bicheno, Hugh, *Vendetta*, 2007.
Bierman, John, *Dark Safari, Henry Morton Stanley*, 1990.
Boyd, Douglas, *April Queen*, 2004.
Boyles, David, *Blondel's Song*, 2005.
Bramly, Serge, *Leonardo*, 1988. A wonderful book.
Bury and Meiggs, *A History of Greece*, 1975.
Calimach, Andrew, *Lover's Legends*, 2002.
Cawthorne, Nigel, *Sex Lives of the Popes*, 1996
Cellini, Benvenuto, *The Autobiography of Benvenuto Cellini.*
Ceram, C.W., *Gods, Graves and Scholars*, 1951.
Chamberlin, E.R. *The Fall of the House of Borgia*, 1974
Cloulas, Ivan, *The Borgia*, 1989
Crompton, Louis, *Byron and Greek Love*, 1985.
Crouch, David, *William Marshal*, 1990.
Crowley, Roger, *Empires of the Sea*, 2008. Marvelous.
Dale, Richard, *Who Killed Sir Walter Ralegh?*, 2011.
Dalrymple, William, *The Last Mughal*, 2006.
Davidson, James, *Courtesans and Fishcakes*, 1998.
Davidson, James, *The Greeks and Greek Love*, 2007.
Davis, John Paul, *The Gothic King, Henry III*, 2013.
Deford, Frank, *Big Bill Tilden*, 1975.
Dover K.J. *Greek Homosexuality*, 1978
Duby, George, *William Marshal*, 1985.
Eisler, Benita, *BYRON Child of Passion, Fool of Fame*, 2000. Wonderful.
Everitt Anthony, *Augustus*, 2006

Everitt Anthony, *Cicero*, 2001
Everitt, Anthony, *Hadrian*, 2009.
Fagles, Robert, *The Iliad*, 1990.
Forellino Antonio, *Michelangelo*, 2005. The most beautiful reproductions
Forellino, Antonio, *Michelangelo*, 2005. Beautiful reproductions.
Frieda, Leonie, *Catherine de Medici*, 2003. Wonderful.
Gayford, Martin, *Michelangelo*, 2013. A beautiful book.
Gillingham, John, *Richard the Lionheart*, 1978.
Goldsworthy Adrian, *Caesar*, 2006
Goldsworthy Adrian, *The Fall of Carthage*, 2000
Goodman Rob and Soni Jimmy, *Rome's Last Citizen*, 2012
Graham-Dixon, Andrew, *Caravaggio* 2010. Fabulous.
Grant Michael, *History of Rome*, 1978
Graves, Robert, *Greek Myths*, 1955.
Grazia, Sebastian de, *Machiavelli in Hell*, 1989.
Guicciardini, *Storie fiorentine (History of Florence)*, 1509. Essential.
Halperin David M. *One Hundred Years of Homosexuality*, 1990
Harris Robert, *Imperium*, 2006
Herodotus, *The Histories*, Penguin Classics.
Hesiod and Theognis, Penguin Classics, 1973.
Hibbert, Christopher, *Florence, the Biography of a City*, 1993.
Hibbert, Christopher, *The Borgias and Their Enemies*, 2009.
Hibbert, Christopher, *The Great Mutiny India 1857*, 1978. Fabulous.
Hibbert, Christopher, *The Rise and Fall of the House of Medici*, 1974.
Hicks, Michael, *Richard III*, 2000.
Hine, Daryl, *Puerilities*, 2001.
Hochschild, Adam, *King Leopold's Ghost*, 1999.
Holland, Tom, *Rubicon*, 2003
Hughes-Hallett, *Heroes*, 2004.
Hughes, Robert, *Rome*, 2011
Hutchinson, Robert, *House of Treason*, 2009.
Hutchinson, Robert, *Thomas Cromwell*, 2007.
Jack Belinda, *Beatrice's Spell*, 2004.
Jeal, Tim, *Explorers of the Nile*, 2011. Wonderful.
Jeal, Tim, *STANLEY*, 2007. All of Jeal's books are must-reads.
Johnson, Marion, *The Borgias*, 1981
Korda, Michael, *HERO The Life and Legend of Lawrence of Arabia*, 2010.
Lacey, Robert, *Henry VIII*, 1972.
Lambert, Gilles *Caravaggio*, 2007.
Landucci, Luca, *A Florentine Diary*, around 1500, a vital source.
Lev, Elizabeth, *The Tigress of Forli*, 2011. Wonderfully written.
Levy, Buddy, *Conquistador*, 2009
Levy, Buddy, *River of Darkness*, 2011. Fabulous.

Lévy, *Edmond, Sparte, 1979.*
Lewis, Bernard, *The Assassins*, 1967.
Livy, *Rome and the Mediterranean*
Livy, *The War with Hannibal*
Lubkin, Gregory, *A Renaissance Court*, 1994.
Lyons, Mathew, *The Favourite*, 2011.
Macintyre, Ben, *The Man Who Would Be King*, 2004.
Mallett, Michael and Christine Shaw, *The Italian Wars 1494-1559.*
Malye, Jean, *La Véritable Histore d'Alcibiade*, 2009.
Manchester, William, *A World Lit Only By Fire*, 1993.
Mancini, *Caravaggio*, circa 1600.
Marchand, Leslie, *Byron*, 1971.
Martines, Lauro, *April Blood-Florence and the Plot against the Medici*, 2003.
Matyszak, Philip, *The Mithridates the Great*, 2008.
McLynn, Frank, *Richard and John, Kings of War*, 2007. Fabulous.
McLynn, *Marcus Aurelius*, 2009
McLynn, *STANLEY, The making of an African explorer*, 1989.
Meier, Christian, *Caesar*, 1996.
Meyer, G.J. *The Borgias, The Hidden History*, 2013.
Meyer, Jack, *Alcibiades*, 2009.
Miles Richard, *Ancient Worlds*, 2010
Miles Richard, *Carthage Must be Destroyed*, 2010
Miller, David, *Richard the Lionheart*, 2003.
Mortimer, Ian, 1415, Henry V's Year of Glory, 2009.
Noel, Gerard, *The Renaissance Popes*, 2006.
Opper, Thorsten, *Hadrian, Empire and Conflict*, 2008.
Parker, Derek, *Cellini*, 2003, the book is beautifully written.
Peyrefitte, Roger, *Alexandre*, 1979.
Plutarch's Lives, Modern Library.
Pollard, .J., *Warwick the Kingmaker*, 2007.
Polybius, *The Histories*
Read, Piers Paul, *The Templars*, 1999.
Reid, B.L., *The Lives of Roger Casement*, 1976.
Renucci Pierre, *Caligula*, 2000
Reston, James, *Warriors of God, Richard and the Crusades*, 2001.
Rice, Edward, *Captain Sir Richard Francis Burton*, 1990.
Ridley, Jasper, *The Tudor Age*, 1998.
Robb, Peter, M – *The Man Who Became Caravaggio*, 1998.
Robb, Peter, *Street Fight in Naples*, 2010.
Rocke, Michael, *Forbidden Friendships*, 1996. Fabulous/indispensible.
Romans Grecs et Latin, Gallimard, 1958.
Ross, Charles, *Richard III*, 1981.
Rouse, W.H.D., Homer's *The Iliad*, 1938.

Royle, Trevor, *Fighting Mac, The Downfall of Sir Hector Macdonald.*
Sabatini, Rafael, *The Life of Cesare Borgia*, 1920.
Saslow, James, *Ganymede in the Renaissance*, 1986.
Schiff, Stacy, *Cleopatra*, 2010
Seward, Desmond, *Caravaggio – A Passionate Life*, 1998.
Simonetta, Marcello, *The Montefeltro Conspiracy*, 2008. Wonderful.
Skidmore, Chris, *Death and the Virgin*, 2010.
Strathern, Paul, *The Medici, Godfathers of the Renaissance*, 2003. Superb.
Strauss Barry, *The Spartacus War*, 2009
Stuart, Stirling, *Pizarro - Conqueror of the Inca*, 2005.
Suetonius, *The Twelve Caesars*
Tacitus, *The Annals of Imperial Rome*
Tacitus, *The Histories*
Thucydides, *The Peloponnesian War*, Penguin Classics.
Turner, Ralph, *Eleanor of Aquitaine*, 2009.
Unger Miles, *Magnifico, The Brilliant Life and Violent Times*
Unger, Miles, *Machiavelli*, 2008.
Vasari, We would know next to nothing if it were not for him.
Vernant, Jean-Pierre, *Mortals and Immortals*, 1991.
Virgil, *The Aeneid*, Everyman's Library, Knopf, 1907.
Viroli, Maurizio, *Niccolo's Smile, A Biography of Machiavelli*, 1998.
Ward-Perkins Bryan, *The Fall of Rome*, 2005
Warren, W.L., *Henry II*, 1973.
Weir, Alison, *Eleanor of Aquitaine*, 1999. Weir is a fabulous writer.
Weir, Alison, *The Princes in the Tower*, 1992. Marvelous.
Wheaton James, *Spartacus*, 2011
Wikipedia: Research today is impossible without the aid of this monument.
Williams Craig A. *Roman Homosexuality*, 2010 – No comprehensive book
Williams John, *Augustus*, 1972
Wilson, Derek, *The Uncrowned Kings of England*, 2005.
Wright, Ed, *History's Greatest Scandals*, 2006.
Wroe, Ann, *Perkin, A Story of Deception*, 2003. Fabulous
Xenophon, *A History of My Times*, Penguin Classics.
Xenophon, *The Persian Expedition*, 1949.

I've priced my autobiography, *Michael Hone His World, His Loves*, at the lowest cost permitted by the editor.

I would also like to introduce what I consider to be my best book: *TROY* and its coffee-table-size edition *THE TROJAN WAR*.